RUSTY'S TALE

Russ Carrington

In memory of Patricia Barbara Ann Carrington.
Born 12th March 1931
Passed away 28th May 2011

Rusty's Tale and Past Imperfect together present a unique slice of Australian history, combining the memoirs of former stockman and helicopter mustering pilot, Russ Carrington and the autobiography of his mother, Patricia.

This is more than just a story of Planet Downs, the family station, but a fascinating insight into growing up in 19th Century Australia, and what life was like for the men and women who tamed the bush.

First edition published 2021

by Stories of Oz Publishing

PO Box K57

Haymarket NSW 1240

ABN: 0920230558

facebook.com/storiesofoz

ozbookstore.com

This work is copyright. Apart from any use as permitted under the Copyright Act 1968, no part may be reproduced, copied, scanned, stored in a retrieval system, recorded, or transmitted, in any form or by any means, without the prior written permission of the publisher.

© 2021 Russ Carrington and Patricia Carrington

ISBN: 978-0-6453511-2-5

Edited by: Greg Barron

Cover design: James Barron

Printed and bound in Australia by IngramSpark

Childhood at Planet

I was born on the 20th November 1958 in Townsville. I don't remember a lot about it but I daresay it was a pretty significant event.

According to legend my dear Mum, accompanied by her mother, proceeded via train to Cloncurry where we were met by Dad. In a move destined to forever warm the heart and moisten the eye, upon the recounting of this momentous occasion, he reached out for me and said, 'G'day little mate.'

Anyway I had a terrific childhood punctuated sporadically by low points of discipline administered at intervals by Dad as and when required, utilising whatever came to hand.

My first real memories are from when I was about five years old. I guess my memory isn't all that good and lots of things I recall are prompted by others, however I will persevere. I remember when my sister Elaine was brought home by Mum. E, poor soul, was born on Christmas Day and thereby consigned to a future of only one cake a year and usually only one present. An extension of this is the tale of the Flying Padre on a visit, innocently asking all of the gathered children who was born on Christmas Day. Mum says he was rather flabbergasted when informed by the gathering that it was "Elaine, Jesus' little sister."

My younger sister, Joan was born in February during periodic flooding. At that time we did not have an airstrip at our station and all aircraft movements were usually conducted at the neighbouring property, Gregory Downs. This homestead was on the other side of the Gregory River and as Joan had chosen to arrive with the river in full flood, it presented difficulties. The vessel used to conduct the transfer was a salubrious craft consisting of a long-range fuel tank that had been used on a Catalina Flying Boat with a hole cut into the topside of it to enable the carriage of passengers. Mum, baby and some cargo were placed aboard. Dad, my Uncle John and a couple of others swam beside and pushed it across the swollen river.

Ah the memories, how they flood in now. When our Aunty Nancy threatened the demise of our cat Twinkle, my brother Steve upended a bucket over the cat and joined in the ensuing search until Twink's tail was seen protruding and all was revealed.

At one stage we had a Mini Moke and I can still see Dad driving the Moke in hot pursuit of Steve after he was sprung lighting fires (a cardinal sin) underneath the Bloodwood tree out the front. Steve could run like the wind and made it to the rough and holy black soil plain which was not very Moke friendly. He then turned north and with Dad keeping pace beside him on the red ground, was travelling pretty well until such time that he was starting to run out of country and it was necessary to make a break for the river. The result wasn't pretty.

I think that while most of the others were taught to drive in the Moke, my tuition was in the Land Rover.

We lived on a small anabranch of the Gregory River that we called the "Runner". Our water supply was pumped to the Homestead at that time from the river itself at a huge deep waterhole called the "Blue Hole" approximately three-quarters of a mile away. The aforesaid Land Rover and I very nearly went swimming in the Blue Hole once on an expedition to shut off the pump engine. I remember Dad once nearly losing the D4 Bulldozer into the water at the same spot. At a guess the river would have been twenty to thirty feet deep with a sheer drop and maybe fifty yards across.

As youngsters we were always swimming and fishing in the river. Our favourite spots were the "Watering Place" and the "Falls", a small set of rapids dropping about eight feet and known to us as "Bumsore".

One of our favourite pastimes was to jump in the water at the junction where the Runner left the river about a mile upstream. Mounted on inner tubes we would ride the rapids down to the Watering Place. This was particularly exciting when the river was in flood. I remember swinging on ropes al la Tarzan and diving in from high trees at the Watering Place.

The Runner re-joined the river here and I nearly broke my neck in later years, diving in from a boat into the murky floodwater disgorging from this creek into the cleaner waters of the main stream. The sediment-filled water disguised a new sand bank, thus bringing about my first flight with the RFDS.

The Arrangement of Things

To get a true picture of my life and childhood at Planet Downs it will probably help to explain the set up.

The place was a pretty successful operation running at its peak around 17,000 head of cattle over two properties being Planet Downs and Kamarga.

It was owned by my father Alex Carrington, his brother John Carrington and their father Ted Carrington. Ted had retired to Brisbane and Dad and Uncle John were the bosses. Both of our families were there at various times. It was a wonderful home. I daresay that their success was brought about by their frugality and a lot of hard work.

Our family comprised Alex Carrington, our Mum Pat, me – Russell, Joan, Steve, Elaine and Jenny.

Uncle John's family was of course himself and his wife Nancy, his sons Glen, Graeme and a daughter Lyndell.

Dad and Uncle John came from a large family of eleven children. Dad was one of twins; his brother William did not survive beyond eight days and he is buried at Planet Downs where they were born. Also in the little grave are the ashes of a cousin of my generation, Lorena Jay Henry.

Another brother, Neville, was killed in a horse accident while attending a muster at Gregory Downs. A photograph of Neville, later in this book, was taken on the morning of his death.

The original property was purchased I think around 1921. The family obtained leasehold ownership over other properties and drew another block in a land ballot to end up with 670 square miles in two blocks.

I believe they were very progressive for their day and were at the forefront in the district, utilising many new ideas and products. The use of a cradle to facilitate the branding of calves as well as the introduction of droughtmaster cattle (in 1958, the year I was born) and Polythene pipe were amongst them.

Playmates and Enemies

We had some great old mates in the Aboriginal families that lived with us at Planet. Fishing and chasing sugarbag (native bee hives) were our favourite pastimes.

A very occasional and risky delight back at the homestead was to prise open the window at the back of the old store hut. A bit of a foray inside and a tin of condensed milk would be liberated from its prison, usually followed in short order by the educating hand of Dad.

Gregory Downs was the neighbouring property. It was then managed by Bill and Wilma Foster. Their boys were our lifelong friends and partners in crime. Gregory Downs was also basically the geographical and social hub for the district. Our airmail service would arrive once a week with the exchange of mail bags carried out usually by Mrs. Foster on everyone's behalf. The RFDS clinics were held there at the Gregory Downs homestead once a month. The Flying Doctor would conduct his consultations and examinations in a small room that was the Station's office.

Unbeknown to all the adults we children had discovered a hole in the floor underneath a bed that looked directly down into the office. Exciting stuff but unfortunately it wasn't possible to actually see very much!

These doctors' days were quite the thing. Most of the matrons of the district would gather and serve a bit of smoko and enjoy some social interaction with each other. It was pretty difficult for women in those days. I recall the little boy of a later manager of

Gregory Downs walking up to all the ladies with something large in his mouth, upon being asked what was in his mouth he opened up and there was a very large green frog. Not too many scones went down the hatch that day, I bet.

Over the river from Gregory Downs station was the Gregory pub, the racecourse and the police station. There was a yearly race meeting, horse sports and in later years a campdraft.

One of my mortal enemies was a boy from a property further down the river who by all accounts could fight like a bag full of wildcats. Butchy and I never mixed it that I remember, however the war still went on and much taking of sides took place amongst the local kids.

On one occasion he left his bag of Minties on the tank stand at the pub and my good self and fellow conspirators proceeded to eat the lot and replace them with small stones carefully rewrapped in the lolly papers. We waited with glee until poor Butchy discovered the crime and then barricaded ourselves inside a vehicle while he stormed around the outside.

It's interesting you know how much that we children actually accomplished in a day. As we had a wood stove our daily chores centred on the servicing of the kitchen. We had to refill the wood box that sat inside next to the stove, gather wood chips and kindling and refill their respective containers, restack the pile of wood underneath the kitchen; cutting and fetching wood from the huge pile that the whole station work force would replenish about three times a year. We had to empty the ash bucket and feed the pigs each day with the kitchen scraps – bearing in mind that this was basically a commercial kitchen feeding around twenty people. There would sometimes be two, twenty-litre flour drums of scraps to be lugged down to the pig sty about three hundred metres away.

Each evening we would yard the milking cows and the goat herd into their respective yards and milk the cows in the morning. The goats were rarely milked and were really only yarded for their protection from dingoes. As well as providing meat for the table they also did service in the rearing of poddy calves. It was quite amusing to see the family of cattle that lived with the goats. The fowls also had to be fed and the eggs collected.

I think it's important that the reader understands how well we lived. Beef was of course always available as well as the pork and goat meat that made the table quite regularly. We often had barramundi as Dad was a keen fisherman. Along with eggs and the occasional fowl, as well as plenty of seasonal vegetables from the huge garden, bread was made pretty much every day. We had a dairy hut where butter was occasionally made but usually tinned butter or lard was used.

Our store was usually replenished twice a year with a truck load from town. Apart from an occasional treat brought by visitors such as a few loaves of Town Bread and maybe some margarine we were pretty-well self-sufficient. Of course things got easier as the years went by.

As we grew older we were entrusted with more demanding tasks. I was twelve when Dad taught me to drive the road grader. This grader was started using a pilot motor, a little auxiliary engine mounted to the huge diesel engine as a starter motor. These pilot motors were very hard to start so Dad would get it going for me and tell me where to go and away I went, terrified that I would stall the engine and experience Dad's wrath. But all went well and he would pick me up usually just on dark, having usually graded about forty kilometres of roads and fence lines.

This grader was the first machine owned by the Burke Shire Council and it was worn out when the Shire got it. I am pretty sure it was used by the Army in World War Two. It came to Planet with an ancient wooden caravan that was used by the Shire operator. One of these poor souls had shot himself inside the van and we children swore that it was haunted.

I don't know if anyone much nowadays knows what a fireplough is, but we had one of those for road making as well. It was made by Comet, the windmill people. It was shaped like an arrowhead with a huge screw at each corner of the triangle for depth adjustment and it was originally towed by thirty-two draught horses. In my era we pulled it with a small D4 bulldozer thank the lord. It's funny you know, but I think that little bulldozer only produced about forty horsepower. Dad won a contract once to plough the road from Burketown to Camooweal with the D4 and the fireplough, a distance of 287 kms in a straight line. On the heavy black soil the little dozer could only handle first gear. God it was slow, you could set it up and hop off, attend to your toilet and walk along a bit and hop back on.

Isolation

At that time it could get very isolated in the Gulf, helicopters were unknown and the use of aircraft very limited. In a good Wet Season, it would sometimes be four months before traffic could start moving. Woe betide the unwary. It amazes me today to see how unprepared the stations are in the event of a disaster.

Our power was provided initially (in my time) by a single cylinder water cooled Lister engine powering a thirty-two volt generator. This grew in time to be a two cylinder air-cooled Lister of 10 kva producing 240 volts and eventually a three cylinder

Lister of 15 kva. We operated on limited power and the lighting plants were only allowed to operate for around 10 to 12 hours a day. Refrigeration was initially provided by a couple of kerosene fridges until the purchase of a large seven door Refrigerator purchased from a hotel in Cloncurry that was fitted with brine tanks to enable it to retain the cold.

The Royal Flying Doctor Service provided a wonderful service to us all, call sign VJI Mt. Isa operating usually on 5110 MHz HF. I was too young to have used the pedal-powered radio but we had one of those as well. In the early days we used double side band HF valve radios and then later on the improved single side band HF valve radios.

I remember Crammen, Traeger, Eilco and then the Codans being the radio types used. As well as the monthly clinics, daily consultations were conducted over the open radio network. The radio operator, at a scheduled time, would broadcast for patients to make themselves known and a list would be formed. The doctor would then work through the list of consultations. His tools were his radio and the medical chest.

This was a marvellous arrangement; the chest was a large container of common drugs numbered to identify each one. The Doctor would say something like take three doses of number 173 twice a day, that sort of thing. There were of course drawbacks but it was all that we had and we made it work. Unfortunately, open radio is not conducive to privacy and your business was everyone's business.

Another great service was the conducting of telegram traffic to and fro. The network would also be open for the all-important 'galah' sessions from seven to eight in the morning and five to six in the evening which were vital to our extended communities. A wealth of business operations was conducted then as well as community, weather and other news (gossip) passed around.

In later years the school of the air used the frequency for most of the rest of the day. Telephones were not known in that country at all. I remember a new stockman asking Uncle John where the phone was so that he could make a call, Uncles reply was 'You have to put your head down and then you put your ring up.'

Testosterone Strikes.

I think I had my first intimate liaison aged about fifteen. The lady in question worked on a barramundi fishing boat that operated out of Burketown and a good time was had by all. She also, as the saying goes, 'Lit me up like a light bulb.'

A few agonizing days later, as my cousin Graeme set off at the usual time of four am to the night paddock to catch the night horses preparatory to mustering the horse paddock, I said 'Mate, have you ever had a dose of the clap?'

Lightning fast he whipped around and said, 'No, have you got one?'

It turned out to be the best move I could have made as Graeme obviously passed the word along. That evening Mum got me aside and asked me if I had some social disease. The best option was of course to fess up and submit for treatment. In the morning this resulted in an embarrassing and humiliating consultation with the Flying Doctor over the open radio network. A course of tablets and a needle a day for three days fixed the problem, however, I can still see my lovely prim and proper mother with a huge grin on her face as she administered the needles, my rump being the target area.

Gotcha the Crocodile

My Dad was an expert with a fishing spear, learned from the same sort of childhood as I had. We would never go off on an expedition without a spear amongst the gear somewhere. I got my first barramundi whilst underwater with a spear. As a young man this grew into spear gunning and I very nearly ended up inside a crocodile.

A party of us young fellows had the day off and were about to jump in the water from a big partly submerged log when we saw a huge catfish circling underneath. I reckon it was about 6 feet or 2 metres long, and at first assumed it was a shark. I decided to shoot it with the speargun and followed it into a deep cave under the bank.

I gave it up when running out of wind and wondered where all the bones scattered around the floor of the cave came from. Three of us then swam downstream and all saw this crocodile at about the same time. Unfortunately I am short-sighted and wear glasses except of course when the goggles are on. I had spotted this big old sunken log and was heading towards it to check on the lee side for fish. It was of course a saltwater crocodile about fourteen feet long. I only realised what it was when it turned its head toward me, no doubt pondering what I'd taste like with mushroom gravy. It was many years before I'd swim in any water deeper than about two feet, I'd reckon.

The original Old Planet Homestead, now the kitchen

The big house Planet 1925

Our home at Planet Downs

Alex Carrington and Grader SN 21F 216

Graeme Carrington erecting a grave marker for George. Pheonix at Punjab Station

Grandfather Ted Carrington with his wagon

Graeme Carrington milking the cows

Grandpa Ted and the Moke

Neville Carrington on the morning of his death

Greg Nicols John Clarke, Steve Carrington, Ian Forshaw
Backyard boys at Gregory Campdraft.

Jack and Anne Carrington

Henry cousins in the Catalina belly tank

Jerry's Wagon Train

Jerry the Tank Sinker was a contract earthmoving operator who did work for us for years. He certainly had a very lonely existence as he never had an offsider and did everything by himself. It was quite a sight to see Jerry's outfit travelling between locations. He had his own little wagon train with his old crawler tractor in the lead, towing, in order: an earthmoving scoop, a huge set of pull along rippers, an ex-army mobile workshop, a fuel trailer, an old Redcliff bus that he lived in followed by a wooden kitchen caravan and a utility last of all.

Jerry would travel directly across country as straight as a die in low gear to the next dam site. But the poor old guy had problems with his elderly tractor and took parts into Mount Isa for repairs. He was never to return, having passed away while in there.

His plant was left untouched for years. Then, a decade later, whilst doing the water run, I took to having a bit of a poke around, looking at how he had lived. To my delight I discovered that his transistor radio still worked. This radio was appropriated to our plant and equipment.

My Uncle John and I were fishing one day, utilising a different type of fishing line that used large square hooks. We were listening to the cricket as we fished and unfortunately in the excitement the boat rolled over with all hands. Spying the radio disappearing into the depths I dove down and recovered it. I wedged it in the base of a small clump of pandanus palms, and as the river was around forty feet deep, with a sheer drop, I then towed the boat and Uncle John across the river to a small ledge where we could get onto dry land.

As we recovered we couldn't understand what this strange

noise was that we could hear. It was of course the radio struggling gamely back to life.

All Hail the Radio

Dad and Uncle John loved listening to the cricket, and whilst the Aussies were in Blighty doing battle for the Olde Mug, they seemed to spend all night giving the team moral support. Any time of the night you would hear the cry, '3 for 254' or similar. They were worse when Grandpa Ted joined them.

The ABC news was listened to with great reverence each evening at suppertime. Any noise or unauthorised talking was banished completely with a very sharp angry cry of 'LISTEN'. I kid you not; it was a very foolish child who drew attention to himself like this.

Old Planet and the Well

The old kitchen that was in use at Planet when I was a kid was the original building that had served purpose as the homestead at Old Planet. This was the small property that the Carrington family purchased from their Aunt, Emily Barret, the proprietor of the Gregory Hotel.

When the family drew the Tagassa block, balloted off Gregory Downs, they dismantled this building and rebuilt it at the present site. The timber in this building was all pit-sawn locally at a spot called the sawpit about four miles to the north of the present homestead. Pressed into service as the kitchen, over time, it would have been awful to work in all day as it was lined entirely with flat tin. With the wood stove simmering away and no electricity for fans the heat was terrible.

The first Planet Downs was a seventy square mile block on which the only permanent water was a well. Saying that it was permanent stretched the imagination fairly well too, when you heard all the trials and tribulations that they had to endure to keep it producing water.

The well was 136 feet deep with two drives following the stream into the sides in each direction. There was a windmill and a steam engine driving a pump jack to lift the water into a small turkeys' nest that was made using a horse drawn scoop. A turkeys' nest is an above ground tank or dam used for water storage that allows the gravity feed of water to the stock water trough.

This water trough was made from a hollow tree trunk sealed at each end with tin, old saddle cloth and tar.

The stories of the efforts to keep the well operating are nerve wracking to say the least. Imagine being at the bottom of the well cleaning the thing out when it started to cave in, only ceasing when it had filled up to your armpits. The Carrington men were known in the district for their knowledge of the work and were called upon to service other wells too. Fiery Downs, one of the neighbours, had a well that was subject to foul air and when you saw the candle flicker you didn't dicker. On Planet Downs I know of two other wells, both dry holes. One of them went to a heartbreaking 240 feet deep.

Other wells that I know of around the district that have been mostly abandoned and lost are of course the four already spoken of with three being on Planet Downs and one on Fiery Downs. I have also found two wells on Gregory Downs, three on Riversleigh Station, five on Thorntonia Station, two on the Riversleigh section of the Lawn Hill National Park. There are two that I know of at Lawn Hill Station and at least three on Herbertvale Station. There are four on Undilla with some still in use I believe and also four on Morestone. I have possibly forgotten some as well.

The Sad Story of the Pregnant Lass

Mum would occasionally employ a girl to help her with the housework, the kitchen, schooling the kids and pretty well anything that was going, a veritable girl Friday. Unfortunately one of these Lasses recently employed and unknown to us was pregnant and decided to carry out a homemade abortion right in the middle of the 1974 wet season. I wasn't present, being stuck in Brisbane but I heard all about it.

You can imagine how distraught this poor girl would have been with the secret of the growing baby inside her and seemingly stuck forever in this very isolated place with no contact from family and friends. So she did the deed not very successfully and started haemorrhaging very badly.

The 1974 wet season was a terrible time for this to happen. At Planet they never saw the sun for forty-one days. It was a record wet of monumental proportions. Mum got straight onto the RFDS and as vehicle traffic was impossible the Flying Doctor decided to parachute down from the aircraft,

This idea was axed after several attempts due to the extremely low cloud and a helicopter was brought in from elsewhere in the state to Mount Isa. The Doctor and Pilot set out for Planet but unfortunately due to dodging storms and also approaching nightfall they ran short of fuel and had to land well short of the homestead.

Once informed of this Dad set off in the Ferguson Tractor in an attempt to retrieve the Doctor and Pilot. To Dads disappointment and due to the deplorable conditions he had to turn around and return but the pair had seen his headlight in the distance.

The next day the RFDS aircraft was able to find the Helicopter and fuel was dropped to them, enabling the rescue to continue. Apparently it was the first Helicopter to visit Planet Downs and we have photos of the machine, a Bell 47J sitting in about four inches of floodwater out in front of the homestead as the river broke its banks.

I believe the whole saga happened over eight days and I thank God for the dedication of the RFDS and their staff. A happy result was achieved and the girl survived, though never to be heard from again.

I flew helicopters for many years afterwards and I can't even begin to imagine the difficulties those poor fellows must have had retrieving the jerry cans of fuel from where they would have become embedded in the boggy black soil and lugging them back to the machine.

To even carry on to the stage that you did not even have enough fuel to take off leads one to appreciate the gravity of the situation. A 4WD vehicle has no chance at all of traversing miles of boggy black soil plains and even the little Ferguson tractor cut a rut about eighteen inches deep.

Watchmaker

Uncle John was notoriously quick tempered and when informed that a long-time friend, ex-employee and Gulf citizen had found work as Head Stockman of Gregory Downs was heard to say, 'Well if he's a Head Stockman I'm a Watchmaker'.

Uncle John was then known as Watchmaker far and wide, in the third person I might add.

Good Horses

I was just thinking of some of the good horses that I was privileged to work at Planet Downs, via Burketown, where I grew up

The Spotted Mare was a wonderful type of horse, a lovely big grey dappled mare. But she had some vices. Getting on her fresh was always a challenge as she used to drop into a fast spin. She would try and cow kick you too as you swung on and you had to use a piece of wire to catch the girth when saddling up. I had her up on the shoulder of a cow once when we were mustering Bottom Kunkulla. Unfortunately, the cow fell and the mare and I rolled over the top of her and when we came up I was hung up in the stirrup iron. She dragged me about a hundred yards and then my foot came free. My Uncle John was about to shoot her. But God I loved riding her, her turn of speed and acceleration was unreal.

Little Pig. Graeme called him that because when he broke him in he would throw himself on the ground and squeal and grunt just like his namesake. But what a horse he was, small in size but all heart and agility. I remember once when we mustered Snake Hole where we used to keep a couple of thousand next year bullocks. We had blocked up the mob in a corner but this big broken baldy bullock that was a couple of years older than the others, and had obviously been dodging the last couple of musters, kept trying to break out.

My cousin Glenn was with us, riding a lovely big grey mare called Redguts. Glenn and I were able to beat this very big bullock as I could get onto the shoulder of him quickly and then Glenn would come up and push onto me. Then, to top it off, my Uncle John who was an artist with a Stockwhip got up behind the bullock and flogged him with his whip so that he wouldn't duck behind us and kept going forward. We did that three times before he chucked it in. That piece of work I remember with pride as I consider it to be some of the best stockwork I have ever been involved in.

Tammy. A really nice bay mare with a star. Tammy was my favourite; she had no vices at all and was always there. She was Mrs Reliable.

Mickey Mouse was an unreal horse. Another one of the famous Planet greys. My cousin Graeme, who is a terrific horseman, took over Mickey Mouse when he was returned to us from Kevin Hanson's plant at Lawn Hill, where he had been worked by a fellow named Arthur Dalavosker. Arthur had him pretty well bombed up as most of their work was with feral cattle. Graeme was able to work his magic on him and settled him down into a fantastic camp horse and a splendid mustering horse

There were, of course, many other horses in our plant, as Graeme would usually break in four or five colts every year, so it's impossible to remember all of them. Some of the best horses, however, belonged to my father, Alex, and Uncle John.

Stockwell was a big chestnut gelding with a blaze face and I didn't really know him but I certainly got told about him. Stockwell was one of my Dad's (Alex's) main horses.

Cousin Glenn told me about a time they had a big mob of cattle on camp at the Five Mile. The Gregory Downs stock camp was attending and they had been going all day cutting out and Stockwell was knocking up. My dad went over to Glenn and swapped horses with him to finish off. Stockwell was still on the bit and had his 'quick and impatient tread' to coin a phrase. Glenn said he was like a shut pocket knife while poking around quietly, terrified that Stockwell would take off after something. Stockwell was well known in the district and thought to be the best horse on the Gregory River.

Little Iodine. This magnificent Taffy mare was another one of Dad's plant. She was a freak in that she could win the cup at the races and the next day you could cut out on her. She was a little low-set mare whose front end seemed to be set a bit too low. She was another magnificent camp horse.

Big Clumper. This splendid grey clumper gelding was one of Uncle John's main horses. He was a magnificent workhorse and suited Uncle splendidly. He was as quiet as a church mouse and Uncle used to get on him and fairly send him. Uncle John may have been known as watchmaker, but patience wasn't his long suit. He would shoulder cattle full pace with no fear.

Big Ian. This was another of our well-known big greys. Big Ian was a bull kicker and also used to strike cattle while galloping alongside them. But he was a lovely quiet horse and suited Uncle John's flamboyant style perfectly.

Some other district horses worth a mention were Pussycat at Gregory Downs, a lovely low set taffy mare, and Bella at Lawn Hill, another wonderful brown mare.

Fiery Ted and Carney the Cook

Ted Templeton was a great character who worked on Augustus Downs. He lived at the Fiery Hut which is on Cartridge Creek. Ted could shoot the eye out of a needle and had made his living as a brumby shooter. He had a terrific collection of guns and carried some with him in his Land Rover all the time. If you chanced to meet Ted out on the road you usually ended up having a great old yarn with him and a shooting competition. Ted's tipple of choice was a foul mixture of rum and chilli cordial with perhaps some water if there was some unlucky enough to be about.

The cook at Gregory Downs at the time was a German fellow called Hans Dross who was nicknamed Carney. Now Hans looked like a really mean version of Sergeant Shultz and was also the model for Tom Quilty's poem 'The Drovers Cook' we thought. Hans had been drinking at the Gregory Pub for a couple of days. Returning for a top-up, he unfortunately collided with Ted's beloved Land Rover. This was a really, really bad thing.

Man the guns, was the cry and a few warning shots (no doubt checking the range) were fired. I was able to bring them back from the brink of World War Three after much difficulty and an unhappy coexistence was established. I think Hans passed away in Normanton in time and I believe Ted spent some great years with his mate Graeme up at Abingdon Station.

Buck Peters

Dad had employed a contractor to convert an old spray dip that we had at Planet into a plunge dip. The contractor had a bloke working for him called Buck Peters. Charlie the contractor must have left Buck to watch the camp while he was away for a while. Buck walked out to the main road about two miles away and caught a lift to the Gregory Pub. He must have consumed a fair bit of alcohol as apparently he went into the horrors. Dropped off at the pickup point, Buck wandered around a bit, then he headed straight west and his tracks were lost eventually. Near the Gregory Downs and Lawn Hill Station boundary fence is the Caroline waterholes which had just gone dry. The Lawn Hill mustering camp discovered Buck's poor old body dead on the fence, all covered in mud from where he must have been trying to get a drink. Dad and Bill Foster recovered the body and brought him back into Planet. They had left him on the vehicle, covered by a tarpaulin down near the goat yard as the smell was horrible, while waiting for the aircraft. We children were consumed by curiosity and sneaked down to take a peek at the body.

As luck would have it, twenty odd years later I was driving a grader for Gregory Downs down that same fence when the machine broke down, right next to where Buck had died. I stayed with the machine for a night and a day and half the next night till someone came looking for me. I don't think I slept a wink and could just imagine the ghost of old Buck walking along and going crook on me for sneaking a look at his body. It also was said that Buck used to work in the railway in Cloncurry and a gang of Islanders gave him a bashing. Buck woke up in the morgue. He had to have a metal plate put into his skull as a result of that.

Jack Mac

Jack MacDougal, the Boundary rider who lived at the Twenty Mile Hut on Gregory Downs, was a wonderful friend to our family. Jack Mac as he was known, lived a very solitary existence and he would visit every week or so. On his visits he sharpened all the butchers' knives and also straightened out bent nails of which there seemed to be drum after drum. Jack was a renowned horse breaker and maintained that he had broken in 3000 horses, thirteen mules and three women. Pretty wicked stuff for our young ears but contrary to the current trend these things were never spoken of in the company of ladies, good manners being maintained at all times. He was also a terrific leatherworker and his bridle was a work of art, all around the hut were examples of this, even the handles of pot plants swinging from the veranda roof had plaited handles.

Jerry and the Dinosaur Bones

Jerry the Tank-sinker was constructing a Dam for us and all these small dinosaur bones kept getting caught up in the teeth on his Scoop. He had a little collection of tusks, teeth and bones that he showed mum and gave them to her. She promptly dispatched them to the Queensland Museum and about six months later, after the wet season, a palaeontologist arrived to check it out. Michael Archer was the palaeontologist and I worked with him up at Riversleigh on the fossil fields there. I do know that the tusk of a Diprotodon from Planet made it into a skeleton at the Museum.

Lenny White and the Buffalo.

On one occasion, up at Planet Downs, one of the men had taken his family fishing down around the Fourteen Mile. Anyway, he spotted this buffalo and had a shot at him with an old .303 rifle. Unfortunately he was only successful in wounding him.

The buffalo disappeared down into the scrubby river bed and was last seen heading across the river onto the island. This so-called island was a scrubby triangle of land formed where the Beames Brook and the Gregory Rivers split apart and went their own separate ways.

About a month after this I took some friends who were keen fishermen onto the island chasing barramundi as it was a pretty secluded spot and often good fish were caught there. We had crossed the Beames Brook at Jack's Crossing in my HiLux and found our way over to the Eastern Bank of the Gregory River.

I parked the vehicle on the northern edge of a little clearing about fifty yards across. The Gregory River at this place had a high cliff-like first bank of about twenty feet and then a low bank of about thirty feet wide and two feet down to the water. I decided I would stay close to the car and the other three blokes set off, walking along the low bank and fishing as they went.

I caught a nice bream and lit a fire, cooked and ate the fish and was just lounging around waiting for the fishermen. Two of the blokes returned with a good barra they wanted to weigh and photograph. We went up to the car and had set the barra up for a photo, hanging off the scales in a small tree. It weighed thirty-five pounds.

As I took the photo of the blokes and the fish I could hear this beast galloping and crashing through the scrub. Next thing you know this buffalo burst out the scrub on the other side of the clearing and came charging straight at us. Well, it was every man for himself, I can tell you! The two blokes raced around the other side of the car and I flew underneath it. The buffalo charged on to the very last thing and then swerved away and disappeared into the scrub heading north.

We waited a while to see if he was going to come back while we worked out what to do. One of the fishermen, Lenny White, was still missing, in the direction that the buffalo had come from. So off we went down on the low bank calling out for Lenny.

After a while we found him up a tree and with a pile of cigarette ash underneath him. He told us that he had heard a large animal moving through the scrub towards him and got ready to climb a suitable tree assuming it was probably a pig. Then he saw the buffalo and scampered up the tree like he was fifteen again. The buffalo came right up to the tree and smashed his fishing rod to smithereens, all the while hooking into the tree and trying to get at Lenny. This continued for quite a while (an eternity if you ask Lenny) and eventually the buffalo took off in our direction. It was time to head for home and fish for tea.

The Old Caldwell-Vale Truck

On Lawn Hill Station, out on the run, stood the remains of a really old truck. I am pretty sure it is one of two trucks that were purchased by a storekeeper in Burketown to cart ore from the Burketown Mining Field to the wharf where the ore was loaded on ships. This Mining Field consisted of all the mines around the Silver King area on Lawn Hill and Riversleigh Stations.

I remember the story of this truck; it had become bogged with a load on, heading to Burketown. It smashed its diff trying to get through a sandy creek. Gordon Smith was a local teamster and he had got the job of pulling it out with his wagon team and carting the ore to the wharf. This truck is possibly the oldest four-wheel-drive vehicle that I know of. It has a huge wooden chassis and an enormous gearbox and running gear. I told my friend Max Gorringe about it when I visited Lawn Hill once while he was managing there. Max shifted what was left of the old truck back into the homestead where it is today.

Sputnik, long may he last.

Sputnik was a crocodile shooter from Burketown who, as was usual in the wet season, had gathered with his cronies for their yearly bender. The story goes that the launching of the Russian satellite generated extreme interest in this camp. The men decided to knock Ivan off his perch and proceed with the construction of their own spacecraft.

A space-going vessel was designed and manufactured by welding two drums together, and our hero Sputnik selected as cosmonaut and skipper. I'm not sure if he got the job because he was the lightest or the drunkest, probably both. An unsuccessful launch was carried out by detonating a stick of dynamite underneath the aforementioned spacecraft.

The skipper survived the launch, but unfortunately his dog did not. Sputnik had an extended stay in hospital and was still working around Normanton when I flew around there in the early nineties.

Memories of Uncle Ray Conlan.

Ray Conlan was married to my Aunt Biddy (Lyle) Carrington. There are some that would say he was the greatest rogue in the back country. I have no doubt that there are plenty of people around who knew Ray far better than I and I stand to be corrected but I want to write down some of what I heard about him.

Horse Breaking: In his younger days Ray was a renowned horseman. No doubt in the years that he got to know Aunty Bid, Ray spent a fair bit of time at Planet. They had a contract to supply the Indian Army Remount with broken-in riding horses. The original Planet horse book, which has the first entry in 1900, regularly shows sales of thirty and forty horses in a lot, sold to the Indian Army Remount.

As I will relate in due course, Ray could ride like the very devil.

In days gone by horse breakers would travel around the large runs breaking in a number of horses, known collectively as colts, usually around twenty or so in a run, depending on the number of camps and so on. Most breakers could turn out around five to seven finished colts a week, ridden outside, shod on all four feet, a going concern more or less. Ray regularly finished eighteen colts a week. The old blokes (Dad and Uncle John) said that he mainly just choked them down and got a saddle on them, got on their back and let them rip, come what may. I daresay the poor old Indian army troopers cursed Uncle Ray for his broke-in horses.

Balance Rider – Ray was a renowned balance rider and a born showman. His party trick was to have an offsider come over once he had gotten on a buckjumper and place a two-bob piece between each of his boots and the stirrup irons. He would then double the whip under the horse and ride it to a standstill. There were the coins still in place.

The Killer and the Copper

Ray and Biddy had the Pub in Camooweal for probably forty years. Also, over time, Ray acquired the lease to the Camooweal town common. Originally a droving town with a clearing dip this was a fairly substantial common capable of running around 1000 head. Surrounded by Rocklands, a large company-held property, any killers taken were usually not Ray's.

Unfortunately, one day Ray was sprung cutting up a beast that wasn't his, and the police started proceedings. The story goes that the evidence, being the head of the beast complete with earmarks and the branded hide, were kept in an open-topped forty-four gallon drum full of brine in the locked police compound, awaiting the return of the district court circuit. Every day the Sergeant could be seen giving the brine a good old stir with a big stick.

Unbeknownst to the long arm of the law, Ray, being a stalwart member of the community, had a spare key to the compound and had in the meantime dispatched a beast of his own to the cold room and substituted the head and branded hide. Imagine the poor old Sergeant's chagrin when discovering the fraud.

1080 baiting (photo credit Athol Foster)

Loading up

Jim Hammond's Camp at Running creek on Wollogorang

A Plethora of Carringtons: Douglas Bunda Campbell, Graeme Carrington, Alex Carrington, Russell Carrington, Henry Clarke, Steve Carrington, John Carrington, Len Carrington
(Photo credit: Henry Clarke)

Aboriginal bird trap (photo credit John Cameron)

Aboriginal painting at the Grotto Riversleigh

Alex Carrington, John Carrington and Bill Foster.

Caldwellvale Truck

George Watson: Legend

Gerald Aplin: a good man.

Grave of Dolly Booth at the Brook Hotel

Grandfather Ted Carrington with his wagon

Grave at Turnoff Lagoon

Gregory Hotel 1908

Gregory River racehorse by Red James out of Miss Planet

Grave of Native Mounted Policeman Calvert Hills

Horse Plant coming up to the camp at Kamarga

John Clarke in Canardly

John Marshall in Hot Pursuit.

The Furlong Post

Earlier on, country racing was carried out by paddocking on grass all the racehorses that were nominated for a meeting, in a secure paddock away from the racecourse, along with horse feed and TLC. Then, for a week before the race meeting, the horses could be fed good feed and trained properly at the track. Time trials of single horses over shortened distances were all the go as no doubt they are today. Ray was the local SP Bookie.

Robey was a local manager who had good horses and participated keenly in the action. Ray went out to the track in the dead of night and dug out the furlong post that was generally reckoned to be the one to start your time measurement at and replanted it a good bit closer to the finishing post. The next morning poor Robey sent his horse around for a time trial and couldn't believe his eyes when the horse produced a blistering run that would give Phar Lap a fright. It was time to regroup and gather as much coin as possible in order to clean up at the races and mums the word. So the next night out goes Ray to reinstate the post to its correct position. The SP Bookie won again I daresay.

Memories of Great Uncle Len

My Uncle Len Carrington was a wonderful bushman, and a very accomplished station manager and drover. Born in 1910, he had started out at Planet as part of the workforce, driving a horse team and running the packhorse mail between Camooweal and Burketown. He had a wealth of stories about his very interesting life. I am very proud to say that he passed on to me his brand AC9 which had been passed to him by his mother Annie Carrington. I still have the original branding iron. In the Old Planet Downs horse book there is a section that details the draft horses branded there with AC9. He told me a couple of stories about things that happened in the Boulia, Birdsville districts.

Dry Stage: It was in the 30's or 40's and a drover named Jack Clark was heading to Adelaide with around 500 bullocks. They had just about completed a ninety-mile dry stage when one of those big dust storms blew up behind them. All it did was send the dust cloud onto the bullocks. They were unable to stop the bullocks that turned around and most died back along the dry stage as they tried to complete it for the second time.

Coorabulka: Len was managing Coorabulka in the forties through a shocking drought. It got drier and drier. The cattle and horses were destocked and all they had left were some mules that they used to pull the scoop to take the sand away that was bearing down on the homestead but the mules died. They built a wall out of corrugated iron to hold the sand back and eventually went up three levels but the sand kept coming. The sand built up against the house and went into the ceiling which collapsed. The homestead was then abandoned.

Uncle Len was the Stanbroke Pastoral Company's first Pastoral Inspector, and amongst his other accomplishments he bred and sold three bulls when he managed Waverly Station for Stanbroke that went for a record price back in the seventies. I believe one of the bulls, Waverly Noel de Manso, fetched $74,000 with the three bulls totalling some $115,000

Shakey the Pilot

I had a pretty wild ride once on a flight from Mount Isa to Gregory in a light aircraft. The passengers were Dennis Bauer and I, Paul Langridge who was a ringer at Planet and Wray Finlay who was an old drover bloke and local identity. The pilot at the controls was known as Shakey. Anyway the aircraft was a Cessna 210 which had retractable undercarriage and no wing struts. It was straight after the Mount Isa rodeo. Unfortunately there had been big rain that had closed all the roads and blocked us from travelling by vehicle, so it was a case of taking the top road home.

Wray and I were sitting in the second row of seats behind Dennis and the Pilot with Paul, who was behind us in the third row of seats, surrounded by a bag of spuds. Wray was a very nervous flier as I remember and he was concerned about how much the wings moved, the aircraft being a 210 with no wing struts. Then, when Shakey lit up a smoke I thought he would have a fit.

Anyway there were a couple of airstrips over at the Gregory station and the main one out towards McAdams Creek but it turned out that they were wet and out of action as they were boggy, so Shakey decided we would land in front of the pub on the road towards the south between the pub and the old Police Station.

Shakey lined her up and down we went, all eyeing the strip with trepidation. As he started to tell the flight service crowd that he wouldn't be able to land some other clown got on the radio and said, 'You can do it Shakey'. So we continued our approach and landed once, twice, three times a bit too far down the selected landing strip. So there we were still continuing past the pub at a great rate of knots heading towards the grid. Shakey is on the brakes something fierce as Wray and I peer out each window watching smoke coming from each of the brakes discs.

Being a retractable undercarriage aircraft it had pretty small wheels and didn't they bump and shudder going across that grid! We staggered to a stop on the other side of the grid and after Shakey shut her down we dismounted. That was it for Wray, he was off for the pub!

The rest of us gave Shakey a hand to turn the thing around and also proceeded to the pub as well after the aircraft had taxied back over the grid and back to the pub. I reckon Wray had downed about three straight scotches by the time we caught up to him!

Malcom Hussein

Malcom Hussein was a legendary Afghan hermit who lived along the remote western Gulf coast of Queensland for many years. In the dry season Malcolm lived right on the Coast effectively as a beachcomber. In the wet season he moved back to the escarpment country and lived in a few caves throughout the hills. I know that he was friends with a friend of mine who has a property in the area.

In return for services rendered Bill was at a loss how to compensate Malcolm and finally decided on a small motorbike. Bill said that Malcolm would ride it 'til it ran out of petrol and then pushed it everywhere.

Dad and a party of his friends usually went fishing in this area once a year. Occasionally they would see him away out on the flats spearing fish, completely naked. They would leave him small gifts of .22 bullets and flour, sugar and tea. In later years my friend Ron and I found his hut on the coast and then later again, as a helicopter pilot I discovered a couple of the caves he had used. A clever setup he had in one of the caves was a stick driven into a small seep of water so that the droplet would run down the stick into a flour drum thus ensuring a full drum of water over time.

Fire Fight

I remember fighting a fire one night when I worked at Gregory Downs driving the grader. I was out on Augustus Downs just through the boundary, grading a break over very heavy black soil just off the fire front. The grader was the old 21F Cat that had come from Planet Downs and the pilot motor had been removed by then so the only way to start the grader was to tow it.

Unfortunately, this machine was an old wrist breaking mechanical-control-box model and it chose this moment to break a blade-lift lever control rod. As I could not get the blade out of the ground I had no choice but to shut the machine down.

Now I knew that our really old original grader from before the war was still at Planet, resting in the salvage yard so, with my offsider who was bringing the Toyota along behind, we drove to Planet (approx. twenty-five miles) and pulled the front off the control box and got a control rod out, went back to the other machine and pulled the front of the control box off, put the second hand control rod in, then pulled the cups off the blade arms, jacked the grader off the arms and then jacked and chained the blade up. All this time the fire was creeping closer. We then had to tow the grader backwards far enough to be able to tow start it going forwards so as not to hurt the engine. Then it was straight back onto the fire again. I reckon I was definitely worth more money.

Time moves on.

Eventually the family partnership failed as Dad and Uncle John grew apart and the property was sold. I am sure that for my cousins as well as my siblings this left a hole in our hearts you could drive a Mack truck through. We, the children of both families spend a lot of time reminiscing and reliving old musters and events. I can't blame our fathers for their decision but wish that they had only realised that we children were their greatest asset. Our lives still seem to revolve around the Gulf and working cattle has always been our passion.

Malcolm Hussein's Cave

Malcolm Hussein's beach hut

Me, David O'Keefe and John Clarke at my 21st

Monument for Sam and Opal Ah Bow at Louie Creek

Old car wreck and house stumps Touchstone homestead

The Boss John Clarke

The Grave of my fathers twin William and my cousin Lorena Jay at Planet Downs

The Cross on the Hill at Lawn Hill

The Landsborough Explorers Tree Camp 6 Carringtons Camp

The rainbow serpent at Lillydale Spring

Tommy Doolan, a wonderful old gentleman, milking the cow at Gregory Downs (photo credit Nev Barnes)

The second Planet Grader SN 21F216

Truck door at Carringtons Camp Planet Downs Social Club

Uncle John Carrington, Watchmaker, with the bullocks.

Washing up duty at Kamarga. Ron Condron, Self,

Uncle John and Victor Jacob butchering a pig.

Well at Ethel Glen Hotel

Helicopter Days

The Mystery of Flight

I learnt to fly in a conservative fashion, as I would save up for a year and then spend it on flight training over the Wet Season. Consequently, it took me a while.

First I gained a Restricted Fixed Wing Licence. This was in, I think, 1982. Training was in a Piper Cherokee 140 at Proserpine Airfield. Next, in 1983 came the Unrestricted Private Fixed Wing again at Proserpine Airfield but I graduated to a Cessna 172. In 1983 I also did a Constant Speed Propeller Endorsement as well as my Retractable Undercarriage and Tail Wheel Endorsement.

Then, in the 1984 Wet Season I switched to helicopters, and at Melbourne's Morrabin Airport did a Helicopter Private Licence Conversion, flying Hughes 300's, and also a Low Level Endorsement.

At this stage I had around seventy hours in fixed wing aircraft, I remember going solo in helicopters at around nine hours and I had a Private Helicopter Licence at forty-one hours. Over the next two years I flew around 450 hours mustering on a private basis at a large cattle station who owned their own machine. There were two incidents of note during this time.

On one occasion I got into a 'settling with power' state (when a chopper settles into its own downwash) at around fifty to sixty feet AGL. I gave myself a pretty good fright before I was able to effect a recovery.

The second incident was effectively a partial engine failure; I was yarding up feral cattle at a portable stockyard and suffered a severe loss of power at about 40 ft AGL. I was able to land the machine onto the ground undamaged with the happy result that the cattle still yarded up ok. The engine was still running when the dust had settled but it would only develop about 800 RPM out of the desired 3200 RPM. I think of these as my lucky years, as the Hughes 300 is a touchy mistress and needed a lot more care than I was able to give it.

I was running the stock camp at this property as well, so all my time was taken up and I did not know anything about caring for the helicopter beyond what was in the flight manual. I could see how to grease it plain enough but knew nothing about dismantling and greasing the short shaft or all of the other things required to operate a maintenance intensive helicopter at a remote location. There were no telephones or access to engineers to ask for advice and contact with other pilots was limited.

As I had by then more than the required 400 hours Pilot in Command time, I was eligible to sit for a Commercial Exam. I attended a theory school first of all and passed the required seven subjects.

Then, at Maroochydore Airport, I did about ten hours refresher training and a Bell 47 Type Endorsement and passed my Commercial Helicopter Flight Test. I also completed a Mustering Endorsement at this stage.

I then started working for a commercial operation in Mount Isa flying Bell 47s. At this operation I was taught how to care for my machine properly and learned the value of paint and polish. These machines were essentially pretty worn out but were extremely well polished. It was amazing how that won over client confidence.

Fossils and Caves

At Riversleigh Station and known to the local population for many years, there is a very large boulder that has tumbled down to just beside the main road. It is known as Fossil Rock because when looking around it you could find lots of small fossils embedded in the rock. Nowadays the Palaeontologists call this D Site and it is the start of a large area of ground known as the Riversleigh Fossil Fields.

With my Helicopter work I assisted a lot with the early work of discovering the extent of the fields and identifying suitable areas to investigate further. On one particular day Henk Godphelt and Sue Hand were on board and I had spotted the entrance to a large cave. Upon investigation this entrance allowed the light to penetrate well back into the cave. Looking about there were quite a few cone shaped piles of loose rocks, stones and soil around the floor of the cavern. I assumed them correctly to be of Aboriginal significance and could also see another arm of the cave disappearing into the depths. This tunnel had a worrisome looking hanging ceiling. We followed this back quite a distance and eventually it broke open into a very large chamber. They found an extinct bat species in this chamber at a later date.

So we flew on, continuing our exploratory work in a very excited state and you would not believe it but I spotted another cave. Now the entrance to this cave went nearly straight down; it being only a few degrees elevated from horizontal. A tree had recently fallen into the entrance and the view below was obscured by branches full of dead leaves. Henk decided to investigate. As far as we could see their looked to be an initial vertical drop from the surface of about five feet and then a gravel-strewn rock slope of perhaps forty-five degrees.

This was about where the dead tree was lodged and we could see some large tree roots which looked like they would be good to assist in climbing down. So Henk lowered himself down to the slope and started shimmying on his backside down towards the tree roots. Next thing he lost his traction on the loose gravel and slid wildly down the slope, crashed through the dead leaves and disappeared into the black void. I am not sure whether he was cleaning his trousers or just regaining his composure but it sure took Henk a while to answer our calls. I was starting to think about leaving Sue there with our Water and Emergency Rations and flying back to camp to gather help and equipment. But all was well, and Henk was able to discover and explore another chamber that he told us was filled with helictites, an extremely rare and beautiful stalagmite type growth.

Further to this tale I was staying at the time with my friend Mick at Riversleigh Station. Mick wanted to see the caves as did his head stockman who happened to have a broken leg. Mick is a pretty wild bloke with a heart of gold and suitably armed with his six-gun and accompanied by Thump-along-Cassidy the head stockman, we proceeded down the tunnel with the hanging ceiling. In my mind's eye I could well imagine a bat fluttering into Mick's face, him letting loose with the six-gun and the ceiling descending upon us all.

I was very relieved when we had seen all there was to see and departed for home. Later whilst doing mustering work for Mick he arranged for me to take a National Parks ranger to the site of the first cave to check it out. This fellow told me that the piles of rock were certainly put there by Aboriginal people as they were full of bone fragments and artefacts. He said that he had left them untouched as they would have to be correctly mapped if it was decided to investigate them. About fifteen years later I was flying past and stopped to have a look. I was very disappointed to see that the stone piles were broken down and picked over, a tragedy indeed.

A Lost Soul

Like many other mustering pilots I was called on from time to time to search for someone who was lost, sometimes with a good result, sometimes not so good.

Once I had to go to Floraville Station to help search for a little three-year-old girl who was missing. This was the daughter of my old friends, the Camp family. She had been missing for around five hours by the time I got there, and my good friend and fellow pilot Craig had already arrived and commenced the search.

Now the Camp family were very old school with their stockwork and did not use helicopters to muster, consequently their children had never seen or had much to do with helicopters.

Their homestead was not far from the Leichardt River. There was a large and deep waterhole with a precarious steep bank down to the water. A saltwater crocodile had also been sighted there recently.

The weather and flying conditions were atrocious with a cyclone bearing down hard on Burketown which is around sixty kilometres away, there was also very low cloud with around a one-hundred foot ceiling, vicious gusts and driving rain squalls, and I was told that the station measured eight inches of rain that day.

So Craig and I searched most of the day in ever widening circles and things were looking grim, the weather conditions had eased as the day went on and the cyclone had gone past.

Meanwhile, the aunty of the little girl was searching down around the causeway about three kilometres away from the homestead and she thought she heard a cry when the helicopters were elsewhere. It was a good result with her finding the little girl cowering behind a conkleberry bush down below the causeway on the saltwater side. It turned out that the little girl was terrified of the choppers and we had inadvertently been driving her further and further away as we searched.

An incident of note is that because it was so cold and wet I was busting for a leak. I landed in the muddy ground and stood on the skid so as not to bring mud back into the chopper. This caused that skid to drive into the mud a bit and when I took off the chopper became subject to Dynamic Rollover. It was only good luck that saved me, it happened so fast there is no way I was able to bottom the collective in time but fortunately the skid broke free and all was well.

A few years later I got an early morning call from Thorntonia Station. One of their stockmen was missing overnight so I went over and picked up Lloyd the boss and away we went to where the man was last seen. This fellow was riding a motorbike, and following his tracks through the hills and valleys we could see that he had really taken a wrong heading and was making in the wrong direction very fast.

After a while we spotted some smoke up ahead and flew straight to it. It was obviously lit by the stockman as it was only a fresh fire but try as we might, flying round and round that fire, we couldn't see him. Then I remembered what had happened at Floraville so I landed on the good flat and gave Lloyd my hand-held radio. I then flew away and pretty soon Lloyd was calling up saying 'Come back, he is here.'

Now this bloke just about qualified for the dumbest bloke in Australia. Whenever the helicopter had got close to him while we searched he would rush to the top of this little hill that was covered in lancewood scrub and wave his heart out. I still remember how he looked, though, with no shirt and his chest and mouth all covered in dried foam. I left Lloyd there and flew him back to the station, and then I returned and picked up Lloyd. We backtracked him and found the bike where it had stopped having run out of fuel. Lloyd switched the tank onto reserve and rode it home!

The Hitman

I had arranged with my friend Johnny Craigie to walk his horse plant up on to the Calvert River in the north western part of Wollogorang Station. The problem was that every beast that we were going to find up there would be a cleanskin and it was too far to walk coachers up from the station and then back again. The original cattle would never have made it as also it was really bad sandy country. My plan was to put a little mob of fresh cattle together and make coachers out of them. I knew I could do this without losing control of the cattle if I had a good understanding with the stockmen of how we operated.

Chopper sunset

R22 at sunset

Claytons on the job (photo credit Lynda Lucht)

Moving stock out of the floods (photo credit Lynda Lucht)

Trevor James: one of the best

Tipperary Station NT

Chopper over water (photo credit Scotty Bridle)

Chopper and station.

I went to Johnny's camp and we all had a real good yarn about what to do. The only radio contact I had was with Johnny's catcher. I don't really remember how many men he had there but there wouldn't have been any more than around four or five men and young Lyman, his fourteen-year-old son (he became a great bull-rider later on).

I instructed the men that they were not to even chase a beast or throw anything but to just ride along in sight of the cattle and to just be there so that the cattle got used to them. Then, as we went along and things came to hand a little better, Johnny would let the men know when to start doing a bit of handling of the mob, all fresh cleanskins remember.

So I flew off and pretty soon put together about forty cows. I spent around two hours educating them, blocking up and starting off, going down the flat and back again. After a couple of hours of this I was pretty happy with how things were going and got Johnny to just sort of park up near to the mob and drive around slowly without pressuring anything, then after a while start to very carefully poke them about. When he could just sort of hold them a bit I quickly slipped away and got fuel, returning just in time to sort out a minor revolution with the mob and bring them to hand again. Then I got Johnny to bring his men up and the fun started. These poor blokes must have been beside themselves with excitement because they just sort of charged the cattle and in no time our entire mob was busted up and scattered and going everywhere. After a few minutes of trying to put them back together I gave up in disgust and flew back to the camp.

Over a cup of tea I had a good yarn with the blokes pointing out how we just couldn't do this in the old style where you would throw a couple of head and then knock them together. Then you would bash a few cows around until you had a bit of a mob and they would be your coachers and you would go from there.

There was too much at stake here and we stood to do pretty well as there were a lot of cattle in the area. The other contractors all relied heavily on portable yards and it was impossible to get a truck up there due to the heavy sand. Johnny had a tactical advantage as he was a really good cattleman and was able to operate in bad country with a minimum of equipment.

Anyway, I jokingly said to the blokes 'The next time I come up here I am going to bring a hitman and the first fellow that steps out of line, we'll take him out'. I flew off to the station to other tasks and to give the cattle there time to settle down for a couple of days.

As luck would have it there was a group of big game hunters camped at the roadhouse. They were there capitalizing on the explosion in the pig population due to the recently complete destocking shootout on the other side of the border. I believe the DPI destroyed around six thousand head so there was plenty of tucker for pigs at any rate. They were there in thousands, mobs of a hundred or more were easily found.

One of the ways that I was able to make some money out of it was to fly along and spot the pigs. When I found a good mob I would call the catchers over from travelling close at hand and drive the pigs at them then get out of the road and watch the carnage, assist in the cleanup and so on. I got to be pretty good mates with these blokes and seized the opportunity to take one up with me to Craigie's muster.

Now this hunter was a large bearded man dressed in camouflage gear all the time. He used some sort of semi-auto rifle and had strapped across his chest on the left side the meanest looking pistol and holster I had ever seen. It was a large stainless steel 44 magnum pistol and even had a red dot sight on it.

He was very reluctant to wear the pistol over to the camp but I convinced him to leave it on and we went and had a cup of tea with Johnny. Now Johnny's men were all aboriginal blokes from Borroloola way and I reckon I can still see them peering around the end of the big wind break staring at the pistol and wearer with disbelieving eyes.

Anyway, the long and the short of it is that things went very well with a good little mob of about fifty head put together, in hand and travelling well.

The pseudo-hitman had a wonderful day and didn't get to shoot anything. He signed the guestbook as Hitman and is probably still telling the story in the big game hunter parts of the world.

Johnny put the coachers in his yard which was constructed of K wire with hessian clipped on it wrapped around a stand of gum trees. It's another story but we continued mustering down the coast to the border then south to the station and delivered 1,600 head of cleanskin cattle all broken in and in hand at the house yards.

This was one of the most significant musters that I have ever been involved with. It enabled me to demonstrate my thoughts on how to handle feral cattle quietly and successfully. Thanks to Johnny Craigie for allowing me the time to develop this. Without his overriding good stock sense and faith in me it may never have happened.

A Friend in Need.

When I first started flying at Lawn Hill station about 1984 the manager got a radio call from the neighbour Kerry McGinnis at

Bowthorn station. She was at the homestead by herself as David and Judith, her brother and sister, were away mustering and she was in urgent need of medical help.

I was dispatched to pick her up and take her to Doomadgee Airport to meet the RFDS aircraft. I can still see the pain on her face when I went into the house to get her. She asked me to open the medical chest to give her some morphine as the pain was really bad but I couldn't find the key so had to abandon the idea.

I got her into the helicopter and headed for Doomadgee. It was dark when I landed and we got her into the RFDS aircraft and away. Apparently some sort of growth inside her had burst and was bleeding.

Rissole Ron

When I first started working at Lawn Hill I was flying the Hughes 300 and also the Cessna 206. The head stockman was a real tough old character whose name was Ron Maher but he was known as Wingy because he only had one arm. His leg got hurt pretty badly not long after I got there and I took on the stock camp as well. Wingy was away mending for a long time and eventually came back as the cook. Now that I have some disability myself I can see how hard it must have been for him. Anyway we used to joke about how he might have made rissoles, the old under the armpit trick was our favourite assumption.

One Hell of a Fright

One of the biggest frights that I ever experienced was in a helicopter.

I was heading from Brunette Downs back to Katherine at around 1000 feet above ground level. The country below me had just changed from open black soil plain to a low turpentine scrub. All of a sudden I encountered an extremely severe updraft. I reduced my airspeed to 'turbulence penetration' speed and lowered the collective until I was in an established autorotation with the needles split. However, the helicopter kept ascending at a frightening rate with the vertical speed indicator showing over 2 000 feet per minute. Once the altimeter showed us going past 9,500 feet I didn't look at that gauge anymore.

I put the machine into a ninety degree angle of bank turn and after a few minutes the machine started to descend. It ended with the machine coming down quite smoothly and I was able to land eventually. I walked around for a while and then continued with my flight. I have Parkinson's disease now and I reckon that's when the shaking started.

Flora

I have always taken a keen interest in the flora species that grow on properties where I worked. There is a clump of timber on Lawn Hill that had me beat for a long time but it turned out to be fairly common, it was that just I had never seen it before and that is boree. Another odd one is the lignum and belailey on Magoura

Station within sight of the Gulf. It usually grows on watersheds that drain inland.

Check Rides

As the Chief Pilot for North Australian Helicopters, one of my roles was to check out new pilots. I was giving Steve a check ride at Mt. Isa in a Robinson R22 and there was a storm brewing just to the north. I could see we probably should start heading in, but Steve really needed a checkout and we all had to depart first thing in the morning. We had just carried out a normal approach and were sitting on the ground while I gave him a quick debrief. I noticed a gust of wind and said to Steve 'Let's just stay here for a bit'. A wise move indeed as the wind increased to sixty knots (108 kilometres per hour) measured on our airspeed indicator.

The wind then moved around and was coming at us from the side. Sheets of tin were getting plucked from buildings, and debris from around the hangars was sailing towards and around us. I had assumed command from Steve and kept the revs at flight RPM with the disc tilted into wind. Steve would call out every now and then as sheets of roofing iron sailed closely by, 'that one just missed the tail rotor' or similar. Then the wind just seemed to get stronger and started to push the helicopter sideways across the tarmac. Fortunately this decreased after a while and I was able to execute a quick taxi and shutdown.

Searching

One of the first searches I was involved in using helicopters was when I was running the stock camp at Lawn Hill in 1984. I had my camp set up near the western end of the 'Blue Hole' and my cook was Danny Ned, an old aboriginal fellow. I got up early, as you do, and there was no sign of Danny.

Now I had noticed that his mood had changed lately and strangely his skin colour had started getting really black, I had seen him also nearly white. I assumed he had walked to Doomadgee, which was about fifty kilometres away, and alerted my boss.

We started searching all the paddocks towards Doomadgee and eventually the army, who had joined the search, found him about one hundred kilometres away, in the completely opposite direction, hiding from the choppers up in a tree. The army observer had spotted the tree shaking and sure enough there was Danny.

The lesson that I learned was that people may not always be of sound mind and they can do completely the opposite of what you think they might do. When organising a search it is good to sit back with an overview and consider this now and then. In later years I was asked to write a section in the AA Company Station Operations Manual about searches and I made this point.

Rats

I was just thinking about the rat plagues that happen from time to time. I remember seeing on the Barkly Tableland this enormous network of little pads about the size of a motorbike track. I thought to myself there's no way that could be from motorbikes as they would have to be going all year to make that many tracks so I had a closer look. The tracks were thousands of rat pads.

The next thing I noticed was the cats. I flew around this turkeys nest enclosure and thirty-three cats went shooting out across the flat. Then I remembered the old fellows telling me about the letter wing kites that follow the rats and sure enough in all the corkwood and whitewood trees were all these Letter Wing Kites. They are a little white hawk about three-quarters the size of a meat hawk. They are very noisy and all around the foot of the trees and under the nests were thousands of rat skeletons.

An Unsavoury Event

I remember just south of Balfe's Creek, two brothers owned a property in a partnership and one poor fellow had died. Everything that they owned had to be all sold up to sort out the estate. The only thing was that their cattle were lifetime trap and lane trained and it was still pretty wet around the paddocks.

The surviving brother was pretty stressed out about the muster and insisted on being in the machine all of the time. He got airsick within minutes of flight and proceeded to vomit for the next three hours. He would not even attempt to put his head outside after a while and just sat there letting this green foam bubble out of his mouth, flow around the back of his head and spatter all over the inside of the canopy of the Bell 47. I landed to shut down at the gate and he crawled to a tree and there he stayed.

A Close Call

I was flying once at Lawn Hill and had taken the boss up for a look at a fire. I came in to land, to drop him off at his vehicle and the only place that I could put down was just past his car down the fence a bit. We had just landed and I was tightening the control locks when this face appeared, looking in at me from the passenger side. He disappeared towards the back of the chopper and an instant later was at my side of the machine.

It turned out that he was an old bloke who I knew from years ago and he was very keen to catch up with me. I got the manager to take him forward until I shut the machine down. It gave me such fright thinking about how close he must have been to the tail rotor that I couldn't talk properly for a fair while after.

Once I was asked to take a girl in to Mount Isa who fallen off a horse and hurt her neck. We made a neck brace from a towel and set off. The air was pretty turbulent over the hills going into town and I did not realise that she was close to vomiting. When I touched down to land I had habitually faced the machine in towards the hangar. Virtually as soon as I was on the ground this poor girl leapt out of the machine and went straight towards the back so that no one would see her vomiting. As soon as I could make the machine safe I also went down the back ducking underneath the tail rotor and easing her away from it.

Loose Horses

One of the things that I could do was catch horses that were loose with the saddle. Horses that had thrown their riders or fallen in a hole, also ones that had not stood when the rider made a hasty dismount to throw a beast. I had a real knack at doing it. I would land if front of them and catch the horse, usually tie him up and hobble him and then fetch the rider.

Legend

A guy I had the privilege of working with was Phillip Kim. Known as Kim he was an unreal pilot. I believe he was trained to fly by the US Army in a special unit of Koreans to fight in Vietnam. I was told he completed four full tours in Vietnam. He used to do some radical stuff and could keep a Hughes 300 going like you wouldn't believe.

Once, at Riversleigh Station, he was mustering down the Gregory towards the homestead and his passenger Mick, another terrific bloke, could hear a chattering sound every time that Kim pulled power. He poked back to the house and they found that the strut that supports the vital H frame part of the drive was broken. Mick found a piece of water pipe and brazed some flat bar into it and away they went, good as gold.

Apparently the engineer didn't think it was such a cool idea.

Serpent

I was mustering the Rankin area at Riversleigh, driving a mob along the river bank when I saw this huge snake deep in the water. I dived down to get a closer look and just before the rotor wash hit the water and ruffled it up I could see it was as thick as my thigh.

I couldn't see into the water anymore as the surface got too disturbed and flew on for around fifty meters so that the water could settle down. I spun around and there was the snake reared up about three feet above the water looking at me. It dropped back into the water and was gone

The Worst Smells

I reckon just about the worst smells that I know of come from helicopters. When the clip holding the cowling around the cylinder breaks and the cowling drops onto the oil return line and chews a hole in it and then the oil drips onto the exhaust, what a stink. When the lower bearing that supports the drive starts to fail and the grease and the dust cover melts it smells a bit ordinary. When the machine throws the drive belts off and they start chewing themselves up the smell is horrible.

An Awful Thing

When you are flying in the bush you sometimes see some bad things. I was flying the manager around Beames Brook after a flood had gone down and we went to have a look at this turkey's nest. This nest used to leak and they had done a really good job of fixing it by lining it with proper polythene sheeting and then erecting a good netting fence to keep the wallabies and pigs out. Unfortunately the flood waters had gone right over the turkey's nest and the twelve plant horses had come swimming along and grounded on top of the nest. When we flew up all twelve horses were drowned and floating in the turkey nest. They had obviously gone in for a drink and were unable to get any traction on the hard slippery plastic sheeting and had drowned.

Skeleton

A mate of mine showed me a photo that he took while mustering down the Cooper. He had landed on this sand hill and there right beside the skid was the hand of a human skeleton exposed by the blowing sand. He took the photo but when he touched the bones they just turned to dust. Apparently the ancient custom of the local Aborigines was to bury their dead in the sand hills.

John White

A fellow I mustered for quite a bit was John White from Hanging Rock and St. Ann's Stations on the Belyando River. Old John really loved his dogs; I have never seen anything like how well those dogs were treated. The kennels were true five-star accommodations. In each kennel was a large comfortable day yard with a drum or a tree for shade, as well as the main individual kennel – a little house made of Besser block with a removable roof and a water dish that was formed from concrete.

Over the top of the row of ten kennels was two roofs, one of corrugated iron, and the other of spinifex. One stockman's job in the morning was to go around and collect all the dog droppings and put them on a big permanently smouldering pile. The smell was unreal. He would drive off to work usually with the ringers in the back of his truck and all the dogs in the front. I quite liked John but he was an odd sort of character.

The old Brumby Yard

I was mustering at Neumayer Valley station, the boss was a really nice bloke called Bill Abdy. It turned out that both Bill and I were reading a book called Beyond the Big Run written by Charlie Shultz about his life at Neumayer Valley and later on at Humbert River station. One of the stories about Neumayer Valley told of running brumbies off the big waterhole. Now this waterhole is about twenty miles long and on the eastern side there is a sort of a low ironstone escarpment about twenty feet high. There were only about two good places along the whole length of the waterhole where horses could easily come down to the water for a drink. Well we looked carefully where the old pads were and sure enough there was the old brumby yard. So we landed and had a look about and there, nailed onto a gidgee tree was a piece of tin with the details of Charlie's brother who had died there while running brumbies into the yard.

Winter Time Mustering in the Channel Country

Once at Tanbar Station it was a really cold morning, just for a change, showing minus two on the outside air temperature gauge. We were putting these bullocks together on a big waterhole called Hookamutta; about mid-morning it had got up to about two degrees and the boys had them blocked up on the hole.

Those old channel country bullocks just turned in and swam the waterhole and the boys had to swim with them and meet them on the other bank. They did a great job of blocking them up and took turns drying out and warming up around a big fire they started.

One other very cold morning George Scott was up with me and he got so cold he was just shaking all the time. His teeth were chattering so much that he couldn't stop it; he was also going a bit blue. I put him down and he lit a fire, I used to come back every hour or so and see how he was. 'No worries mate, I'll be right, you keep going.'

There is this bindi-eye that grows in the channel country they call bogan flea, it is terrible. It is so tiny that you can hardly see it and if your blanket goes off your swag cover and gets some on it you just about had to throw it away. I had a set of long johns that I wore for the cold but by around ten o'clock they got too hot to wear, so I used to find a big smooth log I could get up on to take them off because of the bindies.

Bloody Cold in the Central Highlands

In 1987 I was mustering at Conway Station near Mount Coolon and three mornings in a row it was minus-five. I still managed to get the Bell 47 started but if you missed that first kick you were finished. At Elgin Downs the cook used to start the lighting plant at five o'clock in the morning. We had this asbestos blanket that we wrapped around the engine and gearbox every night and also this little fan heater on a long lead that was plugged into the power and was left positioned pointing up at the sump so that by daylight the engine was warm enough to start. The same year I was mustering Fort Cooper not far from Nebo and we could see snow on Mount Nebo.

I did a lot of work on this place called Conway near Mount Coolon in 1986 and 1987. It was owned by three cane farmer brothers and when the price of cattle went through the floor in the late 1970s they just put it on hold and did very little mustering for ten years.

Then along came the BTEC program. They were about seventy per cent cleaned up when I knew them. That country grew tremendous horns on the brahman cross cattle. The contractor who was there had about ten sets around his walls and one set was over six feet long measured along the horns. I got a set that was over five feet measured along the horns.

The number of dogs there was also unreal. Once I counted sixty-three. There were no jackaroos picking up the evidence here, and you had to watch where you stepped.

A Muster for Sabu

I showed Peter (Sabu) Singh a muster at Wollogorang in 1990 that worked out to be pretty extraordinary. We mustered the Westmoreland valley with three choppers and sent them via the Branch Creek gorge through into Queensland Pocket. This took us all day. I took the tail through the gorge while Steve and Darryl in the Hughes 300s ferried in the ringers and their swags.

They camped on the inside of the gorge lighting fires and firing shots all night to stop the cattle coming back. The next day we mustered Queensland Pocket and took the mob up and over the next range, into the horse paddock at the homestead, and finally into the yard. I believe this muster yielded 1400 cleanskins with 400 grown bulls.

Dalgonaly Muster

I was on a muster once at Dalgonaly Station that yielded a big result. Dalgonaly Station was a growing-out depot staging the young male cattle between the breeding stations and the fattening properties or alternatively the feedlots. The muster took place in Scrubby Paddock before they split it into two paddocks. The manager, Gavin Hoad, knew that there were a lot of bullocks getting missed there and as he had an intake of 2800 steers come in from Headingly Station he put them into Scrubby.

They were in Scrubby about a month and then we mustered them. There was one stock camp and mine was the only chopper. I flew ten point six hours altogether, mustering into coachers on the Maidenhand Bore side of the paddock. I also worked another big mob past the Sedan Dip and down the channels towards Cockatoo Yard.

We ended up putting about 3000 into the yard and another 2000 in the Cooler which we let into the holding paddock and they worked them in a couple of days' time. There ended up being 5300 all together with 647 bullocks over ten years old and another 1800 being seven years and older. I remember one sixteen-year-old bullock that was branded 7TT Milungera from when Australian Estates owned all those places. It was a terrific result.

Shark

On Morestone station just near Elbow Hole on the O'Shannesey River there is an aboriginal painting of a shark. Obviously from a time long gone by as the river does not even run there anymore. I guess it is probably similar to Shark Hole on the Stirling River above Nelson Springs on Limbunya Station where there are sharks swimming around right now. The first time I saw them I thought that they were the biggest Catfish I've ever seen but they were sharks all right, 142 nm (255kms) from the nearest saltwater and above the Ord River Dam which was completed in 1972.

Riversleigh

I lived at Riversleigh Station for a few years and I was able to find the old wagon road that goes from Riversleigh to Camooweal over some very bad stony country. I could see where the old teamsters had stacked the stones on the side of the road by hand and also where they had dug out dirt and carted it on the wagons to cover the bad rock in places.

Bird Strikes and Books

I mustered a particular holding paddock at Lawn Hill quite often and was often charged by a pair of wedge tailed eagles attempting to intimidate me. I was obviously getting too close to their nest but I had to go there all the same. They did a fairly good job at intimidating me I can tell you.

I have had a few bird strikes over the years. Usually it was the kite hawks but a wedge tail I hit once as he charged me. The helicopter blades did not strike its body but severed one wing completely off. The eagle was still walking around and as my leg was bad at that stage I had to get another pilot to come over and dispatch him.

A real bad habit that I and a few other pilots had was to read a book while we were flying along. A really good pilot who owned a large local company showed me a book that he had torn in half when the H frame on his Hughes 300 broke and he had lost his drive. He carried out a successful autorotation but he maintains he does not remember tearing that book apart.

I was travelling along in a Robinson R22 once reading my book and I was startled by a very large bird. I think that it was a brolga diving with widespread wings about three feet in front of the helicopter's bubble. How it missed the rotor disc I don't know; I guess it was diving from just above my flight path and I actually felt the tug as this bird hit the skid.

Early day Choppers

I remember the first few pilots I had anything to do with were the ones based at Escott and Maggieville. Those fellows had a ball, and they were like gods in the late seventies. There was a large feral herd on most stations and their way of thinking about how to muster was very different. The country was just coming out of bad years of a huge slump in cattle prices and no serious clean up mustering had been done for years. The brucellosis and tuberculosis eradication campaign came along and cattle were worth something again. The pilots of the day usually weren't stockmen and most had a hard time understanding the finer points of cattle control. It mostly did not matter as their main work was pushing feral cattle into portable yards. But times changed and most cattle were brought to hand and controlled. With most of the work I did, a lot of time was spent sitting on the ground waiting in strategic spots for the coachers to move into position to take the next intake of cattle that I had set up. I got to read a lot of books and to know my flight manual anyway.

It is really great to learn that a lot of pilots are using their machines more thoughtfully these days. The original Bell 47 style of pilot had little chance to use his machine with the more controlled work that we do today because of the mere fact of a lot less noise and impact. Being able to take a weaner back pretty close to a heldup mob without blowing the whole show away is just great. I did about 2500 hours flying in Bell 47's and at that time in the late eighties the herds were becoming a lot more controlled. It used to really frustrate me not being able to work in a lot closer to the cattle in hand. Bell 47's were great earlier on though with the BTEC shooting work and were certainly a lot stronger airframe. I know that I wish the Robinson tail rotor was as strong as a 47's.

Around the Gulf

My family started out in the Gulf and Camooweal districts as teamsters with wagons carting to and from the stations sometimes to the Burketown wharf. It was great as a pilot to review a lot of their old runs and find again some lost wells and camp sites and places they had been.

Bird Traps and Burials

I used to keep an eye out for those aboriginal bird traps. They look a bit like a stone BBQ. The hunters would cover the top with sticks and branches and hide inside with a lure of some sort out on the ground in front of the hide. When a hawk came down and attacked the lure the hunter would race out and kill the hawk. Around the Victoria River I saw one that still had sticks on it in reasonable condition. They are all over the north once you start looking for them.

In that rough and isolated country west of the Queensland border in the Nicholson land claim along the China Wall once I saw an aboriginal burial on this spur of rock sticking out from the side of a cliff probably seventy feet from the ground. It beats me how they got the little bark parcel up there, quite a feat.

I flew over a spring once, roughly on the Northern Territory - Queensland border. It was about thirty kilometres north of the Nicholson, early in the morning and from deep in the spring timber there was a little plume of smoke rising. There were no roads close or sign of people and there was no way I was going to land and walk in. I have heard yarns there are still wild Aboriginals in that country and perhaps there are, I hope so.

The Border

At Border Hole on Highland Plains, there on top of the hill is a huge cairn of stones that marks the border. There is another one on the north side of the Nicholson on Bowthorn and it is known as the Border Gate.

The Central Highlands

At Conway Station once I had to work feral cattle into a small portable yard they had set at the bottom of a gully in big timber which was all chain sawed down and laying there in the wings. Sometimes I would come to the hover over the stumps and my passenger would leap out and shut the gates and sometimes we could have a bloke hiding there that did it.

Once I had yarded two bulls and went away and came back with one more. By the time I got back, which took about twelve minutes one of the bulls had killed the other. By the time I got back again with another mob in around thirty minutes the same bull had killed the last bull that I had yarded. There was a young fellow closing the gate for us and he said that both times that bull just drove his horn into the others neck.

It was amazing at Conway; I had never really seen anything like the economics of that style of operation. The only thing that came close was the DPI BTEC shooting camps. They had been using a Hiller before I turned up in a Bell 47 and they were quite happy to keep me going all day as long as I could yard at least fifteen head.

I was watching this last patch of Brigalow Scrub going down in front of the tractors pulling a chain at Cassiopeia Station and these old bullocks were hanging in there till the last minute. You should have seen them coming out as the timber was crashing down around them.

Maintenance

Occasionally I have found the odd thing left undone after maintenance; some I recall are the alternator base mount bolts left loose, the main rotor pitch link lock nut on the barrel adjustment loose or the magneto mounting/adjusting nuts loose. I have seen an engine overhauled in America by Lycoming fitted with the wrong gasket on the oil filter housing covering up the oil holes. Also a fuel control unit on a Hughes 300 that was fitted incorrectly causing a massive over speed.

Gulf Border Country

I was doing the 'Across the Gulf' muster with Johnny Craigie and they had been doing a bit of fishing off the beach while waiting for me. Craigie came over to me all ashamed and very bashful and he said 'Mate you are not going to believe what we found washed up on the beach, have a look at this'. All the old dark ladies were giggling away over at the camp and they burst out laughing when Craigie held up a ladies' sex toy.

It was really good mustering at Calvert Hills when Alex Chapel had first bought it off Tom Barnes estate and they had to build the herd and stock up. Paul Edmonds managed the property for at least nineteen years. Paul has a wonderful understanding of how to handle that unfenced rough country. Over the years he established a set of musters that brought the entire herd back to the house yards.

Conventional staff are hard to get up there and they operate pretty well only with backpackers. It used to work incredibly well.

The best bull catching operator that I have ever seen in action is John Marshall. His sense of timing and ability to understand and anticipate cattle was remarkable. I recall times where I would run bulls out for John to catch. I saw him once catch and head-rope to trees fifty-one bulls in four hours of helicopter time.

Personal life, my own little tragedy

In 1985 I met a girl while I was working at Lawn Hill Station. She was staying with her aunt and uncle who were old friends of mine; they operated a Cessna Aircraft on local charter operations north of Lawn Hill. This girl had a little six-month-old son with her. Cupid's arrow struck deep for me anyway, and I was sorely smitten. We set up house together and were married in October 1986. I loved her so very much.

I actually don't have all that much education as I wasn't even able to achieve a junior pass and left the world of academia behind not long after my fifteenth birthday. Life ain't easy for a boy named Sue as Mister Cash maintains and I struggled with my identity and place in the scheme of things as I worked back at Planet for my domineering and at times abusive father and uncle. This potpourri of life was a powder keg of emotion and highly volatile.

Time moved on and the property was sold. I had always had an interest in aviation and was working towards a helicopter pilot's licence. I had been training in fixed wing aircraft as I could afford it and had progressed myself from student pilot to restricted and unrestricted levels of fixed wing private pilot licence. As Planet had been sold, I had taken a job at Gregory Downs as a grader operator. The manager of Lawn Hill Station at the time offered me the pilot's job of flying their Hughes 300 helicopter for the 1985 season. I still have my log book from then and find that what they entrusted me with was phenomenal.

I have had a long and not very successful career in aviation, having been the chief pilot of four operations at different times, operations manager of a large outfit of forty-six machines and the HAAMC as well as low level check and training, mustering training and checking, SAR controller and God knows what else. There is no chance that I would let a pilot of my tender experience loose like they did but thanks to Terry McCosker and Aramis Patti Maia I got my start.

So over the following wet season I trained for a Private Helicopter Pilot's Licence in Melbourne. I went solo at nine hours and received my licence at forty-one hours total helicopter time and returned to Lawn Hill. By the time I had logged forty-three hours total helicopter time I was mustering and putting feral cattle into portable yards. How I never crashed in those early days I do not know.

I had my first emergency at 247 hours total time when the helicopter engine failed as I yarded up into a portable yard. A successful emergency landing was carried out with the added bonus of the cattle I was working still going into the yard. I guess it was actually due to good training and a good attitude. I was not a mug lair, and flamboyant flying has never impressed me. I worked very hard for them and had, I think, one day off in nine months.

The result of all this was that I was treated with a lot of respect and the road to my future was a little clearer. Unfortunately for my wife and growing family my heart kept drawing me back towards Planet and the Gregory district. I lugged them all over northern Australia trying to find a spot where I could feel settled. We had some happy years at Gregory Downs and Riversleigh Station. This came to a savage end with me crashing my helicopter and being severely injured.

I had flown for 16,000 hours by then and apart from one other minor accident had never damaged an aircraft so I sure blotted my copybook. It was a comedy of errors like most accidents. A month previous to this my oldest son had a motorbike accident while visiting a school friend. He had been knocked into a coma and had to learn to walk again. He was still in Townsville General Hospital recovering. My wife was still by his side. I had stayed with them in Townsville for a while and then returned to Riversleigh to keep the business going alone. I was very worried about him and the factors relating to this all contributed to my weariness and state of mind.

I reversed into a tree and the tail rotor had struck a small branch, dislodging the plug of weight in the end of the blade causing a massive and instantaneous vibration. This had the effect of causing the tail casting to crack through and fall off almost instantly. The helicopter then flipped inverted and struck the ground while rotating at speed. My memory of these events are hazy to say the least but I recall regaining consciousness, and struggling to escape from the wreck as I hung badly injured over the seat belt.

I had to cut the seat belt with my knife as I was unable to undo the latch and passed out again as I slumped to the ground. I came to after a while and was able to drag myself out of the wreck with my forearms as my legs would not work. (I had broken my pelvis).

Unfortunately, I managed to spear myself with the knife as well but it was minuscule in the scheme of things. I guess I was at the wreck site for a couple of hours before help arrived. I can mostly only recount my saviour's tales now as it was around four weeks before I was conscious again.

As stated earlier, I had broken my pelvis with consequent internal bleeding. The old heart was still working pretty well and was pumping all my blood into my abdomen, crushing my lungs and anything else that was in the road. I do remember really needing to pee or poop but was terribly embarrassed by it and could not bring myself to let go while surrounded by my rescuers.

This pressure was of course caused by my rapidly filling abdomen. I remember being very worried about the work bookings that I had and went to some trouble to make sure that the clients were advised and alternatives suggested. I believe it took about 5 hours before the RFDS could get to me to take me for my sec-

Goyder River Arafura Swamp (photo credit Pat Davison)

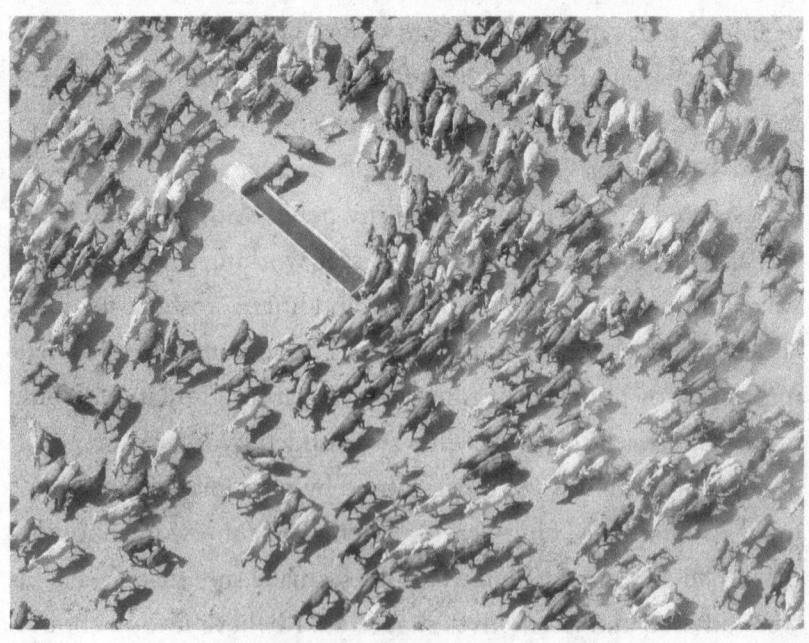
Like ants (photo credit Lynda Lucht)

Coolibah Air and NAH Staff at launch of new helipad Darwin (photo credit NT News)

Lovely flght in the morning (Photo credit Lynda Lucht)

Me with the Lawn Hill 206

Pink Lily Lagoon Elsey Station

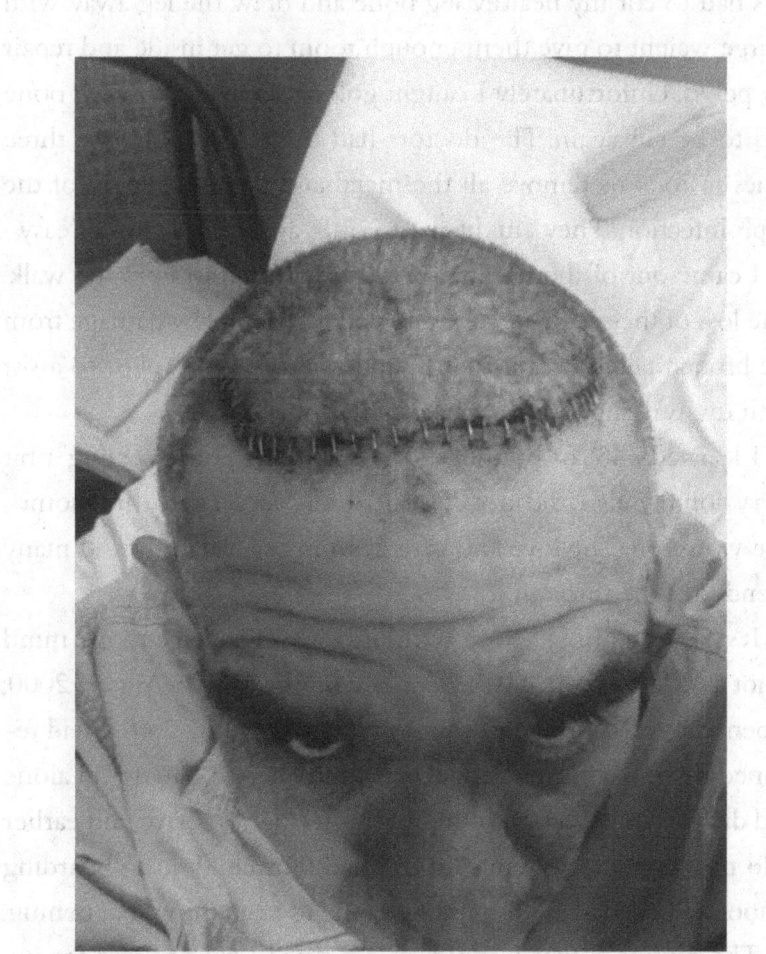
Me after DBS Operation

ond flight with the Flying Doctor. They had to open my abdomen to release the pressure and I believe to get me to Townsville took thirty-six units of blood.

They kept me in an induced coma for three weeks. The doctors had to cut my healthy leg bone and draw the leg away with a large weight to give them enough room to get inside and repair my pelvis. Unfortunately I caught golden staph and that leg bone had to be cut again. The doctors had to go back into me three times in total to remove all the metal and thereby get rid of the staph infection. They taught me to walk again but it wasn't easy.

I came out of the hospital needing a crutch to help me walk. The loss of the sciatic nerve in my left leg caused by damage from the broken pelvis meant that I needed a foot drop splint to assist with my walking as well as a compression stocking.

I learned a lot of humility in hospital. If I got to feeling a bit sorry for myself I did not have to look very far to find someone worse off. The love and care from my wife, family and many friends got me through it.

It's all a long time ago now, things have changed and my mind is not as clear as it once was. I crashed on the 18th of August 2000; I spent around nine months in hospital and by July 2001 I had regained my full commercial licence. I returned to Lawn Hill alone and did the 2001 second round of mustering. As I have said earlier I do not have a lot of education, I had four children in boarding school and needed a substantial income to keep things happening.

The only way that I could see for that to happen was for me to keep flying. So I continued to fly for another 5000 hours. Life as a working pilot in those years was extremely hard for me. The physical difficulties were immense and I also struggled with the decreasing love and affection from my wife.

On the 26th January 2006 my world fell apart when I discovered my wife's unfaithfulness, no doubt the years of following me around and suffering through my recovery had taken its toll on her as well and she had made her own arrangements. But like any cheated-upon husband I was devastated.

So I left her then and moved to another state to a different type of job and lifestyle. They say in life that when one door closes another one opens and that's basically what happened to me. I moved into a position as the Operations Manager for a large and complicated company. I filled lots of roles at this company at various times, either independently or together being the Chief Pilot, Operations Manager and HAAMC.

I felt an enormous responsibility for the forty odd pilots under my care and treated them like they were my own children. I had some success with this company as I taught myself some skills that I had no idea that I had. I had an eighty per-cent success rate at applying for tender documents and contracts. I developed a flight and duty program on an Excel sheet that is still very popular with operators; also on Excel I designed a very successful weight and balance sheet for many aircraft. I set up many procedures that assisted immensely with the running of the business. I was personally contacted by the fellow in charge of the camel shooting operation to congratulate me on the presentation and accuracy of my Reply to Tender. We were audited by a specialist aviation auditing company on behalf of a mining company and the senior auditor told me that he had never seen a company run so well.

But this all came at a cost and the pressure of my life took its toll eventually and I was diagnosed with Parkinson's Disease in 2009. I finished working in July 2012 and I had the Deep Brain Stimulator operation where they insert these probes in your brain.

I don't feel that it worked any good for me and may have over-stimulated my brain. I think it sent me a little bit mad for a few years.

However, I continued living my life at a full pace. I went to Perth and bought a camper bus. I went back up the Gulf and was caretaker at a couple of remote stations for some old friends for a couple of years. I bought a kit helicopter which I built and flew and eventually sold.

The high settings of that DBS device has pretty well burned out the dopamine receptors in my brain and I now have to take some massive doses of Parkinson's medication to get through the day.

Life is not so easy for me nowadays as the Parkinson's has continued its relentless march and my health has steadily declined. I need a Wheelie Walker to support my walking and the disease has also taken my voice away from me. This lastly has been the thing that I miss the most, not being able to have a good yarn with old friends.

Poems and Stories

by Russ Carrington

Mustering time

I wrote this poem while I was Operations Manager at North Australian Helicopters in Katherine.

I felt the poem reflected the changing status quo of mustering operations across northern Australia.

> I am watching the dawn grow stronger as the rotors start to turn,
> The boys are heading out, there's some avgas needs to burn.
> Before the whine of starters broke the morning's peace and quiet
> The scene was quite surreal as the Kookaburras greet the light.
> The mist is slowly fading from a low cover on the ground
> With quiet voices working out a plan, pilots standing round
> And then the engines growling with

the blades all beating down

The rising dust is everywhere, its swirling all around

The choppers are ascending through the rays of morning light

They're off to find the cattle for the time to muster's right

The prices are right up there and the seasons not been light.

The bullocks that are coming in will give the scales a fright

Well they found old Red the piker and the owner gave a laugh

He said if you can yard him boys we'll kill the fatted calf

Well Old Red tried everything, his entire repertoire

But those clever pilots were too good for him by far

And then the day was over and they made it to the yard

Our pilots are back alright, despite the flying hard

And so to the office I retreat, the boys are tying down

Another muster is complete, let's shout the boys a round.

The Hounds of Brinawa

I spent some time at Brinawa Station, caretaking for my old friends, Les and Anne Clarke. I was there for about three months, one of my chores was to feed the dish-lickers every evening.

> Here I am at Brinawa, the dogs my only mates
> I feed them each evening; they are waiting by the gate
> Firstly there is Blackie; he's only got one eye
> He is retired from the job, waiting by and by
> Next comes Miss Merlot, the ginger Huntaway
> She keeps herself aloof, and doesn't speak today
> And there is Penny, she's a little Blue Cattle bitch
> And running down the Wallabies,

she does without a hitch

Then there is Choppy, good looks weren't sent his way

He's got a chequered past, I'll tell you some day

Lastly there is young Redman, a mere callow youth

But I think that I might pinch him, away with him forsooth

The Rockhole

This is a Short Story that I wrote loosely based around a story that I have heard all my life. Apparently, this old miner fellow had a gold mine up the Fiery Creek. The story goes that it was before Mount Isa was a going concern and the assay office was in Cloncurry. Anyway, the old miner chap was found dead after the races in Cloncurry and in his gear was a bag of very rich gold. Old Davey Patterson apparently saw the spring that he lived at with a few old mining tools left leaning against a tree. They say that he used to mine the ore at the location, then load it in pack bags and take it to the spring where he had water to refine it further.

So, I crafted a story around this old legend.

"Well Captain," Ken said to the boss. "Do you think we ought to head on up to the rock-hole and try to catch that mob there? What do you reckon?"

"You could well be right, Ken, so I'll tell you what we'll do. You, Ken, will go for the lead when we strike them and I want you to just get in front of them and go with them for a while before you start to put the brakes on. Now, I'll go for the point on the left side and I'll be there to back you up when you look like being able to turn them. You, Splinter, and you, Steve, will keep coming, spaced out along the left side of the cattle, and I want you blokes to be ready to help with ringing them once we get the mob turned. Now, I really need you boys to keep an eye on the tail and to keep them coming along as well. The important thing for you blokes is to watch that they don't start back down the pad towards the rock-hole or then we will be in trouble. Oh, and Splinter, tell John on your way past the camp to bring the bull-catcher up to the red flat at Policeman Bend. Ask him to keep an eye out for anything that comes off the lead and to roll them for us, thank you mate."

They rode out, just the four of them. The boss was a great believer in the philosophy that he was better off with not enough men, rather than too many. It didn't take very long to get sorted out and trotting along, making their way up over the little pass known as Brumby Gap and heading on up the narrow valley towards the rock-hole.

John, who was also the cook, put a rolled roast in the camp oven and stoked the fire which already had a good bed of Supplejack and Snappy Gum coals. Then he checked the oil and water in the old short-wheel-base Landcruiser that was their bull-catching vehicle, topped up the spare water bottle on the back, and headed off as well. He went around the little range and back up the valley to wait on the bit of good red flat country at Policeman Bend.

It went off as planned, with about 120 head of cattle, of which half were probably cleanskins, starting out from the rock-hole as they came up to them. The boss was not a believer in the new-fangled radios and had the boys trained to watch for his hand signals and a low call if necessary. As these things go they did well to only lose one mad old cleanskin bull off the lead as they brought the mob to hand coming down onto the flat. The revving of the bull-catcher engine told them that John was in position and that the escaping bull would be caught and tied up pretty smartly.

After about an hour spent settling them and shouldering back a couple of younger mickey bulls that needed a tune-up they started off, going gingerly at first until they were able to go a little freer as the cattle came to hand. They made their way down the flat to the creek and around the bend, picking up the bull as they came to where John had tied him to a tree. The bull slunk back into the mob, a very different animal to the one that had taken off charging through the lead. (By that time the mob was in control to the extent they were effectively coachers).

They crossed the creek with the cattle before John boiled their billycan from the tucker-box on the back of the bull-catcher. Steve and Ken came into the little camp for pannikins of tea and a quick spell, while John took Steve's horse and helped the boss and Splinter watch the cattle.

"Hey, Ken, did you see that dead thing laying under that big tree just where that bull decided to go," Steve said.

"What, do you mean that old dead buck roo that was sort of curled round the foot of that Bauhinia tree?" returned Ken. "Well yes, Ken, but I don't think it was a roo at all, I think it was a man."

"Christ, mate, do you really think so? All I could see was a bit of hide and a few long bones."

"Yes I do, mate, it gave me a bit of a start when I realised what it was, but whoever it is has been there a bloody long time. So I thought I'd wait till now before I said anything, because that bloke sure isn't going anywhere, anytime soon."

"Well, Steve, I see the boss and Splinter coming. I reckon John and I will be ok to hold the cattle now, so you tell them what you saw." Off Ken went to where his horse was tied, mounting up and riding towards the boss and having a few brief words with him while nodding in Steve's direction. Then he continued around the settled cattle to where he was able to speak with John.

"So, what's this Steve? Ken reckons that you saw a dead man."

"Yes, boss, I'm certain that I did, and not only that, I reckon it was extremely old."

"Well, that is a helluva thing, Steve; now, just thinking about these cattle. Do you reckon if you told John how to get to it he'd be able to get back up there in the bull-catcher?" asked the boss, as he and young Splinter each grabbed a quick pannikin of tea.

"He could drive to it no trouble at all, boss, there looked to be a bit of an old road that the pad sort of followed though the rocks and it seemed to be heading pretty well straight to where the body is."

"Well, I am blowed if I have ever seen any sign of a road through there before, but I guess that we were usually going flat out, chasing cattle. Anyway, I'll send John back in now and if this mob settles down ok he can slip back up there and check it out properly."

The boss and Splinter then mounted up and rode out to the cattle, while John trotted over to the bull-catcher and gave Steve back his horse. They had a quick conversation about where Steve thought John would be able to find his way through the rocks to the body. The rest of the men had started to get the mob going again. The same old cleanskin bull came out of the mob and Ken was able to shoulder him back pretty quickly. As they were already across the creek and all of the pressure points were mostly behind them the cattle settled down to walk along well.

John called out, "Reckon I'll go back now for a look if you

blokes are going ok." The boss gave him a wave of acknowledgement, so John headed back over the creek and back up the flat.

The boys had walked the mob around the little range and back up the new fence towards the camp and they were lining up for the yard when John got back in time to help with the tricky procedure.

"By crikey, John, you don't mind cutting it a bit fine," Ken called out as John headed back to the camp.

"Wait until we get set up back in camp and then I will tell you all what is there," said John as he left them. He took the roast out of the camp oven and put some potatoes, onions and pumpkin that he prepared into the oven and back on the fire. By the time he had put a fresh damper on the coals, finished cooking the vegetables and made up a gravy, the boys had finished splitting the cattle up between the water yards. Then they washed down their horses' backs and gave them a feed out in the little horse paddock and came over to the camp.

They each got a feed and a pannikin of tea and settled back to hear the yarn. The boss said, "Well John, you had better tell us what you found."

"Do you remember the story that old bloke down at Jotown told us last year, the one about the old miner who used to come down from Sandy Creek every now and then with a big bag of gold?"

"Of course, John," said the boss. "That's a very old yarn around these parts, he went missing they say, but that was probably close to 100 years ago. Do you mean to tell me you think that's him?"

"Actually, I do think it is him, boss. Sandy Creek is a couple of watersheds over from here, and if you wanted to lay a false trail, it wouldn't be too hard to cross over at the top of the divide and drop into Cartridge Creek and come back down here. There is one other reason that I think it is him," said John as he rose and went to the bull-catcher, where he dug around in the toolbox in the back of the Toyota and pulled out an old rolled up towel. Then he returned to the camp table and unrolled the bundle, revealing an old leather bag that none of them had seen before. With the boys all gathered around him John tore the side out of the old rotten bag and out fell about a milk tin of gold-veined ore. There was more gold than rock in the pile.

"Good God Almighty, Holy Smoke," and other choicer expletives were heard as they all stood staring for a while.

"Most of the bones are gone," said John. "His skull is still there though with the temple all stove in. His old rifle, it looks like a 32-20, is there too. I reckon the wild men who used to live in this country might have got him."

The boss said, "John, put that lot back in the toolbox while we have a bit of a think about what we should do. Splinter, put the billycan back on, mate."

The boys were all a bit stunned and were glad of the opportunity to do a couple of normal chores while the boss mused over the best course of action.

"Ok boys, we have plenty of hay left at the yard, so in the morning we will let the cattle back into the big receiving yard and put five round bales in there first. They will probably trample a fair bit of it but they'll be ok. We will start the bore as well so that there is plenty of water for them. Then we will take that four-wheel motorbike and the bull-catcher back over to where this poor old bloke finished up and see if we can bury him."

They drank their pints of tea and cleaned up after their meal, had a quick shower and then settled back on their swags to wait out the long night. About 4.00 am the camp started to rouse as everyone got up and had a wash. The boss was already at the fire and had put the billycan on. He had cut up some steak and soon John was frying the meat on a sizzling hotplate over the fire.

By sunrise the boys had rolled the round bales of hay into the big receiving yard and let the cattle back in there. They had started the bore and the two vehicles had been checked over, the water bottles filled and the tucker box ready. They were all set for a day of adventure.

They headed out, back the way they had come in the previous day, around to Policeman Bend via the road. Up the red flat they went and John showed them where he had gone through the rocks via the faintly discernible old road.

They came up to the bauhinia tree, which rose out of an area of softer alluvial soil at the foot of a steeper slope, and they could see the bedraggled little pile of bones under the tree. John had told them what to expect but it was shocking all the same. None of the boys had seen a skeleton before. Strangely, there was a bit of metal plate which had possibly been worn as a breastplate. That was what Steve and Ken had thought was the hide as they galloped past when the bull broke from the mob.

John pointed out his poor old skull, all stove in on the left temple. "Looks like this is what finished him I reckon, he must have been having a running battle with those old wild fellows who used to live around here."

"I'll tell you what," said the boss, "they aren't all finished either. Rusty the chopper pilot, was saying the last time he was here that he saw a little group of wild men just before dark, up north of the Nicholson, over the border."

With that remark, the two younger men, Splinter and Steve, cast a wary eye over their shoulders and around the hills.

It was only about two feet down through the better digging to solid rock. The boss reckoned that would do the old fellow anyway, as nothing would dig him up because all of his meat and hide was long gone, along with the smell. So they placed another old towel on the ground and put what bones they could find in it before rolling it up. The boss lowered the little parcel into the hole and Ken and John filled it in. They placed the funny looking breastplate against the tree and leant the rusted rifle there also. After a few moments awkward silence, the boss said, "Let's follow this road up towards the rock-hole and see where it comes out."

They travelled along the old roadway that had veered off a little from the pad. The bull-catcher was only just managing to squeeze through between the boulders and larger rocks but they had good sixteen-ply tires on the vehicle and were not concerned. The four-wheeler was travelling along without difficulty. The road swung up the stony ridge along the left-hand side of the little valley and headed for a cluster of larger boulders. As they came up closer they could see a cave opening into the side of the hill.

"Holy Smoke!" exclaimed Ken as they pulled up on level ground. "That's not a cave, it's a proper squared-off mine entrance!"

"And look, there are some more of those breastplate things piled up over here on the other side. Wait a bit," said John as he jumped off and went over to the little pile. "Fellows, you are not going to believe this," he said as he held up a helmet and a sword.

Wordlessly they looked at each other and then back at the mine entrance. They had a couple of good LED torches in the bull-catcher glove-box, so they used them to explore the little mine that seemed to go in about fifty feet with little leaders going off on either side here and there. There was a slightly larger chamber about ten or fifteen feet into the drive, and there they found a little pile of mined ore which was liberally veined with gold. Also, when they shone the bright torches around there were flecks of gold shining everywhere in the rock.

"Well, boys, I reckon we should get together all of the loose gold we can find and head back to the camp for a bit of dinner and a yarn," said the boss, so that was what they did. They took an almost full twenty litre drum of golden ore, which was extremely heavy, with them back to the camp.

"You know something, boys? I reckon I have had enough of working cattle to do me for a long time," the boss reckoned, as he swung the gate and released the cattle that they had mustered the previous day, stepping behind the gate as the old cleanskin bull hooked at him on his way out.

And that is how the Golden Rockhole Mining Company was started.

The Hairy Man

This is another Short Story that I wrote that is basically a true story about a bloke who was working at Wollogorang Station and who appeared to just walk off camp and disappear into the wilds.

G'day, my name is Rusty Cameron and I was a chopper mustering pilot. I'd like to tell you a tale about what happened on a property that I was mustering years ago; a really strange set of circumstances, in fact.

You see, I was mustering on this big Gulf property that lay just on the Northern Territory side of the Queensland border. Valley Downs was its name, or as it was known locally, The Valley. The homestead was on the bank of this large watercourse called Battle Creek, named that I guess when white settlement first took place. The homestead complex still carried some signs of those earlier times of conflict, the old kitchen building was constructed from stone with steel shutters shielding the windows. They even had rifle slots in them.

So what I am getting at is; there was a lot of history and mystique about the place. There were also thousands of rogue and cleanskin cattle, brought about mainly because of the remoteness of the property and the cost factor of conducting full and clean musters.

Anyway, to get back to the story; one of the station workers was this really odd bloke called Charlie. Charlie was a back-to-nature type of bloke who used to spend whatever free time he had exploring the various springs and secluded spots around the station. There was nothing wrong with that except that he always insisted on going by himself and had been spotted in the nude at different times. So, suffice to say, he was a bit different from the norm.

Things came to pass and eventually Charlie announced that he was moving on. He loaded up his old Toyota wagon and caravan and left, heading for the local roadhouse back over the border in Queensland that was called The Caldron.

Well, after about a week, someone came through from that way and we asked how Charlie was getting on. Charlie hadn't been seen and we knew that he had intended calling at The Cauldron as he was mates with Willy, the owner. There was another property between The Valley and The Cauldron that was called Eastmere, where the owner, upon being alerted went for a look down the western side of his run.

He found Charlie's old vehicle and caravan on his main western access road that led into a set of stockyards nestled on the side of a large lagoon. There was no sign of Charlie, however scratched in the dust in large letters was the word HELP. The mystery deepened, the police were alerted and it was found that there was nothing wrong with Charlie's vehicle. It had started immediately upon investigation and was found to be quite serviceable.

The boss of Valley Downs, a good bloke called Bull, was able to track Charlie for a fair distance. His tracks headed westwards back onto Battle Creek. He lost the tracks at the creek, where he found a water bottle and an old rifle that Charlie had obviously abandoned. There was plenty of water about the country and, try as they might, they couldn't find any more sign of Charlie.

To further complicate matters, about a fortnight after Charlie went missing, Bull and I were having a cup of tea at The Valley homestead late in the day when Harry, the local Aboriginal elder, turned up looking very frightened. They had a small community about six kilometres away from the homestead on another large creek called The Backup. Harry told us that they had found a wrecked aircraft. Harry and other members of his community had walked a fair way up the gorge of The Backup creek fishing and had found what they reckoned was part of a wrecked plane. There was still enough daylight left, so Bull and I jumped in the chopper and flew off to investigate. Sure enough, there was a section of the wing of a large aircraft. It had been there for some time though and appeared to have been used as a raft, as there were old tanks and canisters from the parent aircraft tied onto it with old fencing wire to aid with flotation. Local history told us that one of the previous owners of the neighbouring property to the west, Pretty Plains, in times long gone by, had crashed his aircraft in the area. It was supposedly a large aircraft like an ex WWII bomber, which fitted in with the size of the wing section that Harry had found but the location of the wreck was lost in the mists of time. We surmised that this piece of the wreck had been utilised as a raft by the old crocodile shooters that had frequented the area years earlier.

This had the effect of raising the tempo in the district to a fever pitch; what with Charlie going missing and now this semi-explained lost aircraft. The local Aboriginal people were particularly haunted and cleared out for a while.

Time moved on, as did I. Life had led me down various paths and by-ways, mostly associated with helicopters around outback Australia, always working in the bush. So it transpired that about 27 years later I was bookkeeping at another large gulf property.

While there I was told this story about happenings at Valley Downs.

A contract mustering team had seen a 'hairy man'. The ancient figure of Aboriginal legend had been spotted at a spring fed creek up along the Old Coast Road in a remote corner of Valley Downs. The boss's wife spotted it first as she was completing her morning ablutions. She looked up to see this large hairy face looking at her through some bushes. Her wild screams brought the rest of the crew to her at a gallop and a large hairy man was seen disappearing into the scrub. The patch of scrub was pretty big and they thought that was the last they had seen of him, although they gave the scrub a good going over, even looking from above in the chopper. His tracks were found and reckoned to be about a size 17 if you could find a pair of boots that big. They back-tracked him and could see where he had been hiding while watching them but nothing more of him was seen.

Could this in reality have been long lost Charlie? In hindsight, it seems likely. There is plenty of water in this area of Valley Downs and it was rich with fish, also there was plenty of bush tucker to be had. But there was the time factor; it had been 27 years since he had disappeared. He was a bloke of about 40 to 45 at that time, which made him around 70 nowadays. I guess living rough and healthy could keep a man in good shape but I reckon that he would just about be at the end of his run. Perhaps on his weekends away in the bush years ago he had been establishing caches of essential tools and equipment. Clothes certainly weren't a problem.

This reminds me of another story about the 'hairy man' that I heard in my travels while mustering. Out from Kalumbaru on the Peninsular Road, there is a low bridge across the Stanley River which gets submerged every wet season. After one Wet, the Shire Engineer drove out to the crossing to see what work needed to be done on the approaches to get everything right for the dry season. There was a light breeze coming from the north, in which direction he was heading. He coasted slowly down the long low bank into the River and, as he did so, he saw a hairy man ripping up a wallaby that he had only just killed. They spotted each other at the same instant and, in the blink of an eye, the hairy man had disappeared over the bank and was gone.

Now this man was the shire engineer and a person of high credibility. You can imagine how this story swept around the small town of Kalumbaru. I was mustering on a large Aboriginal-owned property that was not all that far from this scene of intrigue. The boss told me that, soon after this event, early one morning he drove out to where the Stock-camp was camped preparatory to a muster. As he drove up to the camp, he was amazed to see the entire camp of men all sleeping in a tight circle, with their wire stretchers all turned onto their sides and set up around the outside of the sleeping men like a portable yard. They were terrified. I think I would have been too.

So that is the story of the 'hairy man' at Valley Downs. Was it really Charlie, the missing man? I'm inclined to think so but it had been 27 years and not a sign of him had been seen in all that time. I'll leave it up to you, dear reader, to decide for yourself.

Waiting for daylight

The stockmen are all around the truck, some have scratched together a few sticks and a bit of grass and they put a match to it. A merry flame flares up with the first rush of fire and the grass is rapidly consumed until they are left with the few sticks of coolabah, too hard to catch alight from this effort but it fills the time and serves to warm the boys as they stand waiting, waiting for daylight.

The ramp comes down with a thud, the drop door with a clang, the batwings screech from lack of grease and the first horse is led down the ramp, shod feet banging and clanging on the steel deck and then we're away, all eight stockhorses are gathered with their riders all about the area as they are waiting, waiting for daylight.

The chopper is parked close by, it's where they left it yesterday evening when it got too late for the pilot to fly. He and the boss are over there filling the fuel tanks from a drum on the back and checking the oil. Thank goodness they got through the gate into the next paddock, the cattle will all be back on the fence, they won't take much picking up and they are waiting, waiting for daylight.

And so the rosy glow appears in the east and grows stronger, quickly now ever quicker. They can hear the pilot say to the boss, "I think I'll start her now, by the time she gets warm it'll be right to fly."

Righto comes the reply, "We'll go through the gate and grab the few standing about for a starter mob and you bring the rest into us. Let's go for I'm done waiting, waiting for daylight.

PAST IMPERFECT

Patrica Carrington

One

A city girl, born and bred, it was my experience to marry a man who lived in one of the remotest parts of North West Queensland. We lived in an extended family situation, on the station. Here we raised five children.

I should, perhaps, explain my antecedents, and my circumstances, as a child, so that the reasons for, and the understanding of why, we had such an interesting childhood, may become clearer.

Mum and Dad married on 9th October, 1926, at Galston. Mum was very clever, but unassuming. She was a real gentlewoman in her attitude, kindness, and with a certain innocence which protected her, and coloured her life forever. Dad was a good deal brasher. He was also single-minded. Having, as a boy, set his heart on a life following the sea, he followed this with a lifelong commitment to the ocean in all its moods, and wherever it took him. Mum's decision was well considered. She had another option, but the other chap was the sort who would never move beyond his immediate circle of family and friends. This was unacceptable to Mum. She was also exceedingly fond of Dad's mother. She actually discussed Dad's proposal with Mrs. Pearse, before committing herself. She had known his family for many years, and obviously felt comfortable with them. She was given her engagement ring, which was a hoop of five diamonds — the valuation described them as of "the first water". I still have that piece of paper. Alas, one day she got home from the Pearse's place to discover a stone was missing. Incredibly, by backtracking her path, she found it again. As the years passed another stone was lost. The ring was then reduced to a four stone jewel. Finally a second stone went, and the ring was again reduced to a three stone ornament. This is how it stands today.

Dad followed the sea, as a marine engineer, with only periodic visits home. The sea became his mistress, Mum was one step behind, only his wife. The family was hit by the depression. As there were almost no imports and exports, Dad lost his job, and life became very hard. In this period they produced three children.

The eldest was Jim. Dad was a firm believer in the rights of primogeniture. Understandably, after all, he was the eldest. His name, Edwin James Pearse was now into the third generation. I am glad that it continued once more, with Jim's son. Dad was very dynastically minded. He obtained untold (and told) pleasure from the knowledge that the name had passed on again. He loved little Jimmy, (Jim's son) passionately. Jim was born on 24th August, 1927.

The next arrival was Sam, named for his maternal grandfather, Samuel Harold Quinn — so Sam was also Samuel Harold. He was born on 5th October, 1929. He was always a steady little boy. He was interested in all things mechanical too.

Next was the first daughter, myself, born on 12th March 1931. Mum told me that she had chosen my name, Barbara Ann, after her friend Barbara Brookes. Ann after her dearly loved, now lost, Mother in Law. After my birth, Grandma Quinn came to visit her in the hospital. While there she asked Mum if she had chosen a name. Mum said that something in Grandma's manner made her hesitate, and say, "Not yet."

"Patricia is a very nice name," said Grandma. Patricia Ruth was the name of her youngest daughter, who had died at two years of age. So Mum, out of affection for her mother, and also for love of the little sister she had lost years before, gave me Patricia as my first name.

Dad was out of work when I was born — he had been taken off his ship in great pain (the doctor thought he had appendicitis. What he did have was renal colic). He was taken to hospital, where Mum followed to see what was happening, shepherding a three-year-old (Jim), a two year old (Sam), and expecting me in short order. The tragedy was, that once Dad lost that job, as the ship had to sail on time, with or without that particular engineer, there was no other work available, because of the Great Depression. Shipping was the first casualty, there being nothing to ship.

We lived for a time in a house Dad built with his own hands, until conditions became too difficult for mum to manage when he was not present. We lived for a period in the cottage at Galston. I was born in a small private hospital in Hornsby. Things must have been bad, because Mum told me, that to her everlasting humiliation (nowadays one would only be grateful), the doctor who attended her, and the matron of the hospital both told her that payment of their fees could wait until funds were available. Dad, full of pride, and a bit of pomposity, insisted on settling the bills immediately. Also, partly because I was the first Quinn granddaughter, and partly to help, people gave gifts of clothing very generously. Mum said I was very well equipped.

We also stayed for a period at Blackheath, in a holiday house owned by Grandpa Pearse. Mum said that because it was so cold I did not attempt to walk very early, not until I was about fifteen months old. In parenthesis, she told me that the doctor paid them a house call one day. Sam had the habit of climbing on anything. In the end the doctor had to ask her to lift him off the dining room table where he was cavorting, because he couldn't stand the thought of the little boy falling.

In the course of time we moved to 41 Falconer Street, West Ryde. I recall much of this period of my life. The house was of light apricot brick, with light-coloured terra-cotta tiles on the roof. To this day, those colours in a house have never appealed to me, and guess what colour are the bricks in my present home? There was a white picket fence in the front, inside of which grew a green and yellow privet hedge. I detested the horned caterpillars which developed and lived on the twigs in that hedge. Fortunately I was too young to have to keep it trimmed – one of Mum's million jobs. She had a pair of hedge clippers, which were both stiff and blunt, to keep it in order.

Entering the house from the front there was a brick verandah on the left, which fronted the main bedroom. The front door led into a hall. On the right was the sitting room, a sacred area, the door kept shut by Mum. On the left was the access door to the master bedroom. Following along the hall one entered the second bedroom – mine, later to be shared with my baby sister. The bed was against the wall, and at night, to entertain myself, I used to pick a small hole in the plaster near my bed. As the walls were kalsomined it could be, and was, repaired at intervals, and repainted – by Mother. On the left was the dining room, where we ate our evening meal. It had a carpet square covering most of the floor. The outer edges were of varnished wood. Jim still has the renewed and improved dining suite, which was second hand when we got it. It had two extra leaves so that it could be enlarged. The table had to be wound out with a crank handle so that the leaves could be inserted. There were four ordinary dining chairs, the seats covered with leather, and two carvers, the same chairs with arms. When anyone had a birthday, he or she was promoted to one of the carvers for the day, and the chair was decorated with crepe paper streamers. The celebrant always had a rainbow birthday cake with candles. One present was given. Occasionally a generous relative would come good with a second gift. Grandpa Pearse used to give the boys additional parts to a very large Meccano set, with which they played obsessively.

Off the dining room, to the right, was the boys' room. Because I was a girl, they flatly refused me entry into it, though their friends were welcomed with joy. The hall ended on entry to the kitchen, in the centre of which was a plain deal table, which had two drawers in it, one for the tablecloth, the other for the cutlery. It had to be kept clean by daily scrubbing with Pearson's sandsoap, in an orange wrapper. I loved doing the table with this and the scrubbing brush.

There was a simple gas stove, and a set of kitchen chairs painted green. Off the kitchen to the left was the bathroom, with a claw-footed bath. Mum tried to keep this in good condition by painting it with silverfrost. Even today I detest that style of tub. A chip bath heater provided the hot water for the bath. Off the kitchen, behind the boys' bedroom, was the laundry, where Mother did the washing. The house was built on a slope, so that though it was ground level at the front, it was high at the back. To get to the clothesline she had to carry a large wicker basket of clothes down the steps.

About three weeks before the due date of Elaine's birth, on 5th December, 1938, Mum was staggering down the steps with the laundry, and fell, bringing the birth forward. The clothesline was of the old-fashioned variety, with four lines strung between two planks. These planks were attached to uprights, held in the ground, and fixed so that they could be adjusted, so that the laundress (never a man) could reach the lines in turn, then shift them up higher. The weight of the wet clothes often pulled the lines too low, so they were supported in the middle by a clothes prop, a long pole which had a fork in the upper end, to hold the lines up, and held at the other end, into the ground, by the weight of the washing.

Naturally, under this system the poles and lines sometimes broke, and a line of washing would need to be done again. No washing machines in the good old days. Washing day was always on Monday, throughout the whole country. There was a clothes prop man who came around the streets, selling this most precious of articles.

We were almost entirely under the care of Mum, as Dad spent most of his time at sea. Aunty Blanche, probably with a good deal of truth, said that not only were we spoiled rotten, but that if Mum had had a dozen children, they would have all been spoiled rotten too.

We had several years of living in Falconer Street prior to Elaine's birth on that momentous date. Upon her advent she was loved and worshipped by us all. Her problem is that, even after sixty years she is regarded in the light of our eyes as our "baby". Whether she likes it or not, she will always be our little sister. She was also born during a heat wave, and she was the most vivid red colour. In a few days this was enhanced by a nice yellow jaundice shade. Fortunately, this did fade after a while.

I was prepared to let her have everything I owned, save only my precious doll, Baby Betty — a mama doll. I even knitted her a jumper. It was much too large when I began it, but it fitted quit well by the time it was finished. Elaine was named for Mum (hence the Marian), but her first name was purely from Mum's love of the poem "Elaine the fair, Elaine the loveable, Elaine the Lily maid of Astalot". What a charming reason to be named. I loved her enough to name one of my daughters after her.

This then, was the family circle into which I was born. Dad was away almost all of the time, so Mother brought us up, with occasional forays home by Dad, where, after a brief honeymoon period, much-needed discipline was administered. Not only did we look forward to his arrival, we also looked forward to his departure.

In this family group was a tender, kind mother, three self-willed, strong-minded children, and a gentler fourth child, made in the mould of her mother.

I do not remember all that much about the back yard, except that it was quite large, surrounded on three sides by a six-foot grey paling fence, as was every yard in that street. There was a path downstairs to the toilet, where we were lucky enough to have a water closet. One of my more interesting memories is the panic stations that ensued when Jim, one cold night, went down there with a book and a candle. He placed the candle on the floor between his legs, and settled down. After a while the heat of the candle and the cold water in the bowl re-acted. It must have seemed like the splitting of the atom, as the centre of the bowl broke out, and water gushed away. Mum was most upset. Grandpa Quinn saved the day. He built a big cement block around the broken area so that it was once again useable. I believe the landlord was not pleased.

We had a lovely loquat tree, the fruit of which we all enjoyed greatly. The council eventually cut it down, when there was a fruit fly eradication programme on. Everyone lost a lot of trees at that time. There was a large and luscious mulberry tree halfway down the back. I was sitting up in its branches one day, when I heard my brothers practising swear words below. Evil words, like dash, darn, cuss, blast, and even an occasional damn figured greatly. Naturally I disclosed this to my mother.

Away down the back was a stand of bamboo. There were some loose palings on the back fence too. In this way the boys exited to a lane, which led to Park Road. We had spurious attempts at vegetable gardens, but we were not consistent. It took too long between planting the seeds and the sight of any seedlings. Only Mum had any reliability.

My real escape from reality was reading. I was lucky enough to be from a family where this was respected, and the fund of books available to me was extensive. I read and enjoyed "Ivanhoe" when I was eight. I fell in love with "Anne of Green Gables" when I was not much older. To me no birthday or Christmas was complete unless I received a book as a gift.

My toys were not extensive. I had a rather ratty looking koala made of rabbit skin. It had a small piece out of its abdomen, through which the stuffing showed. I owned a knitted Humpty Dumpty, with the usual skinny legs. And I had the adored Baby Betty which I would not lay on the altar of sacrifice for Elaine. She was a cloth doll, with a porcelain head, and celluloid arms and legs from the elbow and knee down. I loved Betty passionately, though I carried her around by the neck. Once a year she visited the Dolls' Hospital, as, at some stage, usually through the agency of the boys, her head would be smashed.

My usual recollection of Betty is with her head joined together with silvery Tarzan's Grip, and often with a small piece missing, where my darling mother had patiently re-assembled the broken pieces. She had a number of different heads. Grandpa Quinn made me a wooden stroller which had a shaft of wood out the front, so I could pull it along. He also made me a small scooter, out of the grating from the running board of a car, and four wheels. It had handlebars for steering and was used much as a skateboard is used nowadays, for locomotion. But it was easier to control.

I also had another doll given to me, an elegant female with jointed limbs, neck and head. Her name was Elizabeth. The day after Christmas I was unable to find her, until I put some rubbish in the bin. There she lay, in bits. My brothers had investigated how she worked (with rubber bands, actually) and had been unable to reunite the various parts, so they had taken the easiest way out. She was rescued, but this spoiled any real love I had for her.

At the corner of our street, where it bisected Park Road, was Miss Donaldson's shop. The entrance was on the diagonal, facing the centre of the road, with three cement steps leading up to it. It was there I first saw those delightful thin Nestlé chocolates, at a penny each, which were later joined by the original Freddo frogs. They rested temptingly on the counter. Miss Donaldson had a bun, and an olive complexion, but she was thin. She kept this shop to maintain herself and her mother. (Where was welfare then?)

Biscuits were purchased by weight. Mis. Donaldson kept a row of large Arnotts biscuit tins on the top shelf. They all sported the logo of the rosella — the bird, not the fruit. From these she would take out and weigh, then place in a brown paper bag the required biscuits. But the biscuits occasionally broke, and could not be sold as perfect, so we were, on rare occasions, allowed to purchase a penn'orth of broken biscuits. I remember Iced Vo-Vos. Heaven!

I first saw the small four-piece packets of Wrigley's P.K. chewing gum there. Fortunately I didn't like the sharp flavour much. She also sold cordial and SOFT DRINK, a magical nectar, which we never experienced except on Sunday School Picnics.

My great crime was committed at Miss Donaldson's shop. Surreptitiously I swiped a penny from Mum's purse, and whipped over to the shop. As I was making my purchase who should come in behind me but my mother. I was forced to return my purchase, and the coin was refunded. I still remember my shame.

I don't remember much about Mum's clothes, but I know she always wore a hat, gloves and stockings when leaving the house. When she was pregnant with Elaine she did not go out much, but I recall a brown silk cloak she wore, with fine pleating around the collar, and slits where her hands went through it, when drawn closed. It was a peculiar garment, but it came in handy at one stage, when I had to play the part of a peddler in a school play.

My earliest recollections surround the losing of my right index finger when I was three. I remember going with Sam to the area behind the outside water closet, which had a lattice surround, and where the lawn mower was stored. I know (whether I remember it or not first-hand is a moot point), that Sam told me to feel if the newly sharpened blades were sharp, and that he pushed it. Yes, they were! My finger was severed at the first joint, though still hanging by skin. Mum pushed the top back into place, and walked me several miles to the Ryde Hospital. I was lucky and unlucky. The doctor said the flesh had mortified, and chose to amputate down to the second joint. But at least, by using the flesh between the first and second joint he created a pad, which was not unduly disfiguring, and which saved any phantom pains forever.

What I do remember, without any prompting, is that I was kept in hospital for several days. There was a lady in the hospital suffering from pneumonia. The nurses used to take me to her, sit me on her bed table, and allow her to brush, comb, and arrange my very curly hair. Grandpa Quinn came to see me. He was so distressed that he clenched his hands into the pocket of his coat, and went walking for a long period of time. (I should here comment that Aunt Blanche once told me she was dubious about my claim that Sam had done the deed. Such was the impression of honesty that I emanated apparently, that she thought I could have blamed Sam to get out of trouble myself — who knows? I do know that Sam went to Galston to stay for about six weeks after the trauma because he was so upset.)

There were several disadvantages as a result of being fingerless — minor. I learned to read and write very young, and because my finger was so awkward to use, I had to learn to write with my left hand. Prior to attending school, I once wrote a letter to my father which took him some time to interpret. It read: "Dad, Pat s gud Boys r bad Itin Pat Rtin Rat."

In third class I had a sewing teacher who mocked at my sewing efforts, holding my work up to ridicule to the whole class. I have never forgotten that pain. We used to combine with the boys school for hated folk dancing. The boys, absolutely and forever, refused to touch my mildly disfigured hand.

When I was six I suffered from tonsillitis so badly that it was decided to have my tonsils removed. I was a patient at the Ryde Hospital. After a week I was allowed home. No sooner was I home than I haemorrhaged, and had to be returned to hospital. No ambulances, no taxis — just Shank's pony for Mum. My chief recollection of this incident, apart from having a very good time in hospital was in the operating theatre, being instructed to take deep breaths and "smell the lovely lady's scent," and start counting.

My brothers were also victims of tonsillitis. The preferred solution to the problem in that pre-antibiotic period, was a tonsils and adenoids surgical removal. Hospital care was not free in New South Wales, and thus not available to a struggling family.

Instead, Mum scrubbed the wooden kitchen table meticulously. Dr. Howe fronted up at the house. He instructed Mum in the method of administering anaesthetic (chloroform) — I know she had to allow the liquid to drip onto cottonwool masks. Thereupon he proceeded to remove both sets of tonsils, using the kitchen as his operating theatre. I was banished outside, so did not witness this version of E.R. (as seen on T.V.) Doctors at that time did carry out regular home visits, so there was after care provided.

Two

As a small child I attended Mrs. Pott's kindergarten, the fee being somewhere about two shillings per week. She lived around the corner from Miss Donaldson's shop, in Park Road. I remember she had eight or nine pupils. She taught them the basics, until she became pregnant herself. At this stage she handed over her business to Mrs. Lock, who lived a bit further away.

Mrs. Lock had one son, Don; a bit of a handful, and a close friend and associate of my brother Jim. She had lost her husband. I was told that he had committed suicide by jumping off the Sydney Harbour Bridge when the phantom pains from a leg he had lost became more than he could bear. This left a widow who had to cope somehow. No welfare then. She ran the Sunshine Kindergarten for many years, doing a remarkably good job.

The main room had friezes all around the walls, in grey pastel paper, with the alphabet, suitably illustrated. There was a covered area out the back, where the little ones sat at playtime and lunchtime. The children I recall were Leslie Thorsby, a boy slightly younger than I. He arrived the first day just before me. He had a sister too, Margaret, who was a little older. There was Marguerite Jorgensen, a blonde with very short hair, and a big bow on top; Margaret and Johnny Sefton (Margaret was clever all her school life, and was always the youngest in her class); Margaret (Peggy) Pattison, and her younger sister Wendy, who caught the dreaded infantile paralysis – polio – while a pupil there. She was forced to wear a calliper on her leg after that. Barbara Warneke, and a younger sister too. Patsy Smart lived next door to the school. Narelle Jenkins lived in the street beyond Falconer Street. She was a pretty little thing. In fact, she played the most important shepherdess in "Rendezvous", an enactment of a sentimental song of the period. (I would have died for that role in the school concert at the end of the year. I was Patty Pearse). There were one or two others, including a boy named Brian, and another youngster named Yvonne Billington, who lived in Orchard Street.

I was, even at that age, a natural actress, and usually secured the lead in any play. Those parts, however, did not require the beautiful dress that the chief shepherdess wore. For my most outstanding role my aunt had made me a short white voile frock, with two frills around the hem, puffed sleeves, and a sash. It had greenish flowers scattered over it. It was really pretty, but not as flash as that particular shepherdess's gown. Furthermore, Narelle wore a wig, made of cotton wool, which had curls hanging over her shoulder. I haven't forgotten! My common old shepherdess dress, the same as all the other unimportant girls, was a pink full-length dress, quite a vivid shade, with a pale pink crepe de chine floral top. This was a jacket, which had elbowlength sleeves culminating in a circular frill. It was held together at the front with press studs, and these had black velvet formal bows superimposed on them.

Two panniers were attached to this garment at the waistline, positioned over the hips. These were bouffed out with brown paper linings, which were gathered underneath the panniers, and had to be regularly pushed out to create a very full look. On other occasions I loved that dress, but not at the concert.

At West Ryde school all the girls who owned a fairy dress were allowed to take part in a certain concert item – another concert. I decided to be one of them, so I created my own outfit. I wore the under part of my shepherdess frock and sewed a large sheet of pink crepe paper to the middle of the back. It was bunched together and held there by a safety pin. The two outside pieces were tied to my wrists with pink ribbon, and I fluttered away happily on the stage. These were my interpretation of wings. I did hear someone in the audience commenting on the "little pink elephant". I can't say I blamed her. It mortified me at the time, but now I enjoy the vision it recalls.

Prior to Mrs. Lock's end of the year concert (held in the church hall at Top Ryde), there was drama. Just when she was needed to support the future Oscar winner – Dad was away at sea – what should my mother do, but fall down the steps with her load of washing. This caused her waters to break (we were not even aware she was pregnant — we didn't even know what pregnancy was!). She finished the washing, walked over to Miss Donaldson of the corner shop, because she had a phone, and asked her to ring the Galston police. They then took a message to Grandma, that she was needed to come and collect the family. Only then did Mum go to the small local private hospital the other side of West Ryde Railway Station, where she gave birth to Elaine Marian.

I, poor rising star, was forced to go to Mrs. Lock's home to stay for a few days, so I could carry on in my non-family supported role, as Fanny, in the Sunshine Kindergarten's annual concert. (My only taste of boarding school). I recall the smugness I felt when I strolled out of Mrs. Lock's private quarters each morning, to join the rest of the pupils. Furthermore, my cruel mother, instead of spending time arranging my curls each morning, used to pull my hair back into two plaits. Mrs. Lock, obviously taking advantage of the pleasure of having a small girl for a few days, spent a lot of time, every day, curling my hair, and tying a ribbon in it.

Our next-door neighbours on one side were the McKessars. She would have been well under five feet tall, and she was as round as she was tall. He, and all their adult children, were well over six feet. He used to stoop to pass through a doorway. Their daughter Jean had married a Mr. Poole, who owned the Glaciarium ice skating rink, and we were all very much in awe of his wealth. Their son, Douglas, was a big, kind, single chap, of whom I thought most respectfully. They permitted us access to their place by swinging aside two palings in the fence, to effect entry.

On the other side we had for years, as neighbours, the Newcombes. They had a horse and cart, and had the garbage contract for the area. They had a number of adult children, Robert, Neville, Phyllis, Ronnie (Veronica), Maisie, probably others, and a small daughter, Patty, who was six months to the day younger than I. We were fast friends. There was also fence access into their yard. Occasionally Ronnie would faint at work – it was nothing more sinister than being too late to eat her breakfast before she left. Maisie had committed the terrible sin, (they were faithful members of the RC Church) of marrying Ben Horner, a bloke from our West Ryde Methodist Church, and she attended our services every week! Phyllis was being courted by Hector Goodchild, the milkman, who travelled his rounds each day delivering milk in his horse-drawn van. This had a tap at the back, from which he drew milk for his customers. When he reached the Newcombes' house business would cease for a while, while he did some serious visiting.

If we were short of milk, Mum would send me in next door, to get some milk from Hector, until he chose to carry on.

On my sixth birthday, I had my one and only party. I stood at the front door, where I was handed gifts by my visitors. Patty came empty-handed so I sent her home to get something. She came back with a small coin in an envelope. I had a lovely party. I believe I was the last to leave the table. The cake was a rainbow cake, as were all birthday cakes at that time. It had a pink musk stick in the centre, with six tiny dolls attached by ribbons to the musk stick — a Maypole. I have never seen one I liked better.

On a visit to Patty's home one afternoon we chose to entertain ourselves in the enclosed back verandah which had a step halfway along it. We were refining the art of skipping, by using a shorter and shorter rope each time. I jumped and missed, landing on the bridge of my nose on that halfway step. My nose bled for hours, and my face was bruised and broken for a long time. I still carry the mark where I landed full force on that nose.

Finally Newcombes moved away, and I was temporarily heartbroken. The milk supplies improved because Hec and Maisie got married. The family was replaced by the Bells. Also an interesting family. The belonged to the Closed Brethren — the House of David — and nobody, men or women, cut their hair. The men all wore hats, and their hair was somehow rolled up and secured underneath. The Bells had a daughter, May, slightly older than I. A good little girl, but not half so much fun as Patty.

When Mum was finishing off my garments she would require me to stand on the dining room table, on a cloth, so she could adjust the hem. Once I accidentally knocked the glass lampshade, and it fell down, only to be caught by me on its way to the floor.

We used to eat our evening meal in the dining room. The curtains were not always drawn, and Sam used to sit opposite the windows. Mum noticed him grimacing and pulling horrible faces – he had it down to an art form. Suddenly it dawned on her; the glass had become a mirror at night. Sam was shifted to another seat after that.

The sitting room was forbidden territory to us. Mum said it was the only way she could always have one tidy room in her house to receive guests. It was also our punishment room. If we were due to receive a hiding that is where it was administered. Consequently we were quite happy to keep away from it.

We used to sneak into Mum's bedroom when we were allowed, to share the beginning of the day. One day we looked out of the window on to the frosty lawn, to see our black cat, stiff as a board, rimed in white, and obviously dead. It had been baited the previous night.

The rag man, who would come around with his cart, soliciting rags, never got much from us. There was the milko with his cry, "Milky-ilky-ilko!" each morning as he went his rounds, the baker, who had a van full of fresh tempting smelling produce, and the fisho who had his container on a motor bike, who was trailed by every dog and cat in the neighbourhood. (He had rabbits as well, which he would skin on purchase.) The merchants who had horses and carts were popular, because keen gardeners kept an interested eye on their horses, ready to claim any droppings shortly after they fell to the ground. The butcher and grocer also delivered ... this was actually a necessity, because most people did not have cars, and could not carry their purchases home. The grocer not only delivered, but took orders for the next trip too, so it was essential for housewives to have lists ready for him. The greengrocer used to call, as well as the tinker and scissors sharpener, who also sharpened lawnmowers, as I knew. He also sold clothes props.

With further reference to the milkman. This gentleman had a habit of making his milk stretch a bit further, by the judicious addition of some water. When the milk began to look a bit thin, and take on a bluish tinge, someone complained to the health authorities. An inspector was sent to investigate. He approached the milko, who realised what was about to happen. Apparently a very quick thinker, he turned the tap on at the back of the van, climbed into the seat, geed up his horse, and trotted away from the unfortunate health officer. He hurried after the horse and cart, which had milk streaming from the open tap. The last anyone in our street saw of the incident was the sight of a baffled inspector, unable to obtain the proof that the milk was a bit light on.

Over the road from us in Falconer Street lived the Hughes family. They may have had other children, but the one I recall was a youngster the same age as our baby sister. Her name was Patty Hughes. She had a mass of tight very short fair curls on her head. They were allowed to play together, and visited each other with delight. We have a photo of the two mites sitting on a step, side by side, both with their pinafores on. Mrs. Hughes wore glasses and I was repelled by the thickness of the lens. She must have been very short-sighted. The glasses had pink composition frames, and the edge of the lens was reflected and duplicated ad infinitum. Guess who ended up with the same sort of specs?

Once Mrs. Hughes had a black eye. I have no idea how she received it, but the doctor's treatment shocked me, in fact it still does. He attached a leech to her lower eyelid, to remove the bruised blood. Apparently he had a supply of leeches for this purpose. It still gives me shudders to think of it. Small boys used to catch leeches in local streams, and sell them to the doctor.

Mrs. Lewis lived on the same side of the street as us, about three doors up. I never knew why Mum was involved, but several times every week she would go up to see Mrs. Lewis and help her. It was whispered that Mrs. Lewis had a dreadful disease – I am certain it was breast cancer—Mum said it was as if a thick rope came down from her shoulder, and into her breast. I suspect she may have dressed it for the older lady, because of the regularity of her visits. The Seftons lived a couple of blocks up from us, on the same side, as did Peggy Pattison.

Twice a year we went to the city where Mum bought clothing and other necessities. Because I had a twisted small toe, and wide feet, as well as somewhat pigeon toes, Mum always bought my shoes at David Jones in the city. The shoe department had an x-ray machine. When I tried on a shoe I had to stand up next to the x-ray machine, and place my foot, or feet, underneath it. The shop assistant would switch it on, causing a green light to beam down, to show which way the bones were lying inside the shoe. I could thus see whether it fitted or not. Usually it didn't. Mum favoured a style known as a college shoe, which had a strap across the instep. I thought it was ugly, but it was an improvement on the other school shoe which was favoured – a black or brown leather lace-up. I was fourteen before I had a shoe I liked. They had a fairly solid adult heel, were white, and had a roll of leather on the front, being well-suited to a middle-aged matron. However they fitted, and I was happy, even though they looked like boats. My next pair were for winter, and were a fairly low-heeled pair of brown court shoes, which really were attractive.

Most of our clothes were home-made, boys and all, and Mum was no seamstress. She bought my dress patterns from the "Young Misses" section of the pattern book, and did not discover until Elaine was growing up that there was also a section for teenagers. She was very careful with money, which included saving on dressmaking. If a pattern instructed her to buy three and a half yards of material, she would only buy three yards. Ignoring details like the grain of the material, or the way a pattern was running, she would use up every piece of material, and join two pieces together to fit the pattern onto the material. It was unfortunate if a striped weave didn't run properly, but she had saved on half a yard of fabric, so that was considered a plus.

At Christmas time we were taken to see Santa Claus at one of the big department stores. Mark Foys had a wonderful window dresser, who could make anything out of an uncut bolt of material. Grace Brothers had a myriad of Christmas lights, as did Farmers. But the ultimate festive window dressers were Anthony Hordens, and David Jones. Everyone turned out to see the Christmas windows in the city.

We would also go to the pantomime. As we grew older this became the Gilbert and Sullivan Savoy Operas instead.

I clearly remember "Aladdin." The Dame was Madam Twanky, Aladdin's mother. Aladdin was a girl. For some reason the principal boy was traditionally played by a girl. The magician was evil, out to destroy anything and everything, while the audience watched. We had to shriek out to Madam Twanky to stop him whenever he appeared.

My favourite panto was Cinderella — not just for the magic between Cinderella and Prince Charming, but the array of other characters was so entertaining. There was the Demon King (bad), and Buttons (good). The ugly sisters and their mother were delightful. Ethel and Maude were two bulky men. It was wonderful to watch them preparing their toilette for the ball. They washed themselves, then poured the contents of the basin of water into a chest of drawers to dispose of it. They used a flit gun as a deodorant, they had Cinderella lacing up their stays, they had pantaloons, outrageous wigs, and were as crass as it was possible to be. They flirted with a ghost, thinking it was the Prince, and altogether had a wonderful time. So did the kids in the audience. We shrieked and yelled, fully participating in the action. There was also a wonderful sunflower. Buttons planted it, and it grew a foot or so every time he watered it. Naturally the Demon King felt it was his duty to destroy it. We had to summons Buttons onto the stage to save the flower. It worked every time.

Growing up more we were introduced to the Savoy operas. I wish I could have seen all of them. My repertoire was The Pirates of Penzance, The Mikado, the Gondoliers, H.M.S. Pinafore, The Yeomen of the Guard and Iolanthe. Sam displayed his love of music very early, and was permitted to attend an operetta while the rest of us went to the panto. We had a book full of the librettos of those musicals, and I still know most of the words from the ones we saw.

Street photographers were everywhere at that time, and people would be snapped as they walked down the street. There was one delightful family photo of all of us, dressed in our Sunday best. Even Dad was with us, and we were going to the Theatre Royal for Gilbert and Sullivan. When Dad brought this photo home he would say, "Look, there we all are, Mummy, Daddy, Jim, Sam and Pat. All together." Then the youngest member of the family would expostulate: "I'm there too."

"Where?"

"Look, down among the legs.".

That pink shepherdess dress was used on yet another occasion. There was a school fancy dress ball at Top Ryde. For some reason I was taken to it. During the evening there was a competition. This consisted of all the children in turn reciting a nursery rhyme. As soon as one missed a turn he or she dropped out. The numbers were rapidly depleted. Finally I was the winner. The only difficulty was that I still knew a number more rhymes and I intended to say them. It was hard trying to get me to stop.

Three

When I left Mrs. Lock's school I was sent to Eastwood Primary Girls School. I spent one unhappy year there before I was transferred back to West Ryde School and my old friends. The idea of Eastwood was that I should be friends with Shirley, my cousin. Unfortunately this was not a goer. Shirley was a year older than me, she had her own friends, and each age group had a different part of the playground in which to play. I have always regretted that I never knew her as a friend, when we were children. After I grew up I found out how pleasant and friendly she really was. Mine was the loss.

While I was at Eastwood the health department of New South Wales started a vaccination scheme, to help prevent tetanus, diphtheria and whooping cough. Unless excused for some good reason, every child in every school had to attend the nearest hospital to have a series of inoculations. We were bussed to the hospital and lined up like cattle going through a dip. Dozens of us at a time. As our line shuffled forward a nurse would swab each child's arm in turn, ready to be presented to the doctor, who was waiting with a syringe at the ready. Almost my turn. The girl ahead of me offered her arm, and suddenly the needle broke off in her flesh. In appalled horror I watched as the embedded needle was removed, replaced, and the girl re-injected. The youngster concerned could not see anything as they shielded her. But I was next and saw the lot. I fronted up, then my imagination just got too much for me. I bailed up!

My punishment was awful, but very much of that period's thinking. I was stood to one side and had to watch as everyone else received his or her needle. I was given mine last of all. As a result, I still have a fear and horror of anything connected with injections. I suspect the doctor was overworked and fed up, but that didn't help me.

One day while still at Eastwood I was walking towards the railway station when I saw a three-year-old girl, with blonde curls, run out onto the road. Horrified people tried to stop her, but she was too quick. As she darted out a lorry came trundling along the street. It struck the youngster, knocked her to the ground, and passed right over her. When it stopped, the driver tore round to see what he had done, and the little girl got up, and ran back to her mother. In those days vehicles were quite high off the ground, and there had been sufficient clearance to not damage her, as she lay still on the ground.

In winter our footwear often became soaking wet, and would have to be dried off ready for the next day. Once when this happened, Mum put our shoes in the oven to hurry up the process – all three pairs. Time passed. At some stage we were alerted by a strange smell. Our shoes had been dried all too well. They had shrivelled up, and were totally unwearable. I presume we wore our good shoes to school until they could be replaced.

Back at West Ryde school I was happy again, although I preferred Mrs. Lock's school. I made my dearest friend there – Joan Wendy Levy. All Mrs. Lock's old pupils did well, particularly Margaret Sefton and me. Never one to allow for emergencies I was inclined to just get to school on time.

Once I realised I had missed the bus, and had to walk. It was a long way, and I was desperate and late. At West Ryde station I saw a line of taxis waiting for passengers. I had one coin in my possession. I climbed into a cab – the first time in my life – and asked to be taken to West Ryde School. As we got closer, I got a bit nervous, and got him to stop just before the school grounds, I got out, and went to pay him. I handed him my sole coin, a sixpence. He nearly exploded. I could not understand why. It was a lot of money to me. He took it, roused at me, then showed me the meter fare. Flag fall alone was one shilling. At least I wasn't late. When I went into school I was met by a throng of other children, who had seen me in the cab. They all thought we had won the lottery.

My good little mother deplored gambling, including the lottery. Once, someone to whom she had done a kindness, gave her a lottery ticket in appreciation. She was on tenterhooks until it was drawn, and she found she did not have a prize. We used to ask her what she would do if she did win. "Give it to the hospital." The hospitals were the main beneficiaries of profits from the lotteries, which is why she said this. She would have too.

I remember fifth class with pleasure. Mrs. Naughton was my teacher. She was a big bosomy woman, who affected to dress in white all the time, and who carried a burgundy-coloured parasol to do playground duty, so that her face was bathed in a puce light whenever she was outside. When the year started she called the roll. We had to respond with "Present Mrs. Naughton," and state our birth dates. Betty Doig replied, "Present Mrs. Naughton, 10th March."

My heart tingled with delight because Mrs. Naughton said, "Why, that is two days before mine, Betty."

In due course I was called, and I was able to say, "Present Mrs. Naughton, 12th March."

"Why, that is the same day as mine, Pat."

Life held no greater bliss. For the only year in my life I was the teacher's pet. Each morning I was sent out to purchase a raspberry slice and an apple for Mrs. Naughton's morning tea. I pressed my mother for some money to buy Mrs. Naughton a birthday present., and on the great day I went to the shop, and bought her six raspberry slices and six apples, because I knew what she liked. I sometimes wonder what she thought. She, in turn, gave me a pretty little cardboard box. Inside was three yards of three-inch wide, heavy pink satin ribbon – to tie up my bonny brown hair. She could not have chosen a kinder gift. We could not afford wide ribbon. I used to envy the other girls at Sunday School who flaunted big bows, and now I had my very own. I could hardly bear to cut it to size.

Fay Cheetham went to that school, as did Beverly Dawes, and Lydia Malishkin, and Klara Shershoff. One day the girls were racing through the toilet block, playing chasings, when a swing door closed on the finger of one youngster, cutting it off. We were all shocked, but Lydia picked up the dismembered member, and took it to the school incinerator, where she disposed of it. We could understand her bravery. She was of a white Russian family which had migrated to Australia, so we knew she must have suffered torture and cruelty – we had read about this in books – and a minor thing like this would of course, be of no problem to her. Klara was also of the same background – but had she shown the same savoir faire? Actually Klara was a very nice girl, when I came to know her later on. Lydia was swarthy, and wore her straight brown plaits slightly to the front of her shoulders, giving her face a rather flat look. She also had rosy cheeks (no doubt from the frozen Russian steppes – well, that's what we thought!)

Once – only once – I was invited to make the headmistress's morning tea. Actually Miss Best, who was wheelchair bound, always had orange juice, which the privileged pupil had to squeeze into a glass jug, which should have been waiting for her to do so. I was told this, I found the orange, I found the squeezer, but nowhere could I find the glass jug. The only glass item I could see was a clear glass round bowl, in which I placed the juice. In hindsight I feel that it was actually a sugar basin. When I told my mother about this she told me an even more interesting tale.

When she and her friend Dot Hubery had once been given the same privilege at Methodist Ladies College in Burwood, N.S.W., they had been requested to make a jug of cocoa for the staff room. They did so without trouble, but on the way from the kitchen to the staff room they spilled some of the liquid. Already delayed, they spotted a vase of flowers. Dot poured some of this water into the jug to make up the right amount again. This mixture they delivered to the staff room. They also were once only cup bearers.

Joan Levy's father was the Principal of West Ryde Boys School. I was very much in awe of him. (Mr. Michael Charles Ivan Levy (Ivan to his friends, Sir to the rest of the world.) I felt honoured to be allowed to become Joan's friend.

This was the school at which it was discovered I was shortsighted, and that severely. The school nurse picked it up. I always had to use a front desk to see the blackboard. So periodically I went to visit Dr. McIndoe, an eye specialist in Macquarie Street.

I went to school in my new glasses — pink composition frames, the cheapest available, and discovered that glasses were a disadvantage, even if you could see better. I must have been the despair of Mum. I know I broke a number of pairs over time, and certainly they had to be upgraded into stronger ones each year. I hated them. I was different. I was encouraged to eat fish, brains (ugh), and other white meats, which it was thought might improve my sight.

At this stage Fifth Class was gathered together to take an intelligence test. Apparently all Fifth classes in the Metropolitan area were to do this test. The purpose was to pick and choose a couple of groups of elite pupils to be placed in special classes, to do advanced work at selected schools. A small number of girls (and I presume boys also) had to attend special classes. I was one of the chosen. Our communal school was the Eastwood Public School. To add to the interest, we had a classroom in the boys school, so actually we attended Eastwood Boys School. As it adjoined the girls school we still had to use all the girls' school facilities.

Norma Jenkins was in our class — she had a disfiguring naevus, which divided her face symmetrically. One girl was Erina Matheson. She was a pretty blonde. We could never understand her selection as she was incapable of doing the work. She was submitted to a number of tests throughout the year, each of them revealing her as having the highest I.Q. of us all — genius rating. (And that was in a class which included Barbara Houlsby and Joan Baker.) Nowadays I would say she was probably a true dyslexic. It must have defeated the purpose of a lot of the class however, because there were times when the whole class had to slow down to include her. It was here that I discovered, and disliked, projects and assignments. Basically I think I lacked true ambition — the purpose was not there. I certainly did my homework — 10.30

to 11:00 each night, and as I got older, it never got easier — but I lack that drive which takes one to the top. Barbara had it. Joan Levy was a member of that class too, as was Joan Baker.

Joan Baker's mother had been friends with mine at school, and they rediscovered each other through our friendship. Joan's mother, Freda, could neither sew, knit, nor crochet. When she found she was expecting another baby when Joan turned eight, it was Joan who knitted the whole of that baby's layette. I don't know where she learned. I recollect Barbara to, doing a similar sort of thing. She knitted herself a full dress on one enormous circular needle, each morning in the train on the way to and from school. She was in her early teens at the time of this effort. Like most of us, she still had lots of puppy fat, and would have been well advised to choose a garment other than a figure-hugging frock, but what an achievement for a young girl. Joan Baker and Barbara were both brilliant women in their careers later on.

At this time I had my first crush on a boy. though he never knew it. John Denny learned the violin, and at a concert, where Joan Levy played the piano, John Denny played "Danny Boy" on the violin, and I fell in love from a distance. I could work up the courage to ask for his autograph, but that was the beginning and end of the romance. Not only that, but I lost the revered signature before I reached home.

I bet Joan Levy has never forgotten the day when several us were standing under the eaves of the Boys' School. A pigeon dumped its message on her shoulder, spilling the subsequent mess both on the front and back of her tunic. At this stage the bell rang. Both Joan and I were excused until we could clean her up. She told me of her family friend, a teacher at Singleton School, who made the mistake of looking upwards as she was speaking and had a similar hit from above into her open mouth!

From being one of the "big" girls in primary school, I found a cultural change when I was promoted to secondary school. I was once again at the bottom of the ladder, a "little" girl at Hornsby Girls' High School.

First of all, there was the uniform; a navy double breasted tunic, combined with a white, long-sleeved blouse, a tie striped in navy and putty, an appalling combination, black stockings and shoes. For my sins my mother favoured strapped college shoes. There were also navy gloves, and a felt or Panama hat — if one was lucky enough, she had a velour hat — round the crown of which was a hatband in the same offensive colours and sporting the school badge on the front. When the weather was cool a navy, vee necked jumper, and/or navy blazer with the school emblem on the top left pocket could be worn. Although this was a Public School, and although it was wartime, uniform regulations were very strictly adhered to. Consequently, our school had a remarkable pride in itself.

During my first year there, the school came up with the idea of a summer uniform. This was a putty coloured dress, in my case, very home-made, as Mum was no seamstress. It was buttoned from neck to waist, with a collar which had rows of navy stitching around it. The dress had to conform to a certain respectable length, a fact which worried me not at all, as I was not interested in, nor did I understand fashion. Others who cared, hitched up their dresses over the belt, sneaked half an inch here or there, and achieved a more attractive look. I greatly envied Yvonne Billington, who had her dress made by an expert. This, combined with a good figure, made her stand out. We were able to wear ankle socks in leaf mould colour with this outfit, which was much more suitable than the heavy serge uniform.

In winter, of course, out came the tunic. I expect most people were like me. I had one uniform only, but two blouses. Each afternoon, when I arrived home, the uniform was taken off. After pressure from my mother, I would sponge off any dirty spots, then with a steam cloth (usually a man's handkerchief) I would press the pleats back into the tunic, and hang it ready for the next day. My long-suffering mother usually saw that my blouse was ready. I would not have put it past me to wear the same one for days.

Again, in winter it often rained. This meant that one's shoes were frequently damp. It was necessary to stuff them with newspaper to keep their shape. Then they would be stood in the oven long enough to draw most of the moisture out of them. One appalling day, when both of my brothers and I had shoes drying in the oven, we forgot them. These twisted up, small, hard shoes came out. They smelled pretty horrible too.

Strangely, I do not remember the outcome, as we each had only one pair of school shoes. I suppose we wore our Sunday shoes instead.

During the war it was not easy to obtain decent quality items. It rained particularly heavily one day, and we all got drenched on our way to school. Once there, fires were lit in the various rooms, but as this was such a rarity, a great deal of smoke belched into each room, and it was not an entirely successful move. Moreover, on this day, we were allowed to remove our saturated stockings and shoes (in fact some girls even had to change into their gym uniforms), and the discarded clothing was draped wherever it could be placed to dry. To our delight, and Joan's horror, her legs were bright green — the dye in her stockings not very stable. It would have happened to other girls too, but Joan was our prime source of interest.

Who could forget some of our wet weather gear? So many things were unavailable that we had to take alternatives at times.

Most of us wore poncho-like oilskin capes. Not only did we fit under the capes, but so did our school bags. We must have resembled walking eggs! Or watermelons! The rain would drip down from our hats, and run in on the back of our necks. At least, in Queensland, the rain is warm, even if creating a sticky situation.

To travel to school involved some timing. My train left Denistone for Hornsby at six minutes past eight in the morning, taking twenty-five minutes to reach its destination. I was chronically tardy, which always meant a last minute rush. I would cross the road, walk down the street, past a couple of houses, turn off and follow a narrow dirt track, just wide enough for one person. This went through a tract of bushland, which descended to a narrow creek. This had to be negotiated, then up the other side, through the bush, until it joined a concrete pedestrian path (and the way I should have gone) which led to the station. My train left from the platform on the other side of the railway line, so I not only had to get to the station, but to the section where the First Year, Second Year, Third Year etc girls had to enter the carriages. This was nearly always a scramble.

There were strict rules of behaviour on the train. There was a proscribed carriage for girls in each year to use, and a train prefect in each carriage to observe that we behaved ourselves. These prefects had the privilege of issuing Order Marks, which were credited not against the sinner, but against her school house. For honour's sake we behaved.

I only missed the train twice by some miracle. There is little worse than having to wait twenty-five minutes for the next train, and be the object of curiosity to other travellers, especially when you know it is your own fault.

There was one attractive girl, a year ahead of me, who also caught the train at Denistone. One of her eyes was milky and sightless. I understand that acid had been accidentally dropped into it, instead of eye drops.

Four

As I grew older my sight troubled me more, and the eye specialist recommended that I do little, or no reading. This was, to a born reader, a terrible hardship. Every day in the train, on the way to school, Joan would read to me. Her book of choice was about the adventures of Mildred Cable and Evangaline French, missionaries carrying out their work in New China.

One day we went to meet these two redoubtable ladies in the city. "How nice to meet you again," said one. A faux pas — this was our first and only meeting with them.

Out of the train at Hornsby we formed into lines, according to our year, and marched to school. We all had season concessional passes. Woe betide anyone who lost, or forgot, hers!

We would assemble in front of the school in our classes, when the bell rang at eight forty-five. After regular formalities we were marched into our classrooms. In the first year our room abutted that of the Headmistress's office, a fact which guaranteed our behaviour on the whole.

Miss Muriel Violet Morley was the Principal. To me she was a commanding and august figure, very upright, with snowy, closely-curled hair, and a very regal mien. As she swept along the corridors she would keep an eagle, beady, black eye out for unacceptable behaviour. One sin was to walk in pairs or groups along the hallways. I can still clearly recall a haughty voice saying, "Single file in the corridor, please, gels!"

One one memorable occasion the whole school was kept in. At the weekly assembly in the hall there had been undue restlessness. In a rash moment Miss Morley threatened to detain everyone. When the restlessness continued she had no option but to keep us all in. A number of teachers were seated on the stage behind her, as Mis Morley reprimanded us. Then she stood aloofly, watching for any misdemeanour, and waiting for sufficient time to pass when she could release us. As she was holding sway over six hundred pupils she was doing a remarkable job.

She had a small crystal bedroom clock on the table next to where she stood so erectly. Every few minutes she would pick it up, look to make sure it was still going, then shake it, until a satisfactory lapse of time had occurred when she could release us with dignity intact.

Those weekly assemblies in the hall were impressive. The staff, in their academic gowns, were seated on the platform in front of us: the headmistress reading the notices, the admonitions, the praises and the criticisms as they flowed in.

One musical pupil had the task of rendering the National Anthem each week, as we roared it out. One day she was absent. Miss Morley (which means I was in First Year) appealed to the school for someone to accompany the singing. I very much wanted Joan to offer, after all music seemed comparatively simple to the musical illiterate. No, she wouldn't. Nor would anyone else. In desperation I stood up, and offered my services. I was willing to play the air, picking my way with one finger — a feat I had taught myself on Grandma's piano. My offer was abruptly, and unkindly, declined. Miss Champion eventually took over.

Our own English teacher being absent one day, Miss Morley, to our horror, took our class. She led us to the oval, announced that the sundial on the flag-stoned path beside the oval, was an altar, and that we were Grecian maidens coming to honour the Goddess, Diana. We were then sent to stand behind the poplars which edged the playing field, while Miss Morley read out the poem "Ode to Diana". As the words: "Queen and Huntress, chaste and fair," were proclaimed we were supposed to shimmy out from our poplars and head towards the sundial.

Her immediate successor was Miss Hansen, who was of a somewhat gentler mould. She lacked the gimlet eye which produced such reverential awe and terror created by Miss Morley.

In first year Miss Martin, our French teacher, produced one of many interesting memories. April Fool's Day was upon us, when Miss Martin disclosed that the French greeting on that day was "Avril Poisson," (April Fish). French was the first subject on the 1st of April, so we pushed up one blackboard, and scored the magic words, then drew the upper board down over the lettering. Along came Miss Martin, pushed up the board, and there revealed were the words,"Avril Poisson". What deflation!

We had some wonderful teachers. English was my chief inanimate love, so I flourished under such women.

In a music period I was unhappily seated in the front row of the class. Miss Champion, who had not yet assessed my musical inabilities, was trying to teach us something about music. Suddenly she started dipping her head at me. I had not the foggiest idea of what she was trying to convey. As it turned out, she expected me to leap to my feet and turn the page of the sheet music she was following.

Miss Noel had the misfortune to have a droopy face, and she combined this with a hair style from the early thirties. Altogether, she had an element of droop about her. She also had the habit of sitting on the right hand corner of some girl's desk when she wanted to make a point. With the fiendishness that children so often disclose, we chose one day to thoroughly ink the rim of every inkwell in the class, so that if she chose to practice this habit, she would be rewarded. Well, she did, and she was. To our horrified delight, when she rose from the corner of the desk, a clear round inkwell shaped stain decorated the rear of her dress. Absolutely nothing was ever said about this incident.

Miss Lever had grey hair, which she livened up with a blue rinse. She taught the sciences. I was informed (allegedly reliably) that she was a member of the Lever & Kitchen soap manufacturing clan. I have no reason to disbelieve this fact. It has certainly made purchasing soap products more interesting over the years. Even now I cast an enquiring glance at all soap products as a result.

Miss Falconer was under five feet tall. Also a greying lady, she took great pride in her appearance, having beautifully coiffed hair. She wore what I considered to be the most beautiful clothes. She favoured, and could wear well, georgettes, crepes, gathered skirts and bishop's sleeves on her frocks. I remember her peachy complexion, and one deep green georgette dress with bishop's sleeves, which I thought was enchanting. As I grew older and she figured in my school life more, I was amazed, in my final year, to find that she liked me too; big, bumbly, clumsy and immature as I was. When I was leaving school I followed the trend of seeking autographs, and I sought hers. To my amazement she gave me an autograph book which had been hers, filled with lovely little paintings and sentimental quotations. I treasured it for many years.

In my autograph book, was one which still amuses me. Barbara McGinnis had sketched a picture of a frightful old hag, hairy warts and all. She had inscribed it with the immortal words, "They say beauty is only skin deep. Then, for goodness sake, skin her!"

I had yet another which entertained me, partly because it was written by Joan's mother, who must have had unplumbed depths. It ran, "Naughty little cuss words, such as "dash" and "blow", often lead to wuss words, and then to realms below."

Who could forget Miss Cora Ruby Buckley? She also favoured the hairstyle of her girlhood. This was a mistake, as it lengthened her face, and her glasses obtruded — they were fairly heavy. But she proved to be a good teacher for me. I recollect snippets of the poem which was written about her in the Gay Day Book. A group of us was once invited to the A.B.C. Studios to broadcast a session of a class having an English lesson and discussion, live. I was one of the elite half dozen who had been chosen. When the affair was over Miss Buckley generously took us to Grace Brothers to have afternoon tea. At this stage one of my memorable foot-in-mouthers occurred. We had dainty sandwiches, and an assortment of sweet cakes and slices. As I gazed at this impressive array I commented,"Isn't it a good job that the waitress realised we are girls, and not old women of fifty?" I knew I had offended as soon as the words were out of my mouth!

She was very fond of poetry, and succeeded in passing her interest on to her pupils. She tried to make a responsive poem out of "Sweet Content." Half the class would utter "Art thou poor, yet hast thou golden slumbers?" and the rest would reply "Oh, Sweet Content." I'll give her this, I still remember the whole poem quite clearly to this day.

She also had great admiration for the works of Dame Edith Sitwell, an eccentric English aristocrat and poetess, who was convinced that one could perform ballet to words, as well as music. We had a poem of hers to study too, "When Sir Beelzebub, called for his syllabub, In the hotel in Hell, Where Persephone first fell, Blue as the sea were the Gendarmerie, Rocking and shocking the barmaid."

Miss Friedrich was also a vivid teacher. One dramatic day she showed us the effect of a vacuum created in a tin. There was a wonderful bang as the last air was withdrawn, then the buckled and twisted container. There was also the vivisection of the unfortunate frogs, which we each had to bring in for the ultimate sacrifice. My specimen was a bit spindly, and instead of drawing it in a stylised fashion, I drew it as it was, a poor, pathetic specimen if ever there was one. As a result, in spite of its realism, I did not achieve top marks for that drawing. There was also the frog that nearly got away. Coming out from the ether, it revived enough to hop away after dissection.

To our group of innocents Miss Friedrich explained, in biological terms, the mysteries of sex, from the amoeba through to plants, to animals and humans. She announced that we were to learn about S E X. I couldn't have cared much less, especially when we learned that it was just the means of reproduction for everything.

As a result of my studies under Miss Friedrich, when I cut up a bullock's brain, sliced and dissected a kidney, and other pieces of offal, I have always felt a distaste for those foods, even though I cook them for my family. I was appalled at the enormous quantities of tubing through which urine passed in the filtering system of the kidney. When I lived at Planet Downs, I used to look at these organs, brought in with the killer, and think back to Miss Friedrich, and my biology classes.

Thursday afternoons were devoted to sport. I had never been any good at it, and was never selected for any team event. About this time volleyball came into vogue. It was planned for the hopeless athletes like me. I actually enjoyed it, I expect because I could see the ball. It was non-competitive. Years later I was vindicated in my lack of co-ordinated skills. An eye specialist said to me: "You have never been any good at sport, have you? I bet you always missed the ball, in any sport?"

I acknowledged that this was so, feeling rather ashamed that so long afterwards it was still apparent. Then he explained that my vision was the problem, and would always be so. I could have kissed him!

In summer we used to go swimming, not a very common school sport at that time. We would travel for half an hour on the train, from Hornsby to Milson's Point, to attend the Olympic Pool — the only one of that size in Sydney. Here we would change, plough through a trench of water, to cleanse our feet, over which was a flowing shower, to cleanse our bodies, then into the water, to swim. While there we trained for our Lifesaving Bronze Medal. Somehow I received one on each of two occasions, as well as our Lifesaving certificates. It was a real effort duck-diving to the bottom of the deep end of the pool to retrieve a brick, particularly with a great audience keeping an eye on one.

Swimming carnivals were also starting about this time. Once our group went along as cheerleaders for our school. Here, for the first time, I saw a girl doing Butterfly stroke. There was not a separate race for this, so it was included in with ordinary breaststroke. It seemed extraordinary. That girl won the race by a mile. Quite a few of us caught plantar warts from the swimming pool, and tinea was often a result of walking around barefooted on the damp open surfaces there.

I never discovered the intricacies of vigoro or softball. I certainly wished I knew something about basketball years later when I went to Mary Kathleen to teach.

Cloncurry, Mount Isa and Mary K had a tournament, arranged by the Headmaster. He worked on the principle that every woman must know about basketball. He was wrong. As the only woman teacher present I was told to referee the games. I solved the problem in an unusual manner. All the girls who were playing knew the game, so when I saw them glance at me to see my reaction to some play, I blew the whistle. Sometimes they even stopped, awaiting my whistle. I then gave it to them. Those must have been the most self-regulated games ever conducted. But it was hell on earth for the ref.

Once I visited Linnea Jonsson's home. She took us in to look at her father's studio, where Radish, the infamous racehorse, and the characters from the Smith's Weekly cartoons were created. We were introduced to her father, who was very nice to us, and I learned that Joe can sometimes be spelled "Jo".

Joan Levy's father terrified me. He was so important, and I was merely a weak link at school. One year he took Mrs. Levy and Joan to Port Arthur, in Tasmania, for a holiday, because he was writing a thesis on the subject, for his Doctorate in Literature. It seemed almost the end of the earth to us. How small the world is now for travellers.

A fashionable hairstyle during my high school days was the pageboy cut. It looked so sleek and pretty on other girls, sometimes turned inward towards the neck, sometimes flicked out, but always smooth and attractive. I was keen to have such a style myself, but was limited by very curly, and extraordinarily long hair, which I was not allowed to have cut. Finally I tried to achieve the unachievable. I brushed and combed my hair, tying a ribbon around the bottom of it quite tightly, then I turned it under, bringing the ribbon over my head, then tying the ends together under this enormous mass. I even wore it for part of a day. I also wanted to be able to put my hair in rags, as did many of the girls, to achieve a certain look.

At home I ripped an old sheet into strips, then painstakingly put my wet hair in curls. I slept, (or not, as the case may be) that night in this arrangement, then proceeded to unfurl it the next morning. There were bits of thread mixed up with hair, bits I had to snip out, because I could not possibly untangle the cloth and the twisted hair, and the final result??? Many years later a short Afro hairdo became fashionable. Mine was a long Afro hairstyle. My unfeeling mother made me wash it out, and I attended school with two heavy, soaking wet plaits all that day.

Joan Baker was extraordinarily clever. Unlike Barbara Houlsby she did not need to study, but held things in her memory without effort. If Barbara didn't come first in any subject, Joan Baker did. It is just as well that they had some different subjects to challenge others. Barbara topped the year in her Leaving Certificate. Joan came second. Like Margaret she was younger than the everyone else, but that did not affect either girl's ability. Margaret, even as a quite young girl, gained my endless admiration when I discovered she could solve cryptic crossword puzzles.

Can I forget my misery at high school, as I felt my close friendship with Joan Levy being eroded, as she found equally good friends in the school? If only she knew the heart burn she cost me, when she confided secrets, but explained that I was excluded from them.

On the other hand I felt extremely important, as having an

almost personal interest in Joan's sister Bessie, when she had her three babies — the third a complete and total surprise to the doctor and nurses as well.

Five

With the war on, travel had become difficult. Most of us did not go anywhere much, but sometimes something special happened requiring travel. Bessie Levy was an army nurse. She fell in love with Alf Betts, also in the army. With all the emotions generated by war, and the possibility that neither might survive battle, they chose to marry. The wedding was to take place in Queensland.

Unfortunately, all travel between states was banned. Therefore, the Levys decided to "Hop the border". After all, Mr. Levy had to give the bride away, and Joan was to be the only bridesmaid. They caught a train as close to the border as they could, and were transported the rest of the way by vehicle, without being challenged. We, of course, waited with bated breath for the family to be arrested.

The bridal couple were married in uniform, and the bridesmaid wore a pink short dress, unlike the romantic ones we all dreamed of. Ultimately the triplets I mentioned were the result of this union, the only children they had.

Other than school, the church provided most of our social life, both before leaving Falconer Street, and when we lived at Ryedale Road, Denistone. I used to walk to Sunday School, which meant I had to walk down our street, turn right along Park Road, then turn down Mrs. Lock's Street for a block and a half, then right into another street. Halfway along this street was a square park, which was bisected by two diagonal cement paths. I would cross this, come out into a road, turn up beside the Commonwealth Bank, then turn left into Station Road, past Mr. Bowe's Cafe, Adams Rich Cake Shop, past the newsagent, grocer greengrocer and toy shop. At Mr. Birch the Chemist's shop I would cross the road, go over the railway bridge, down the other side, follow a footpath down into the Main Parramatta Road, Victoria Road, cross this, then walk a few houses up till I came to the Methodist Hall and Church.

We were abuzz with interest at one time. A house was being built in another street of our suburb of a wonderful new material. Curious about something so unusual, I diverged from my usual routine and took another path so I could examine this wonderful house. As far as I knew all suburban houses were made of brick or weatherboard. When I saw it I wondered what all the fuss was about. It was the normal shape and size, although lack of building materials owing to the war prevented the addition of any verandah. It was being constructed of fibre cement, something we had never heard of till then.

When I was smaller I used to go to Little Sunday School in the Hall. We belted out hymns and choruses, learned the Christian story, learned texts, handed in our offering — 1d in little Sunday School. We sang Twinkle, Twinkle, Hear the Pennies Dropping, If I were a Beautiful Twinkling Star, Jesus wants me for a sunbeam,

Now Sunday School is Over, I am H A P P Y etc, and then went home.

I graduated into Big Sunday School, which was held in the Church itself, and I was given 3d to put in the plate. Mr. Bowden was a wonderful superintendent, and he inspired us. His father had been declared bankrupt. Mr. Bowden took his father's debts on and paid them all off. He was a solicitor in civilian life. Then he joined the armed forces. I was heartbroken — fortunately he had a son, Tony, about my brother's age. At no time did he display the slightest interest in me, but I had a severe crush on him.

I can remember that we once had a visit from the Temperance League at Sunday School. I remember two interesting things. 1. The speaker produced two bottles, one full of alcohol, one of water. He lowered a worm into each. The unfortunate in the alcohol, twisted and shrivelled up in short form, the one in water swam around obviously still in good health. This was enough to convince us that alcohol was unsafe. 2. He then urged us all to sign the pledge, and after the demonstration in those bottles we all signed happily and eagerly.

Upon Mr. Bowden's departure for the war, Mr Annabel came out of retirement to become Superintendent. We did not like him — no one could equal Mr. Bowden! He used to urge us to close our eyes during prayers, then he would open his own to check on any disrespectful sinners, whom he would then name. He appeared to us sanctimonious.

Once a year we had a whole new outfit of clothes, from shoes and socks to ribbons and hats. These became our good clothes for the next year. And we first wore these clothes at Sunday School Anniversary.

One year, when the war was becoming desperate, the people of the church met and decided to go without new clothes for the next year. Instead, they would give the money to the war effort. Mum, with her husband away at sea, did so. She gave the money as decided, and took us to church in our one-year-old clothes. When we arrived we were the only ones who were not sporting new outfits, even the Minister's children were bedecked. We were noticed all right. Mum was so upset that for about three months she felt unable to take communion, because she could not forgive the other communicants.

Sunday went along these lines: 10 a.m. Christian Fellowship — I went but it never engaged my interest much: Church 11 a.m. Mum was usually home, cooking the Sunday dinner, so we were the family reps: Home for a joint of meat (corned beef, a leg of mutton or a roast of beef): back to Sunday School at 3 p.m. Mum attended church at night, if she hadn't gone in the morning. Once a month there was fellowship tea, where each person had to supply some contribution to the meal. One girl always brought along a copha chocolate biscuit cake — I always positioned myself near that cake, I would have eaten the lot, had I the opportunity — that was Lorone Ellis. Her younger sister Judith had one ambition in life, to own and run a sandwich bar (I wonder if she ever did?) Then at 7 p.m. there was evening church.

On Tuesdays after school there were the Rays for pre-teens; the Comrades for older girls; and the Order of Knights (O.K.s) for the boys. They were also in cubs, scouts, and later Rovers. Occasionally Mum went to morning church. Once Sam and I decided to stay at home, to give her a surprise and help her. While she was out, we got to and did the whole family wash, boiling up the clothes, washing and rinsing them, and hanging them out to dry. We were so proud to have helped her. As she walked home she became aware that of all the houses in the street there was one that was different. Her own! Sunday had been blasphemed. Poor thing, it mattered so much at that time. She was humiliated and upset. She said later how sorry she was that at that time she had been too bigoted to recognise the goodwill behind our effort.

For all Churchgoing families Sunday was set aside. We were never allowed the Sunday papers, nor were we allowed to sing anything but religious songs. As we did not know too many others this wasn't such a hardship. We were never allowed comics except Ginger Meggs and Mandrake — why they were acceptable I do not know. No housework was done on that day except making beds, meals and washing up. We all had a thorough bath that day too, but my hair was washed on Saturday because it took nearly all day to dry. We did not have a shower. I knew no one who actually had one in the home.

One Sunday (I was under ten at this time) I was, as all too often the case, late for Sunday School. I did not want to face the humiliation of walking down the aisle for everyone to see, but I knew I had to attend. My solution was simple. I went all the way to the church; then I slid under the little Sunday School Hall to wait for the proceedings to finish. At this stage I proposed to slide out from underneath and join the crowd of youngsters going home. Unfortunately, I did not bargain on the open windows of the Church itself, or the sharp-eyed teacher who spotted me crouched below the floor. I was forced to come out and join my class, later than ever!

Our path to Sunday School led us past the tempting cafe run by Mr. Bowe. He sold ice cream! We never entered his shop. Then I conceived a bold plan. From my brothers I extracted tuppence of each of their threepences for the offertory. Thus they still had money for the plate. I put in my bit also, and on the way home I used this cash to enter Mr. Bowe's shop and buy ice creams, which we consumed. However, as usual fate worked against my nefarious schemes. A city-bound train pulled in at the station, which was close by. Out stepped our aunt, on her way to visit our mother for the afternoon; we were caught in the act.

The West Ryde shops were like most other average suburban shopping centres, including the grocer, greengrocer, newsagency, produce merchant, hairdresser (Miss Isle), a dress salon and a chemist. The chemist often took the place of a doctor, as he didn't charge for advice, just for his wares.

Neil Olsen's father had been in the First World War. As a result he had become deaf. The doctors had not been able to help him. Mr. Birch, however, had a look at his ear, and felt he could help. Each afternoon, on returning from work, Mr. Olsen would call in to the chemist's shop, and Mr. Birch would gently syringe it out. This continued for many months. One day Mr. Birch had his usual good look inside, removed a heavy plug and also extracted a tiny piece of shrapnel. It was a miracle cure.

The grocer upset me on one occasion. I had been sent to purchase some sugar (using coupons). It was raw sugar and looked very dirty to me. I commented on this to the storekeeper. With an eye to his audience of several shoppers he gravely told me the best thing to do would be to wash it carefully. This would remove the grot. I thanked him for his advice and left, wondering why everyone was laughing. Only later did I realise the dissolving quality of sugar, and the fact that he was having a go at me.

Our move to Ryedale Road took place when I was ten. It was within walking distance of our home in West Ryde. Consequently we shifted a lot of stuff ourselves — in the baby's wicker pram. The bird aviary with the two canaries in it was trundled along the streets, for instance. The final move involved a removalist's van. All the gear was piled into the van. Mum and Elaine walked off with the pram, loaded, and the boys and I were assisted up on to the top of the cabin of the van, and drove around to the new house.

This house was slightly above the ground, and when the previous owners (McBeans) moved out, they left some rubbishy bits behind in the underneath area. Naturally the boys scrounged around there, and came up with one interesting find — an ice-cream churn.

To us ice-cream was the ambrosia of the Gods. Rarely, because we lived a good distance from any shops, and because we only had an ice chest as a cooler, rarely did we taste this superlative dish. I was envious of the orphans in the book "Daddy Long Legs" because they had ice cream each Sunday! But occasionally — I am talking of say, once in three years — we would have some. The boys would be sent to West Ryde to purchase an ice cream brick, which was well wrapped in newspaper, and carried rapidly home. It was only its size and shape that allowed it to reach home in one piece. It would then be evenly divided by Mum, the only one to be trusted to give equal shares, and then eaten.

The ice-cream churn created other ideas. We were going to make our own. It had a narrow central cylinder, which rotated by turning a handle on the top. The ice-cream, in our case custard, went in there. This cylinder was surrounded by a larger area into which was placed a mixture of crushed ice and salt. Then the whole thing had to be turned and turned and turned. When the mixture was half frozen it was taken out, stirred, and put back in. The turning was then repeated until hopefully, it was frozen hard. I cannot remember the actual result, just turning that abominable handle.

After a few goes at this, I knew why the churn had been left under the house.

The iceman called each weekday. Carrying a block of ice on a four-pronged set of tongs, he would come racing up to the side front door, and leave the block on the doorstep, where the money for it was waiting. A billycan and money was also left out for the milkman to make his daily delivery.

It was necessary to bring the ice inside as soon as possible, so there would not be too much ice melted before it could be used. The block was placed in a metal lined box at the top of the ice chest, with drainage holes allowing the melted ice water to rundown the internal metal walls of the ice chest, to keep things inside cool. Then it would fall into a baking dish placed strategically below, to catch the drips. Quite often people did not understand the principle on which an ice chest worked. They would try to keep the block of ice as long as possible, by wrapping it in newspaper before installing it in its box. This would defeat the purpose of allowing the melting ice to distribute the coldness to the internal cabinet.

Jelly was a common dessert. Mum used to set it in the coolest spot she could find, often outside, but never in the ice chest, in case it melted the ice too quickly. We had all the usual desserts of that period, rice pudding, macaroni pudding, junket, golden syrup pudding, all accompanied by custard.

Sam, from an early age, had the work ethic. He obtained a job with the local produce and coal merchant. Every Saturday he would fill bags of coke, or coal, on a commission of sixpence per bag. He once went away for the weekend. To make sure no one else got the job he sub-contracted the work out, at threepence per bag, to me. The produce merchant was astonished to find a small girl, absolutely filthy, filling bags with coke, when he had expected a slightly older brother on the job. I never found out if my mother was aware of this job sharing before it took place. She would certainly have known afterwards, by the state of my clothes.

I can't remember much about medical treatment. I do recall the kerfuffle when the dentist, from North Ryde, arrived at our house, in his car, followed shortly by the baker, in his horse and van, to tell Mum that Sam had been run over by a bus, and was even then in hospital. Mother assured them they were wrong — Sam was in his bedroom, absent from school because he was ill. The poor innocent went inside to investigate. They were wrong, Sam had absconded through the window, and had gone off on his bike.

He had parked behind the bus stop at North Ryde, and the bus driver had backed over him. His bike was unhurt, but Sam had his head spilt open, a broken collar bone, and a dislocated shoulder. He spent a few days in hospital. Although he was still a child (eleven), as the children's ward was full, he was put in with the adult men, most of whom appeared to be that group of temporary Australians, who owned motor scooters or motor bikes.

After that, all he wanted was to own a motor scooter. Grandpa Quinn would blandly promise him one in the future, much to Mum's horror.

Jim also got into trouble with the bike (the same one); but in his case it was the bike which was brought home in two pieces, while Jim was OK. All his life Jim seemed to fall on his feet.

Jim and the Muir boys (I think another youth was with them too) once ran away, up to the Blue Mountains. I think they proposed to live off the bush. Fortunately it was fairly cool when they embarked on this adventure. I have always understood that it got so cold in the bush that they crept to the Railway Station waiting room, to share the warmth of the fire. Ticketless, they were challenged by the station guard, who flagged the train down as it passed through, put them on it, and sent them back to Sydney. My memory is a bit blurred because it caused such great distress, but I know Mum was summonsed to collect him, and pay the return fare. We talked in hushed voices of a severe hiding being administered by a policeman, as Dad was away from home, but if this actually eventuated I do not really know. I believe the Muir boys got their just desserts from their father.

Six

During Mum's last pregnancy I was attending West Ryde School. Unhappily for me the doctor's surgery (incidentally most doctor's conducted their surgeries from their homes, in the front of which shone a red light, twenty-four hours a day) was on the final turn off to West Ryde School. Once a week I had to leave a medicine bottle containing Mum's "specimen" at Dr. Howe's consulting room. How I hated it. Without chilling, the bottle was warm to the touch, and although it was well-wrapped I used to fear that the bottle would leak amongst my books and lunch. I knew nothing about the baby until she arrived, and even after Dad would say "Where's the lump where Mummy used to cut the bread?" I never understood. Several years later, when I did find out the basic facts, I used to embarrass my mother by loudly commenting to her on every large woman I saw, young or old, being absolutely sure they were carrying a child. I spoke loudly because I wanted them to understand that I knew their delightful secret. Sisters all!

When Elaine was three she hooked her plump little leg over the kitchen cupboard door, then fell over, ripping open the fatty tissue behind and on the inside of the knee. She was most agitated, "Look, my brains are falling out!" The good old days — no husband at home to help, no cars, no direct transport service to the doctor's surgery, no phone to call a cab or ambulance, and no money for one anyway. Mum picked up the three-year-old, and slogged it out to the Doctor's. It was several miles from where we lived. He stitched the little one up, then Mum slogged it back, still carrying the child. I expect she then had to carry on with her work.

Jim, Sam and I always argued over the washing up. We did not have much to do around the house, mostly because of school commitments, and homework, but we did have two jobs to be shared among the three of us. The washing and drying up. Washing up was always preferable, because you cleared away, then washed up: The good old method — a tin dish full of hot water, which you had to boil up, and with soap as a lathering and cleaning agent, the clean dishes being upended on to a tray. Then there was the drying up, and the putting away. Because of the putting away, this meant that this slave finished last, while everyone else moved out of the kitchen. A roster was in place, but all sorts of reasons altered it, and certain persons — male — would conveniently forget it was their turn. I was inclined to take an urgent visit to the loo. Sam was much more reliable than Jim, who would get out of anything if he could. Sam liked to use really HOT water, because of the results. He has always been good like that.

We had a delightful small pot-bellied stove in the back room, the glass verandah, at Ryedale. It was a two hotplate stove with a small coal fire inside. In cold weather there would be soup or coca ready for us after school. As it was often wet in winter, we loved this comfort. One day Jim came bounding home — he was by this time old enough to have graduated to long trousers at school — and, as was his usual practice, he sat down on the nearest article. On this occasion it was the pot-bellied stove, which was going. He didn't get badly burned, but his pants did.

Talking of this room, reminds me of how we loved it. It had been an inspired extension to the house at some stage, so it was a step lower than the rest of the building. It had a lino covered floor, and we ate in there much of the time. Mum also sewed there, and kept her sewing machine beside the sliding glass window. The cat used to love to sit on the closed machine, and watch the world, in particular the dog, or the neighbouring cats go past. Prince would snarl and hiss at them from his protected perch, but when he stalked outside with Mum to hang the washing, he felt safest if he could seek the protection of her legs.

Along the window ledge, under the glass, there was a row of cup hooks. From these were suspended the camouflage nets in the making. Once a week Mum would go to Top Ryde, and with all the available ladies of the district, would make camouflage nets for the war effort. Through the week she would work on the one at home, taking the finished product back with her the next week. I became quite proficient at netting too. She also knitted socks for the soldiers. Everyone knitted squares for blankets. Sam proved to be a good knitter of socks too, even able to turn heels. Balaclavas would also be made. She was given a silver brooch to wear, with a bar suspended from it, and a star to represent her man at war. Some women had several stars, indicating husbands and sons also. Dad made her a small netting needle and width measure, so she could make string bags. They could hold an enormous amount.

One evening we were seated in the back room, finishing tea. The sliding glass window was open. Suddenly a hat came flying in through the open space. Bob Levy had arrived. He had had a row with his father, and as usual on such occasions he had come to us for solace. He was a good companion for Jim — they spoke and understood the same language.

Mum took me to the Home for Incurables Hospital, "Weemalah", on one of her Ladies Church Guild visits. It was tragic. Those who went there knew there was only one way they would leave. There were people ravaged by cancer, others with whole bodies twisted out of shape by rheumatoid arthritis. A twenty-one-year-old was a resident there. She had a cancerous tumour on her brain, and a twisted body also. Her name was Nancy and she wrote poetry.

Who could forget "the fight"?

The two boys were involved in an altercation. Why? I know not. This time it was serious. The peace of Saturday morning was disturbed by the heroes wrestling and fighting near the back porch. This was a small roofed area shielding the back door. It was supported on two sides by the house walls. Diagonally opposite was a green supporting post, cemented into position.

The flow of battle took Jim and Sam right past the post. As Sam was busy upending Jim, the latter reached out and seized the post with both hands. Because he was being clutched around both ankles, this meant that Jim was now elevated sideways to about two feet six inches from the concrete path below. He would not release his grip. Neither would Sam. As a consequence Sam proceeded to walk Jim round and around the post, jerking the enemy as he did so. When the post began to loosen in the cement it looked dangerous. I watched in fascinated horror. Mum tried to pull them apart. Doubtless she succeeded, as the house was still standing that evening.

About this time I heard about the naming of the granny smith apple, because Maria Smith was commemorated at the North Ryde Church, in the area where the apple was developed.

I possess a delightful memory of a baby show held in Maria Smith's church.

Sam, Jim and I loved Elaine passionately, so we cajoled Mum into entering her in the show. She was by this time a toddler. Aunt Blanche had knitted her a pretty, lacy, pale green short-sleeved jumper, which Mum combined with pleated skirt on a bodice in cream viyella. White socks and black patent leather shoes completed the ensemble.

Elaine was not blessed with a thick head of hair at that time, and any breeze whipped what she had into a straw-like effect. Her section was to be judged last. The babies were displayed in rows, on trestle tables. To keep Elaine entertained we took her outside to the accompanying fete. She had a toffee apple, a cordial, fairy floss, and for added excitement, her brothers would hold her by her hands and twirl her around, as they themselves spun around. She shrieked with delight. Then time came for her judging. Proudly we escorted her in and placed her on the bench. Along came the judges. Do you know? THEY JUST WALKED STRAIGHT PAST HER!!! We could scarcely contain our indignation. Our baby not win? I am certain that if there had been a prize for the most loved child, we would have had the biggest trophy of them all.

We never minded looking after Elaine. She had a large wicker pram, with a hood. We would blithely take her to the top of Ryedale Road hill, where there was a crossroad which led over the railway line. These excursions used to take place in the middle of the road. I would stand at the top, holding the pram, inside which sat an eager three-year-old. Standing beside the pram was Sam, the family athlete. At the bottom of the hill stood Jim, waiting.

On orders I would give the pram a shove, it would take off down the hill, with Sam pacing it, ready for any emergency. At the bottom was Jim on full alert, ready to catch the pram, so that it did not hurtle past him. Fail-safe! By a miracle no damage was ever done, and Elaine thought it was wonderful.

Just around the corner was a short No Through Road, which led up to Roly Poly Hill. This was a heavily grassed, very steep hill. I don't know if it really was as steep as I envisage it, but I think it was. At the street's end three-quarters of the way down the hill, was a stiled fence. This just had two uprights with a squared bar of wood separating them at the top. At times the boys would take the bike to the top of the hill and freewheel it down to the bottom. The fence held no problems. They would simply flatten themselves along the strut of the bike, and fly under it, continuing down the street, to where it joined Ryedale Road. We had a freedom that children cannot now have.

The boys used to take the backs of broken bentwood chairs, and turn them into sleds. They would attach some sort of seat, grease the underneath, and use this to career down the hill. Often they (and I) fell off, but no serious injuries seemed to occur. I may say that their friends joined in all these pastimes too.

Talking of injuries, someone always seemed to be getting a stubbed big toe. With no Band-Aids we used finger stalls or bandages to cover our wounds. Grazed knees and elbows were also common. Nosebleeds were a fairly regular occurrence. Our usual bandage was ripped up, worn out sheets. No one, but no one, went to school barefooted.

To save money Mum would purchase unbleached calico or fine duck sheets. To whiten these, they were dampened, then spread out on the grass for several days to be whitened by the dew. This treatment, followed by regular usage, gradually got them a proper white.

As was the normal practice in most households, each Monday the bottom sheet and pillowslip would be removed for washing, the top sheet would go to the bottom, and a new sheet placed on top.

Sam and Jim went to Top Ryde Public School. In Sam's class was a girl who had paralysed arms. She used her toes to hold her pencil. Sam was strongly left-handed. At that time the school system insisted on a right handed culture. The teachers tried very hard to convert him, but he developed a severe stutter, which did not cease until he was allowed to revert to left-handedness again.

Dad was only a passing influence in our lives. We loved the excitement of his arrival home, but within a couple of weeks we became restive at the much-needed discipline being administered, and we would be surreptitiously asking when he was to go again.

I was already showing that I liked food. Mum's theory, which I like because it excuses my indulgences, was that her first two children were such picky eaters that, when she had a child who ate without effort, she kept feeding me everything, and I got in the way of it. My parents decided to give me responsibility for some food. The Americans had given Dad a small carton of tropical chocolate bars. I was to be in charge of it, and at certain times I was to hand out a bar to family members. It had to be hidden in case the heroes found it. I kept it in my drawer, under my clothes. All too handy.

At intervals I checked the chocolate bars, and, just to make sure they were still fresh, I would eat one. The only problem, as I got towards the bottom of the box, was that I had no means of replenishing the supply. Sooner or later I had to be found out. Always inclined to feel guilty, even when I was innocent, I suffered great qualms of guilt until my secret was eventually discovered. I will draw a veil over the rest of that incident.

And speaking of feeling guilty when innocent ...

Galston and Selhurst were wonderful places for a child to have in his or her background. There were loving relatives, such as grandparents, loving, but authoritative relatives such as Aunt Blanche and Uncle Frank, and the kind, but less omnipotent person of Uncle Sine. (Interpreted, their names were Blanche Emma Quinn (crossed in love, she had been engaged to an Arthur Wilkie, who had developed diabetes before there was a means of control. The romance was renounced and they parted. Later after a treatment was found, Arthur married another lady and had a family of his own. Blanche remained single for many years.) Uncle Frank had been christened Frank Kingsley Cooper Quin, and Sine was Sinclair Arthur Mellar John Ruskin Quin. Grandpa didn't do anything by halves! Another brother, Uncle Bill, had married and moved elsewhere, so he wasn't a Galston resident. Bill was my mother's best loved and closest friend all her life.

Back to my story, and the guilt complex. Uncle Frank had a tool room down at the shed, which he wisely kept locked.

His enterprising nephews, my brothers, had discovered that a couple of planks could be moved to one side, and they could get in. To Sam this was like the discovery of Aladdin's cave. Unfortunately for him Uncle Frank was as the magician, seeking to protect his tools from eager, but amateur hands. He once chased Sam, who, to escape annihilation, sallied up a tall pine tree near the woodheap. Uncle Frank sat at the bottom of the tree for a good while, until he had the brilliant idea of picking up the axe which lay nearby, and putting a couple of solid chops into the trunk. A good case of lateral thinking.

But the guilt impulse was something else again. Frank had a leather razor strop in the bathroom. This time the boys must have taken his cut-throat razor, and tried to hone it on the strop. After a few chunks of leather had been removed they gave up the attempt, and tried unsuccessfully to hide the evidence. I had absolutely nothing to do with this, but, by the time everything had been discussed, and we had been threatened with a visit from the police (naturally to take our fingerprints, to discover the criminals) I would cheerfully have confessed to the crime, except that everyone knew I was innocent. I hid under the house where I could hear the adults talking, so I could find out when to expect the police.

Another incident in the food line stands out in my mind. Dad had done some sort of an exchange with the sailors of an American ship. He had brought home for Mum twenty-four pairs of Denier nylon stockings for Mum, in a variety of hues, including red, blue purple etc. Why, I cannot conceive, because she was a most conservative dresser in a very conservative world. She always declared that he should have married someone from the Tivoli Theatre, as he liked red fingernails, dyed and set hair, and modern clothing, as well as the sophistication of women smoking cigarettes. He also had a full carton each of sweetened condensed milk, and tinned sliced peaches. These Mum tucked into the back of the linen press, to be used on very special occasions.

Then Dad received some pre-embarkation leave in Melbourne. He asked his wife to join him there. She did so, as I thought, taking Elaine with her. My eyes were green again. Jim, Sam and I were considered old enough to cope for a few days. Recently I discovered that Elaine, in reality went to Galston.

Sam and I, mindful of our mother's concerns, really did try to be good. However, Jim, who must have had similar tastebuds to myself, must have regarded this scenario as an emergency. He dived into the secret cache of food, and kept his appetite at bay, by a judicious selection of tinned peaches and condensed milk, which he shared with his pals.

Jim burned his leg very severely at Galston. If my memory serves me correctly, Jim was poking the open fire in the sitting room, when a log rolled out and landed on the inner thigh of his (I think) right leg. He was not yet a teenager. He bore this horrible scar for many years.

For us children Galston was the enchanted land.

My grandparents lived at "Selhurst", Bevans Road Galston. The house was originally owned by a family named Bevans. There was fifty-eight acres of farmland, some of it under cultivation, as orchards; some devoted to free range poultry, some to a small herd of dairy cattle. A portion was still virgin bushland, and there were a number of small grazing paddocks.

The whole was surrounded by hoop pine trees, all very well grown, about sixty feet tall. These would shed their pine needles like a carpet underneath, so that walking on them was silent, and when the wind blew the trees would sough a mournful song to the sky. There were several more of these giants on different parts of the property — all ideal for children to climb. I used to love lying on my bed on the verandah, listening to the sighing of those trees.

The house was one which had been added to at various intervals, so it was of great interest to us children. The kitchen had been a large farmhouse once, separate from the house. Years before it had been linked to the house by a room known as the "cage" verandah. One stepped down from both the house and the kitchen into this room, which had a wooden floor, close to the ground. Occasionally a broody hen would nest under there, and if she abandoned her nest, the eggs would eventually explode, leaving a rich smell of sulphuretted hydrogen behind. We children would be despatched to crawl into this space to remove the debris. Ugh!

This room had a very large rectangular table alongside of which were placed long stools, which seemed to be able to seat everyone who turned up for a meal or a visit. The house and kitchen created two walls. The third wall was glassed in, where Grandma raised the most beautiful maidenhair ferns I have ever seen, three or four tiers of them. I have had a lifelong love affair with such ferns ever since, but I lack the right spot, or the green thumb Grandma obviously possessed.

The fourth wall was chicken wire, with a chicken wire door also, which opened into a courtyard created by the house, the kitchen and the cage verandah. There were two galvanised rainwater tanks on low stands in this area. Each was dripping with ferns and other potted plants. Behind the tanks, and abutting the house was a "greenery", also lovely and Grandma's pride. Between the tanks was a door which led onto the verandah of the main house.

Opposite this was the bricked stove recess of the kitchen; the back of it poking out into this area. Between the chimney stack and the cage verandah was a wired in area. Here lived Cuthbert, a cranky Major Mitchell parrot belonging to Uncle Frank. I was present when Cuthbert, who carried quite a bit of age, bit a piece clean out of Grandpa Quinn's brand-new Stetson hat. When Grandpa had been prevented from murdering Cuthbert, he mended the hat with a piece of felt, which he somehow attached underneath. It was a slightly darker shade than the rest of the hat, so it always showed out.

One Christmas I was given a toy stove. Dad had made it, and it actually worked. I could light a fire in it and use my toy frying pan on top. While this novelty was still being enjoyed there was great excitement in the household. Cuthbert, who must have been about twenty, laid an egg. We had never before had any reason to suspect his sex! Obviously the egg was infertile, as Cuthbert lacked the opportunity for it to be otherwise. I was given the egg, which I fried in the frying pan on my little stove. My stomach wasn't so sensitive in those days, and for the sheer pleasure of preventing my brothers from doing so, I ate it. The egg was perfect, with a small yellow yolk, surrounded by white albumen.

The kitchen was, as are most kitchens, the heart of the house. It was a very large room, which held two enormous tables. One of my chief memories was of doing the washing up on the table nearest the dining room entrance. A huge metal tray was placed on it, beside a tiny dish of very hot water, obtained from the fountain which bubbled eternally on the side of the large wood stove. The washer up then lathered the water, using a wire soap holder, and the dishes were washed, then placed on the tray to drain, while those drying up strove to keep up with her.

These trays had another use also. When a fowl was executed for eating, after it had hung for a while, it had to be drawn and plucked. This had a horrible fascination. I would watch (if allowed) my aunt plunging her hand into the fowls innards, and hauling them out. The gizzard, liver (giblets) and feet were saved for soup, as was the neck. There was always an unpleasant smell attached to this duty. Thankfully, I was never conscripted to this job. I did have to pluck out pin feathers. When a duck was killed, all the down was kept to stuff pillows and eiderdowns. This was messy but enjoyable.

Off the far end of the kitchen was a small room, which had been a larder, but it was then the egg sorting room. Each day, as the eggs were collected, they had to be packed into boxes of several dozen, supplied by the egg board. Grandma would wipe them over with a damp cloth to clear off any muck, and carefully slot each egg into its slot. As her sight began to fail, Aunt Blanche would have to check them, as it was not unknown for Grandma to carefully slip in a passionfruit instead.

The second table in the kitchen was used for general working purposes. In the stove recess was the wood stove, for which kindling had to be collected each day, as well as the larger billets of wood. On the side of the stove was the water fountain, which was always needed in a kitchen of this size. There always seemed to be some very young chickens or ducklings in boxes beside the stove, being revived after the trauma of birth, or near drowning in the fowls' water, or perhaps from being almost crushed to death in amongst the other chicks.

At the end of the room were two great dressers. The crockery was kept in the glassed-in top cupboards. The top of the bottom half was a large area, covered with gauze shutters. Each morning, after milking, the strained milk would be carried into the kitchen, then poured into several very large enamel bowls, each as large as a baby's bath. These would be placed on the side of the stove. The cream would rise and clot (I believe it was Cornish clotted cream), then the bowls would be placed under the gauze for the cream to set, and be carefully lifted off. This was the source of our butter. We beat the cream with wooden spoons until it separated into butter and buttermilk; then washed and salted it. At times we were allowed to use the butter pats, to make delightful curls of butter. The skim milk which was left was used to feed the poddy bull calves down at the shed. I abhorred the feel of a calf's tongue curling around my fingers, as it was taught to suck from a bucket. Everyone who was not doing another job was seconded to help feed the calves.

Just inside the door, near the stove, was a wooden vegetable box Grandpa had made. One cat at the farm just loved pumpkin, and he would eat this vegetable if it was not put quite out of reach. There was also a perforated zinc safe, where butter, cream, and other perishables were kept away from cats, rats and mice. No refrigerators or ice chests there!

There was always at least one dog. The best of all was Jeff, followed by the scruffy but loveable Mike. Both were sourced from the R.S.C.P.A.

Around the house was the wide verandah, which always had several beds on it. We children always slept there. It had the lower half enclosed, and the top half was covered by chicken wire. At the end of this verandah, which went around two sides of the house, was Uncle Frank's room. He commanded a certain respect, so his space was never violated. Adjoining his room was a bathroom, which was also an addition. A cupboard — the first linen cupboard I had ever seen — had been constructed around the chimney in the adjoining room. An intrepid explorer could actually crawl around the outside of the chimney, inside the cupboard; it was as if there was a secret passage in the bathroom.

The spare room was entered via the verandah, through French doors. Uncle Frank, who was very handy with tools, had given it a fibro ceiling, which proved of great interest to the family. Apparently it interested Sam even more than the rest of us, because he climbed up through the manhole and gave it a close examination. He even tested it for strength. A pity, as it could not hold his weight, and he came crashing through. As long as I can remember afterwards that ceiling remained broken.

The toilet was the old pit style. It had latticed surrounds for privacy. Over this lattice grew a banana passion fruit vine. I have never seen a similar one. The fruit itself was slightly elongated, with a soft yellow skin with a matt surface. It was delicious when peeled. The skin could be just peeled off, and there was this wonderful sweet passionfruit centre, which held together, not spurting everywhere like a normal passionfruit. I wonder if the location of its planting had anything to do with the bearing qualities of the vine?

Around the side front verandah of the house was a small room, which may have been a bathroom at some stage. In my time it was a storage room. In this room was a wooden chest, and in that chest were books. Books, those wonderful places where anything could happen! Officially I was not allowed in there. This did not stop me creeping in on odd occasions to read. It was here that I found my mother's copy of "Anne of Green Gables", which I read so often that I can still recite practically any section of it. As well as this source of literature, in the sitting room was a collection of National Geographic Magazines, which I used to read avidly.

The sitting room was also forbidden territory. It housed a three-piece genoa velvet lounge suite, the footstool, and a China cabinet which I coveted all my life. In this cabinet were a collection of ornaments and bric-a-brac belonging to Grandma. Many of these were souvenirs from Grandpa's overseas travel, when he was a marine engineer. One was a little silver rickshaw, which I was fortunate enough to be given after Grandma's death. There was also a pair of tiny red brocade slippers, beautifully embroidered. They were the type of shoes worn by Chinese women early in the century, while the practice of binding their feet was still the norm. I used to drool over this very sensibly locked cupboard for years. So much so that, in my turn, I have created a similar one for my grandchildren to observe, and peer at, and occasionally I allow them to touch the objects inside.

Outside the house was a formal area. There was a lawn, which was kept trimmed. Alas, bindi-eye had taken it over, and it could not be walked on by anyone with bare feet. Beside the lawn was a path which looked like a capital P. I felt that I owned this path. In the centre of the P was a strange tree. This was a sour, miniature orange tree. After becoming a northern resident I now realise it was a cumquat tree. There was also a shrubbery on the way from the front gate to the house.

Seven

When I was ten my dearly loved grandfather died. This was a distressing event, although I really did not have any broad idea of its implications. As was the custom, a door was lifted off its hinges, and Grandpa lay in state on this, balanced on the arms of the three-seater lounge, until it was time to bury him. I was led into the sitting room to pay my last respects, and found him there, cold. He was clad in his blue-striped pyjamas, his eyes were closed with two pennies holding them shut, and around his head was wound a bandage, to keep his jaw from becoming slack and open. This created a white frame for his face. The service was conducted in the formal dining room, before heading off to the Enfield church, where he was laid to rest beside his infant daughter.

Many years later Grandma also passed away at home. She was by this time a very old lady. As I was teaching at Camooweal, I could not be there. She must have felt that her time had come, as Mum told me she actually laid herself out on her bed. She was straight on her back, with her hands crossed across her chest.

Our family move to 171 Ryedale Road, Denistone caused many new experiences in our lives. One such experience was the telephone. The previous owners, the McBeans, had had in the hall, a wall telephone, which was mounted on a dark varnished board, and this was attached to the papered wall, (which was to give the illusion of dark wood panelling.) On the board, over a number of years, had been lightly scratched many telephone numbers. My dear brothers conceived the idea of ringing every number on that board. Naturally this took place when Mum was not present, and in the very limited time before the phone was disconnected and removed, as we could not afford the luxury of a phone. Mum was very perturbed when she received a bill for phone calls she knew had never been made after Mc Beans had gone, because she had instructed the P.M.G. Department to cancel the phone before we moved in. In any case the P.M.G. never got paid! I cannot recall any of the conversations which took place between the boys and their hapless victims, so I don't think it could have been too serious. I was ten at that time.

There were three entrances to the Ryedale Road house. The commonly used back entrance, the side front entrance and a formal front entrance through the single front gate (very rarely used). From the gate a cement footpath led to some tiled stairs, flanked on either side by two large cement pedestals, made to hold large formal pots. Ours were never graced like this. What they did have was me, and Joan Levy. When the troop trains used to stop on the Ryde Hill, to take on a second engine to pull them up the steep gradient, the young soldiers used to hang out of the carriage windows, waving streamers of toilet paper. (I hope their stomachs were O.K. for the rest of the journey north). They shouted joyously to anyone who cared to listen, and sometimes threw out packets of chewing gum or small coins to the interested local children who would gather around.

I should explain that our house fronted the road. On the other side of the road was a fence, behind which was a heavily grassed area, then the railway line. We were on the Main Northern Line.

Forbidden by Mum to enter the railway grounds, we were unable to glean any of the harvest which was cast forth. So Joan and I would stand on the two cement pedestals, and pose like Grecian statues, until the forces of nature would remove us. I bet we stunned the soldiers, provided they even noticed us.

The house was built on a slight slope, so that the back was ground level, but the front was about three feet six inches from the ground, necessitating the steps of which I spoke. They led up to a brick and tiled verandah, and a proper front door. This opened into a small foyer, and this in turn led into either Mum's bedroom, straight ahead, or to the left into the lounge room.

The lounge room was fully carpeted. It had a bow window at the front, and a picture rail around the walls, about eighteen inches below the cornices. Some of Mum's treasures were displayed on this rail, and the pictures were suspended below. A three-piece lounge suite in autumn tones, the heavily stuffed variety favoured at that time, completed the room. Cream lace curtains hung there too.

The room behind the lounge was the formal dining room. It was divided from the lounge by frosted glass sliding doors — the first I had ever seen. The dining room had the seven-piece dining suite we had brought from the previous house, a sideboard, and a traymobile and Mum's sewing box, both made of wood by her father. It had a carpet square on the floor and was also curtained over the large side windows. It was a dark room, made so by its situation, and the large trees outside. I was allowed the use of this room to do my homework, uninterrupted by my less studious brothers. They had to do theirs in the back verandah room.

The dining room opened into a hall (the one where the telephone had been). This hall ran parallel to the road, and led from the side front entrance to the other rooms. At the side front door there was also a small tiled porch, and two tiled steps, down to the side driveway of the house, which led on past the back of the house, culminating in a garage (without any car).

The dining room and sitting room could be joined by opening the sliding glass doors. This became the perfect venue for concerts — not that we had many. The boys would set up shadow shows, mostly medical ones, where a patient was being operated on and body parts were drawn out. They also learned to shape their hands into animals, such as rabbits, dogs, and snakes. One night, when Uncle Bill was visiting, he gave the star performance of all time. He gave an extempore monologue on his job. He claimed to be a dustman, carrying his lunch in his pocket. The dustmen used to hurl these big heavily-loaded bins up on to their shoulders and then throw the contents into the back of the garbage truck. In Uncle Bill's version liquids ran down, smells were powerful, and he had a most enjoyably flavoured lunch. Years later I asked him about that starring item. He said that kids are earthy little creatures, and enjoy a bit of blood and guts. I think he was right.

Opposite the hall was the bathroom — fancy a bathroom in the middle of the house — what a novel idea! There was also a door to the right leading to my parents' bedroom, so there were actually two entrances into their room. They had large windows too, as well as a dressing table and two wardrobes. One of these was completely for hanging space, the other had some drawers and shelves as well. There were also bedside cupboards. The design on the wardrobes was a rounded circular disc on each of the doors, about the size of a dinner plate, with a carved plaited wooden tassel curved around these discs, hanging like braids below them. They furniture was made of maple. These were also repositories for Christmas presents until the big day.

The hall turned at right-angles. On the left was the entrance to Elaine's and my shared room. This was papered in such a pretty closely-covered apple blossom pattern in shades of pink. I used to lie in bed and pick out shapes, figures and designs from among the blossoms.

My bed and Elaine's were on opposite sides of the room, and the wardrobe we shared was a creation of Grandpa Quinn. He had made my bed too, and I delighted in the knowledge that stamped into the wood, on both articles of furniture was my very own name. The combination wardrobe/dressing table had four deep drawers, two of which were set aside for me, with two for Elaine. The wardrobe had limited hanging space, but after her birth it was also subdivided. There was a pretty lino on the floor too.

Elaine loved her dolls passionately, and each night she would take them to bed with her. They took up so much space that there was hardly any room for E. During the night she would move in with me, and so would the dolls. The dolls took up so much space, then Elaine would be tucked in. Finally I would be on the outside hanging over the edge of the bed.

Occasionally I would tire of this, and try to prevent the nightly invasion. So I invented the Big Bad Chook, which was lying in wait under my bed, ready to pounce on the visitor. This would only inflame Elaine's fear, until she would finally work up enough courage to gather her babies together, and take a quantum leap into my bed.

We were at Lake Macquarie once when the police contacted

us to tell us that our house had been burgled. We had to go back home and check it out. I recall my personal shame when I was unable to say if my room had been done over or not. I was appallingly untidy, and never kept my drawers neat until forced to do so. Eventually I did discover that the 2/6 which I had been given for Christmas had been stolen (it had been shoved in the back of my drawer amongst my clothing), and the gold watch which had been Grandma Quinn's had also been taken. Other things had been stolen from the house, but nothing major.

The next Christmas Aunty Blanche gave me a dirty clothes bag, which I resented very much. Naomi had instead received a charming pin cushion and feather duster in a pretty pink shade. Years later I asked Blanche about this. She said she had felt so sorry for Naomi, who was by now motherless, that she had bought this pretty knick-knack for her. Believe it or not, I used to envy Naomi, so slender, so graceful, with a delicate appearance and gently plaintive voice — the epitome of all I would have liked to be. The fact that she was a motherless girl didn't count in my book. I must have been appallingly selfish. Yes, and everyone seemed to like her better!

Opposite my room, the hallway led into the kitchen, quite a reasonable sized room. It even had an enamel sink, and a stove with an electric oven and gas burners for stovetop cooking. Naturally the ice-chest was ever present. The ice was always left on the side front porch for collection. From the kitchen there was a single step down into the glassed-in verandah room. At the far end of this was the green enamelled pot-bellied stove. The sewing machine, an old "White" brand, had a long shuttle instead of the round disc used today, and it stood against the glass windows, near the back door.

Jim had the back bedroom, which opened from this verandah

room, and nearer the kitchen Sam had a very small room, which must have once been the laundry, but which he claimed as his own. It barely fitted his bed, his chest of drawers and his junk. But it could be, and was frequently, locked.

The back door opened on to a little porch, and as one went outside, and turned to the right, the path led to the laundry and the outside toilet — much closer than in Falconer Street. Once there was a serious drought in metropolitan Sydney. Each householder was given stickers for the toilet walls. They were printed red, on a cream background, and read "Flush only when necessary. Do not flush after each minor use of the W.C."

Out the back there was grassed area, where the clotheslines stretched, and behind this was our pride and joy — the tennis court. It was rarely used as such, but it was a wonderful playground for us.

In the McBeans' time it had apparently been let out to a local tennis club , because they approached our parents with a view to continuing the arrangement. In a house with four active children and no home and garden maintenance because of an absentee father, this was impractical. We actually needed the space for the family. It gradually became more and more neglected, but it was always a memorable place. There was a beautiful Virginia creeper, growing over much of the high fencing, glorious orange trumpet-like blooms, with a sweet smell, and nectar filling the tail of the trumpets. Naturally we sucked this out. There was also a tennis club house, which was variously a playhouse for me and Elaine, and was frequently used as a meeting place by the boys. Once we stood there and watched the Grahams next door doing a complete cleanout of their cupboards, burning the rubbish as they did so.

Elaine, who loved dolls as if they were humans, saw one about to be burned. She pleaded with the Grahams to save it, so they gave it to her. In honour of the previous owner Elaine named her "Chrissie", but the rest of us called her "Wall-eye." She possessed only one eye. The missing member Elaine replaced with a marble swiped from her brothers. She had also lost her hair and was a very battered individual indeed. The new owner obtained some rope (she would have been four at this time) and assiduously unfurled it, combing it out. Then she patiently glued the strands onto the skull of the unpretty Chrissie. She became a very striking looking doll, loved only by her new owner. On the same orgy of burning next door, we watched in horrified fascination as a French kid doll was consumed by the flames. The kid retracted in the heat, and a squirming body and limbs gave the impression that the doll was alive.

The tennis court was the scene of many activities. At the far end of the court was a raised and stone pitched area where Jim kept a few fowls (Need I say who fed them? Poor Mum.) He went to Paddy's Market in Sydney once, bringing home a chicken which was raised into a big healthy cockerel. He lorded it over his harem until they began to suffer. At this stage he was banished to the Galston farm. His name was Jacob. In due course his earthly reign was over, and he was selected as part of the Christmas meats. He was stuffed and placed on the table for us all to enjoy. At this moment Jim looked at the carcass and said mournfully, "He was a good father." It was too much — only the men felt able to continue to eat the fowl.

Because public transport was almost the only way to move around, people carried the most extraordinary things on trains. Fowls were transported by placing them in a hessian bag, then making a hole in the corner of the bag, so the bird's head could stick out for breathing purposes. Such was the way Jacob moved

Sam, Pat and Jim Pearse

Pat, Jim and Sam Pearse

Patricia as a young woman

Patricia and her brothers Sam, Jim and Elaine

Sam and Jim Pearse with their mother Marion holding baby Elaine and Pat on the right

"Fair Isles" the Townsville house Patrica lived in.

Jim Pearse, Edwin (Dad) Pearse, Patricia and Marion Pearse, baby Elaine and Sam Pearse

to the farm.

As the war progressed Dad came home occasionally on leave. He conceived the idea of purchasing a lady's bike. This was a black, heavy vehicle with a skirt guard attached to the rear mudguard, a carrier basket attached to the handlebar, and a pillion seat behind the rider. I was able to ride a bike, so Dad took me with him to Eastwood, where this abomination was purchased. I had to ride it home.

He had decided that Mother needed some form of transport to do the shopping, and this was it! Mum could not ride, so for many days she was coaxed and abused as she struggled to learn the mastery of the bike — a Malvern Star. Round and round the tennis court she would go, with Dad or one of the boys holding on to the seat while she tried to attain some form of balance. As soon as they let go she would crash. Once into the net post, another time, as she crashed she broke her glasses. She was never much good. The bike was so heavy that it was never a pleasure to ride, and I didn't know how to patch the tyres anyway. This would only be done when one of the boys, mostly Sam, decided to do it.

The tennis court was used for other purposes too. Sam and Jim were keenly interested in training — I do not know if they ever actually played football or cricket outside school hours, but they trained. They would run around and around the court training for football (or it may have been running). But I was co-opted when they wanted to train for cricket. If they wanted to bat, I would have to bowl (mostly Molly Dukers, as they were the only balls I could cast hard enough to reach the other end of the prescribed pitch.) If they wanted to bowl I was the hapless batsman. It's no wonder I never liked sport.

One time they were bowling, and I was up in front of the wicket. A forceful ball came down the pitch, and caught me fairly on the front of my foot. I dropped the bat, and hopped inside, in agony. My foot went black, and remained that way for weeks. Then I discovered that there was now a small piece of bone on the top of the instep of my left foot that I could wiggle about. It was there for many years, and it always made it difficult for me to wear lace up shoes (I loved court shoes as a result). Now I have a bony outcrop of spurs on that area, which swells and gets painful at intervals throughout the year. I am still not fond of cricket.

Neither am I fond of hockey.

When I went to Hornsby Girls' High School I had to choose a sport. I selected hockey as I knew Mum had an old hockey stick from her girlhood in her possession.

The boys were interested. At last I was displaying the right spirit, so they would train me!

Mum's hockey stick was fetched. It was given to me to hold. Then they paced me around the tennis court. As one boy would tire the other would take over from him. Round and round I went. round and round. Over thirty-two times.

I then collapsed. They decided I had had enough training for one day, so they sent me into the house to have a bath. I was by this time bright red. I staggered out of the bathroom, still in a state of collapse, and found that I had become deep purple. That was the start and finish of my hockey career.

Seven

During the war the government had become increasingly concerned about Sydney being attacked. Air raid wardens were appointed and these men patrolled the streets at night, seeking any chinks of light in suburban homes. It really was difficult, because Dad was always away. We cut up strips of a crinkly fawn coloured paper, and put these diagonally and straight, in cross formations on every window. Then special blinds were made, to fit the windows closely, and all curtains had to be drawn at night.

Not infrequently a knock would be heard at the door, and an air raid warden would be there, to tell us that a chink of light was showing. All street lights were doused too. I really do not know how cars managed, as we did not own one, nor did we ever travel in one, except on a few, very isolated occasions.

One of these occasions was when Naomi stayed with us, and Uncle Bill, her father, was visiting. To be precise the visit took place at Galston, and Uncle Bill had a car. We were to be taken on a picnic to Ku-ring-gai Chase. No seat belts, nor any rules as to how many people were in a car, in those days. We drove through the Galston Gorge, and eventually hit the Ku-ring-gai Road. To us Uncle Bill seemed quite old, but he can only have been in his mid-thirties, and he still had a light-hearted attitude to life.

Ahead of us was another car, which accelerated as we drew near. Hanging out of the windows we shrieked encouragement to Uncle Bill to overtake the car ahead. He sped up quickly, and pass we did. Then the road became like the scene of a duel, or more modernly, a drag race. The other driver joined in the game, and with continuous urging the two cars passed each other again and again. The scene only ended when the cars diverged in different directions. A memorable picnic, that one. I vaguely remember a picnic once at Fuller's Bridge, so named because there was a deposit of Fuller's Earth below it — a commodity which was used to dry clean many items, including felt hats. We collected some that day.

Naomi was our dearly loved cousin — Uncle Bill's only child. He was married to Annis Brickett. She was beautiful, with a gorgeous complexion and the most wonderful red hair, which had a sort of transparency through it. I was not aware of it at that time, but Aunt Annis had tuberculosis, for which there was no cure. She stayed with us once, and she had the girls' bedroom. Mum, for the duration of her visit, kept a boiler on the stove. Every item of crockery and cutlery used by Annis had to be steamed. After she left, the room had to be sealed up, while sulphur burned in the room, to fumigate it.

We had Naomi living with us for a time. She was like another sister, and behaved like one. She was a dainty child, with a delicate voice, and a fragile air. While she was with us her mother was in a sanatorium at Leura in the blue Mountains. The treatment sounds appalling. The patients were exposed to the cold weather as much as possible — bracing. After many months Uncle Bill collected her and took her back home. During that period Mum faithfully took Naomi up to the Blue Mountains once each week, to visit her mother.

When Naomi was twelve her mother died. It must have been a terrible time for Uncle Bill. Then Naomi became very seriously ill with pneumonia. I know it was thought that she might not survive, a because she proved to be allergic to the wonder drug of that period, sulphanilamide. Penicillin was not discovered then. Mum took Elaine with her, and went to Armidale to nurse Naomi. Fortunately she pulled through. When she was well enough, I was sent up to Armidale to join Mum for a short period. My greatest thrill was early each morning. Uncle Bill would bring me — ME! a cup of milky tea, with two paper thin quarters of buttered bread on the side of the saucer. I felt truly grown up.

While in Armidale I went to a house and goods auction. I had never been to anything like this before. I came home with a very old fashioned, elegant, beige lady's umbrella with a crook at one end, and a long point at the other. It was fully lined in black. I also bought a pile of books.

Back in Ryedale Road I had one hair-raising experience in the darkness. Our house was situated close to the railway line, but quite a walk away from the station. It was a station manned only by a stationmaster in daylight hours. We were supposed to approach it, either the official "long" way round, walking uphill along Ryedale Road, then along a cement pedestrian path, over a wooden bridge, through bushland, until we came to the station. Alternatively, we could take the "short-cut", a dirt track which wound through the creek, and bushland, parallel to the railway in, only many feet below it. This path joined the main path just before the station.

I had the misfortune to snap a tooth in two, one Saturday afternoon. I had bent down to shut the double iron gate, and had struck my mouth on the iron frame. This had left the tooth in two vertical pieces, both still in the gum, and with the nerve exposed. Ours was an entirely residential area, so the next suburb, Eastwood was where we had our dentist. I had to endure this until Monday, go to school, then get off the train at Eastwood on my way home from school to visit Mr. Bain — the dentist. As I had no appointment I had to wait until he had finished for the day, then he attended to me. Without anaesthetic he pulled out the back part of the tooth, then he took a little corkscrew-like instrument of torture, wound it into the nerve and jerked it out. He was anxious to finish up, I imagine, and did not want to wait for anaesthetic's numbing effect. He did not tell me this, but he said I might as well get it over as quickly as possible, as I had had it so long anyway. He then put on a temporary filling and sent me on my way,

By this time it was dark, and the trains ran about hourly. I waited for the train, caught it, and was the only passenger who stepped off a Denistone. It was now pitch black, with neither street lights, nor a torch, because of the wartime restrictions. I walked along the station, up the stairs, and past the closed kiosk. Standing near the very subdued light there, was a man with a moustache. I have never been particularly good at faces, but I thought I recognized the father of one of the girls who lived further along our street. I said "Goodnight" as I passed, and stepped out onto the cement path, intending to take the shortcut home, as it was quicker. Suddenly I heard footsteps behind me. I quickened my pace. So did the footsteps. I abandoned any idea of using the short-cut, and continued on the cement path, as it was slightly more open. I hurried, so did the footsteps. I ran, so did the footsteps. I reached the wooden bridge, and before I was off it, and out of the bushland, I heard the footsteps echoing on the other end of the bridge behind me. I ran harder. It was a steep incline up the path, from there bridge to the road — I began to gasp in fright. At the road I turned and ran down the street — but there were no streetlights. I could hear my pursuer almost upon me. Beside me was a driveway without a gate, but open, trimmed with a thick privet hedge. I burst up the front stairs, and knocked. No one answered. I fled down the stairs again, and dropping to my knees I crawled along the side of the house to the back. Here I banged again.

Mercifully the door opened, and someone drew me inside. I explained my predicament. The man of the house looked outside, but could see no one. He then escorted me home. The sting in the tail of this story was that the next day Mum reported the incident to the police. I had had good reason to fear. A man answering his description had been arrested later that night for molesting a woman in a nearby suburb.

During the war we had an air raid shelter. Our house was built on clay soil (good for the hydrangeas, but not much else.) It was consequently hard to dig, and retained water well. The boys, who were strong little beggars, decided to build us a shelter. Out the back, towards the vacant allotment next door, they started digging. Eventually a sizeable hole was constructed. Naturally I had a reluctant part to play in this. When, and only when, they could force me to do manual labour, I was called on to help remove the buckets of gluey clay, and tip them in a pile beside the hole. It was deep enough for an adult to stand up in, if he didn't mind striking his head on the roof, and a bench seat was carved into the structure. Then wooden planks were placed across the top. These were covered with pieces of galvanised iron, and this was covered with the enormous pile of clay which had been removed. There were even several steps, constructed on the same principle as the bench seat. Only one thing had not been allowed for. Drainage. It would have worked if you didn't mind sitting knee deep in water, and cold water at that, as rain usually fell in winter in Sydney. It was also a wonderful breeding place for mosquitoes. At times Sam, never Jim, would empty it out, and it would be useable again.

My memory does not extend to a final refinement the boys placed in the shelter. They introduced electricity, I understand. I also understand that when they turned it on, it blew every fuse in the house. They were lucky they weren't blown to kingdom-come themselves.

Alas, on the only occasion when it could legitimately have been used — the night of the REAL air raid, it was full of water again. We were inside as usual one evening, when the air raid siren went off — not a practice — a REAL one. Unable to use the shelter we remembered the next instruction.

Get under a heavy piece of furniture, and stay there. We all tumbled into Mum's room, dragged a mattress from another bed, and jammed ourselves under the double bed. Five of us. It was much too good an adventure to waste time sleeping. After some hours of this, when absolutely nothing appeared to be happening, Mum climbed out from under, took Elaine with her, and settled into bed again. We spent much of the time pushing the underside of the mattress with our feet. It was morning before the All Clear sounded.

When we eventually read the paper, we discovered that three midget Japanese submarines had breached the boom net stretched across Sydney Harbour, by the simple expedient of going through, under the Manly ferry, when the net was opened to let it pass. They must have been brave, if ill-advised, men. One of them had let off a salvo, which hit a flat in Rose, or Double Bay, and had wrecked the kitchen. One of those subs is now on display at the War Museum in Canberra. One is still undiscovered, and one was blown up.

There was an engaging little ditty, which we frequently sang to Mum to cheer her up from time to time. Because of Dad's job qualifications he was often required on certain vessels, and he would have to be flown to join the ship. The song went: "What's the matter with Father? He's all right. What's the matter with Father? He's all right. He went up in an aeroplane, never came down to the earth again. What's the matter with Father? He's all right." Mother's little comforters …

At that time an aeroplane was such a rarity in the sky that as soon as one was heard overhead, people would dash outside to see this miracle of modern science. Even at school we were permitted to go out for a look, and to see if we could find it.

We used, sometimes, to see the great searchlights sweeping across the night sky, criss-crossing each other, in search of planes. That, I think, was to me, one of the real indications that there was a war on.

Dad's absence, at the war, did not affect us as much as it must have affected many children, because we were already used to his long absences, and we had established a life that rarely involved him. What we had was a relationship with our mother much closer than the average child. She was our rock, and our salvation. She had strong Christian principles and a high degree of true morality, which she bred into us, and we were none the worse for it. Mind you, we had to hide a lot of our sins from her.

Sunday School picnics were an annual event, which took place on Bank Holiday, the first Monday in November. Once Mum made me a new dress especially for this picnic. It was an Irish green cotton frock, which buttoned down the front, and had matching bloomers, with a pocket in them, for my hanky. For years we went to Watson's Gap, for this wonderful picnic.

A ferry would be hired, and we embarked at Watson's. We sailed down the Parramatta River, into Sydney Harbour, then over to Watson's Bay, the Gap, and the picnic, near South Head. As soon as we entered the boat, we would line up for a piece of fruit, such as an orange. I remember wedging mine into my bloomers' pocket, and the slight dragging feeling I had all day. We each had a mug tied on to a piece of string, slung about our necks, swaying with every movement. Before we disembarked we lined up again for a sticky bun and a bag of boiled lollies. We then had to assemble in a large ring up in the picnic ground. We would remove our mugs from our necks, hold them out, and nectar like red cordial or Stone's ginger beer was poured into the mugs.

I loathed the foot races; I always came last. One year there was a stir. The Gap was a notorious place for suicides. It was also a prime, if dangerous, place for rock fishermen, who would climb down iron rungs which were set into the cliff, in order to reach the dangerous rocks below, where they would fish, and take their chances with tides and rogue waves.

Naturally I tore up with everyone else to see what was happening. It turned out to be my brothers. They had both climbed the fence, and were scaling down the fisherman's ladder to try to reach the rocks below. Mum, thankful that she could have a rest, did not move. Little did she know of the drama on the cliff top.

The following year, and thereafter, the Sunday School hired a bus, and we would all go to Bobbin Head. It was never quite the same. On one of these trips I was taught two interesting songs, very suitable for good Christian kids.

"Drunk on Saturday night, Sick all over the floor, Cleaned it up with my toothbrush. Don't clean my teeth much anymore." That was the first charmer. The other involved the death of the "Pyjama Girl," her ultimate identification, the revelation of her killer, and his ultimate punishment. It was sung to the tune "Funiculi, Funicula."

"My name, she is Antonio Agostini; I'm inna some strife. I killa my wife. One day, in Surrey Melbourne, I losa my head. I shoot her dead. And now, I'm in a penitentiary. Nineteen fifty, the Judge will set me free. So if you want to escape from worry strife and strain, Just liquidate your wife, and shove her body down the drain."

Belonging to the Methodist Church as we did, some of the teens had a realization that no dancing was permitted on Church premises. A revolt set in. A hall was hired from the Presbyterian Church at Eastwood, and a dance was arranged. As I commented earlier, Mum was no seamstress, and materials were hard to get. Somehow, she obtained a quantity of deep pink moire taffeta. She made me a full length dress, with a sweetheart neckline, a matching dip in the waist of the bodice, large puffed sleeves, slightly ruched at the cuff, and a large pale spot in the centre of the front of the top of the dress. She had pricked her finger, a drop of blood had fallen at that spot, and she had tried to remove it. At that time, waterwave taffeta could not be washed, so she had used a spot of spit to remove the blood — a hint she had heard of beforehand. Certainly the blood went, but so did the colour. In its stead was this large pale circle. Fortunately I was not very clothes conscious, and I went off feeling beautiful.

I was an active member of the "Rays" who met each Tuesday afternoon at the Church. The Rays were little Rays of Sunshine.

They were lively while I was with them, let me tell you. I was at one time the secretary, and Mum found the minute book, and read it. Just as well, because she found that I had undertaken to donate a container to hold all their gear. Where I would have acquired it I do not know, but Mum gave me a large cardboard suitcase so I could honour my promise. Another day the club held a social in the church hall for Mothers' Day. I know that a large number of mothers turned up, and we played games and fed them as well. I was at this time the president, and all of twelve years old. I made a speech, presumably of welcome, in which I came out with the phrase "When I was a child". It brought the house down. The Comrades was a club for the senior girls, and I enjoyed this club too. I can't remember myself as a leading light in it, until we got to Townsville, but that is another story.

The O.K.'s – Order of Knights — was the boys' group. Sam figured in this much more than Jim. Sam was, on the whole, always dependable, and steady. Jim was much more of an unknown quantity.

Neither of them thought very much of me, I was inclined to be tubby, and had the misfortune to be named "Pat" which rhymed with "fat". I do not think I could have been as fat as I was convinced I was. It is hard to describe how inferior, gauche, clumsy, and ugly I felt. There is a photo of myself standing next to our cousin Shirley. She was so neat, tidy, and nice, while I must have been called up from boisterous play. That epitomises just how I felt about myself.

I had another nickname which I despised: "Bolobah." I always understood that Grandpa Quinn had had a friend named Patsy Bolobah, and this was its origin. My brothers never called me anything else, except the shortened form "Bol" to the degree that if I hear it today, I would almost certainly respond to it. I must have been inclined to be sulky, because I used to jut out my bottom lip, and I would be unmercifully teased over this. "Verandah Lip" was my misnomer for this situation, and a cheery little ditty which went: "She's got an India rubber lip, Like the rudder of a ship, And I tell you she looks grand."

Eight

Galston was the enchanted land and was always the setting for mainly delightful memories. To reach the farm, one used to catch a bus, which waited for its passengers beside Hornsby Railway Station. One needed to hurry up the overhead bridge at the station, find the ticket, which always seemed to disappear just as it had to be handed in to the ticket collector. Then we had to gallop down the road to the waiting bus, which also seemed to be just about ready to leave. With luck, there might be a seat right down at the back. There was also a rear vision mirror, the full width of the bus, so the driver could observe any misdemeanours. (Incidentally, once my mother was seated about halfway down the bus when she happened to glance up into this mirror. Her first reaction was "Oh, there's Mum on the bus too." What she was seeing was her own reflection — which gives some idea of how much they resembled each other.)

The bus trundled along the road, gathering and dispersing passengers, until it came to the Galston Gorge. Here the road wound down the hillside, taking in a series of seven hairpin bends. It was too narrow to manoeuvre the bus around the corners, so at each bend, a kind of reverse three-point turn would take place. The bus driver would drive forward as far as he could, then back over the edge of the road (which of course was winding down a steep mountain), where the back of the bus would be suspended in space, and the passengers hoped like mad that the rear wheels would not go that little bit too far. Then a couple more shuffles and the bus would again be pointing in the right direction. This took place seven times every journey. At the top of the gorge we used to get out. The bus would head off to the left, and the village. We would set off to the right, and Selhurst. I don't know that Aunty Blanche was as pleased to see us as Grandma was, but we didn't care. It was like a second home.

Once I was with Grandma, and we had missed the bus — the last bus. So we walked, Grandma and I. Seven long miles. At the gorge I used to take a shortcut from one level of the road down to the next, plummeting through scrub and bushland, rattling stones underfoot as I moved. It must have done wonders for my school uniform. As I reached the lowest level and scrambled on to the road a car stopped. I knew all about not getting into a car with strangers. Some people who knew Grandma had picked her up, and were now trying to take me too. My unfortunate grandparent nearly had to get out and complete the journey on foot to accompany me, when I weighed up the evils of accepting a lift against the walk up the other side of the mountain, and I joined the motorists.

The whole fifty-eight acres of the farm were edged with enormous hoop pine trees. If you walked on the fallen pine needles, your footsteps were drowned in silence. The slightest breeze caused the trees to sough and moan, which was fine in the daytime, and eerie at night. I was so sad when I learned that they had perforce been cut down.

For many years there was no electricity or town water. Even when electricity came to the district the cost of having it put on was too great for a number of years, so we enjoyed lamplight and candlelight for a long time. There was little more frightening to one with a vivid imagination, than the shadows cast by flickering lights, especially when one had a couple of brothers who were quite prepared to play on such fear. The farm succumbed to town water around 1943 and power some time later.

Up at "the Top" (of the farm, close to where one caught the bus) were the peach orchards. Among those orchards was an old cottage, which was quite primitive. It had a corrugated iron roof, on which the Shell Oil Company had emblazoned its name, and a lean to out the front. It was slab. Inside the walls and ceiling had been created out of hessian, which had been covered with paper, and this had been whitewashed. I can recollect someone in it, but rarely. This was right next to the peaches.

Normally we were not trusted to pick peaches for the market, but when they were desperate for labour we were called in. No such thing as a sense of responsibility existed in my mind. Aunty used to harness Baldy, the draught horse into the dray. He would mooch along between the rows of trees, heavily laden with fruit. At this time fruit fly was still a problem in New South Wales, and one had to be wary in separating fruit which had been stung and that which was in good condition. My grandmother used to cut out the bad bits, and bottle the flawed fruit, in her vacola preserving set.

Because peaches were delicate they had to be put down gently in the dray to prevent bruising. This did not always happen, especially when we were helping. They were pleasurable, lazy days, with the sun kissing our faces, and the freckles which were always there in spite of broad brimmed hats. (Please note that they disappeared when I was seventeen, to my delight!)

There were also a few cherry trees. I loved the blossoms — but even more I loved gathering in the clusters of cherries, and hanging them over my ears like earrings. Frequently they were in pairs, sometimes three on a cluster, and very rarely, three or more.

Closer to the house were the orange and mandarin orchards. Below the house, nearer the road, were the navel orange paddocks. In amongst these were two fascinating trees — the blood oranges! These looked like ordinary fruit on the outside, but were not commercial propositions because, when opened, they revealed blood red juice sacs. They were sweet and delicious, but obviously off-putting to customers. Up at the bus stop there was a stall where, in season, reject fruit was sold at ridiculously low prices. I was never allowed to tend this stall. (I would probably have eaten the merchandise.)

We were allowed one privilege. We were permitted to eat the windfall oranges, when and how we liked. We used to tear in and out amongst the trees, swooping on fallen fruit, and frequently using them as weapons. I recall being in a fight involving the fruit.

There was a gravity water tank, which arose on its stand, well above the house. It rested on a platform, with the four squared corners projecting out from the circular galvanized corrugated iron tank itself. It appals me now to think how we would scramble up the runged ladder to reach the tank stand platform, then perch on the little triangular corners, stretching our arms around the tank, and wriggling around to the next projection. No one ever fell, but I don't know how they didn't. While we were up there, at the time I mentioned, Joan Levy and I were armed with oranges. Down below were Sam and his friend, Don Sheppard.

We proceeded to hurl missiles at each other, without any serious damage, but doubtless with much vocalising. I sometimes wonder if our innocent relatives were aware of some of our entertainment.

Beside the gravity tank was an earth tank. This fed the high structure, with a hand pump, which had to be worked backwards and forwards manually, to fill it. Rain from the house roof provided the water for the earth tank. It was covered with a series of protective slabs of wood, and we could see the water below through the cracks in between. Over the earth tank was a pipe, which shifted the water from the roof to the tank. Although it was strictly forbidden, we delighted to balance along this pipe from one side to the other, in the delirious knowledge that it was possible to miss one's step, and fall into the tank below. Naturally the boys did this many times, I less often.

There were also a number of fowl runs — in fact one of them was in the navel orange orchard. They were the original free-range chooks. It was easy to assemble them in the evening. After about three thirty in the afternoon, one (usually Grandma) would take down the wheat, scatter it in the fowl pen, and call out "Chook, chook" in a loud voice until all the birds came running in. At this juncture they would be secured inside from predatory foxes and hawks.

It was always interesting to collect the eggs. The fowls were not released for a run until after lunch, because most of the egg laying took place in the morning, and in the proper nests. However, there was always some renegade, who would lay eggs elsewhere, and it would be up to us to find these nests. Broody hens were the worst defaulters. At times a proud mother would lead a clutch of yellow downy chicks back to the fowl yard after a prolonged absence.

There was an egg incubator at the farm. Owing to the activities of the few roosters who were permitted to live in the fowl yard, the eggs were nearly always fertile. Sometimes a nesting hen would refuse to leave the nest when we were required to collect the eggs. She would give a sharp hard peck at the hand or arm which dared go too close and remove her eggs. They were not very bright. They would happily nest on china nest eggs as well, if these were mixed up with the others. Occasionally they would sit on a round stone if it could be manoeuvred into the nest.

At certain times the incubator would be loaded with rows of eggs. It was kept warm by a kerosene flame. There was a lever which had to be shifted twice a day, so that the eggs would rotate, and the chicks would not be deformed. After twenty-one days the eggs would crack, and dozens of baby balls of fluff would appear. Wet and bedraggled as they climbed out of the shells, in no time they would be fluffy and sweet.

Outside there was a shed — two sides of which were made of chicken wire. In the middle of this was a brooder. This was a circular flared hood, low to the ground, heated also by kerosene. Under this the chicks gathered for warmth and comfort coming out for food and water. Sometimes a chicken would be crushed underfoot in the mad rush for sustenance, or maybe it would be trodden on in the shallow water dish. Time and again Grandma would collect such a hapless, pitiful body, take it to the kitchen, and pop it into a box filled with soft rags, set beside the kitchen stove. Almost always the victim would rise to fight on another day. To me it was like a miracle.

The fowls were fed a mixture of wet bran and pollard each morning, buckets of this mush being carted down to the feed troughs. We were delighted to help when we stayed over. On the way back, Grandma, who always wore an enveloping bib apron, would stop by the wood heap, to gather kindling for the wood stove, then lug it back to the house using the aforesaid apron as a carryall.

The wood heap was also the execution post for the roosters when their allotted span was cut short for culinary purposes. The victim would be held by the legs. Thus immobilised, his head would be placed on the chopping block, and with one blow his life would be over. He was then hung upside down on the end of the clothesline upright until he was ready for plucking. At one stage Sam graduated to the post of executioner.

My imagination ran riot — suppose he missed — or even worse, suppose he only half missed? Distressed at this thought I hid in Grandma's bedroom to listen. One chop, then another... then another. The sound of the axe falling echoed seventeen times. Poor rooster. Actually, the first blow had done the deed. The other sixteen sticks were Sam making the most of an opportunity to officially, with adult approval, use the axe to split some wood. I did not really mind plucking. The carcass would be dipped into hot water, then it was placed on a very large iron tray in the kitchen, and the feathers would be pulled out. All the fine feathers were kept, to be later washed and use as mattress and pillow stuffing. When we helped a white snow of down was almost certain to lightly blanket the whole kitchen. Next Aunty Blanche would gut it. This process also took place in a large tray. She would make an opening near the tail, then pull out the innards. At times the smell was quite offensive. I never really liked eating chicken until the frozen fowls became popular.

One day Grandma had become very upset — why I know not, because she was an easy-going lady. Evidently Mum and Aunty Blanche became very alarmed. They called me in for a backup. Far in the distance her small black clad figure could be seen, stepping out towards the top of the farm and the bus stop. She must have been fed up. Just as certainly, she must have had some plan of action. I was sent to chase after her. When I finally reached her, I had to sweet talk that poor old woman into coming back. For my sake, she did. I was quite prepared to go with her if she didn't return, because I loved her dearly.

We celebrated Grandma's seventieth birthday in style. In the morning she was up a step ladder in the mandarin orchard beside the house, picking some fruit into a bucket. It was suggested that, due to her age, she should consider not using the ladder any more. This was too much! Up she climbed onto the flat top of the ladder and proceeded to jump up and down a few times to demonstrate that she was still agile.

There was also the birthday cake. Blanche was a whiz in the kitchen. She had made this wonderful cake for the birthday. All the family had gathered to honour her. Seventy candles were placed on the top, and four people had the job of lighting them, assisted or not, as you care to consider it, by all the grandchildren. This culinary delight was then carried to the dining table in the cage verandah, and the proper song was rendered with great gusto.

As with most women of her age group and generation, Grandma usually dressed in monochrome prints — soft greys, lavender, moroon, navy and other deep shades. Never brown or autumn tones, and never pastels or bright shades. There was no glamour about their footwear, either. Slippers were always a safe Christmas or Birthday gift. Naturally they all wore hats and gloves, carrying baskets or shopping bags when they went out shopping. Nowadays it is often difficult to pick a grandma, because their lives have changed so much, and for the better.

The farm sheds didn't hold much attraction for me. However,

at one stage I heard about the BOX, which was tucked away in the far corner of one of the sheds. After Grandpa's death, a long time after, one of the adults recalled it, and it was decided that it should be opened.

Many years before, the stewardess on a ship in which Grandpa was serving as a marine engineer asked him to mind a box for her, until she sent for it. Her name was Mrs. Conybear, and no message ever came, so the box remained where it was, and was gradually forgotten.

To my regret I was not present at the opening, but I saw some of the contents later. There were some cut glass and crystal items, some clothing, other things about which I recollect nothing, and the things which delighted me most — dance programmes. These charming little cards were printed with the list of the names of each dance to be performed at a ball, and on the right hand side there were blank spaces for each gentlemen to enter his name, and secure his partner for a dance before someone else beat him to it. Each girl had one of these. At the top of the card a small pencil was secured with a tasselled cord. Dances usually were themed around one colour, and the cards, cords and pencils repeated this shade. There were a lot of these cards in the box, and I thought they were wonderful. They set off dreams in my head of past glories and balls. I had read my Georgette Heyer stories, and I knew what they were all about.

In another box, in a small room at the end of the verandah at "Selhurst", I discovered another of my passions. All my mother's old story books were there. I found her copy of "Anne of Green Gables" and "Mrs. Overtheway's Remembrances". I knew where to hide when I had committed some sin. I don't think this hiding place was ever discovered as my escape hatch, for no one else ever used it.

Galston seemed to be the land of plenty — copious amounts of fruit, plenty of cracked eggs (the good ones went to market), homemade butter, when there was some to spare, bottled fruit, and milk, provided there were not many poddy calves. It was not, until years later when Elaine told me, that I realised their life was hard. All the men at war, or in war-related occupations. Grandpa was dead, and the two women struggled on alone, on a farm that had carried three men as well in better times. Elaine had read a letter written to Mum by Grandma, which said that they were managing with fowls — tough old boilers, I doubt not — for meat, and whatever produce they could spare from the markets for themselves. There was no electricity to make life easier, nor was there any town supply of water. They had to fill up the gravity tanks by hand pump themselves.

There was one job, however, in which we, as children excelled, particularly as we were not afraid of heights. The roof at Galston, especially the section near the wood heap and several extremely tall hoop pine trees, was both corrugated and remarkably steep. The trees used to shed their needles on to the roof, and these would drift or wash down into the guttering. At intervals my brothers and I were called on to climb onto the roof, slide down the iron, following the lines of roofing nails, and edge along the gutters, cleaning out the pine needles as we did so, by the simple process of throwing them onto the ground below.

A nervous mother would come out at times to supervise this, but her presence would stimulate the heroes. They would think up a few interesting activities to alarm her further. With all the men folk gone, even our father, and no chance of getting help elsewhere, we had a legitimate reason to carry out this task. Nevertheless, I was really rather frightened of that roof, though I would never have admitted it.

Nine

When Uncle Frank was living at home, before he had to go away for the war effort, he decided to breed pigs. He obtained some sows, which were placed in a sty below the lower fowl runs. Then he either bought or borrowed Barney, a large boar, whose job it would be to supply the future piggery with progeny. Having fenced Barney in Uncle Frank then ran a light electric wire around the yard in which Barney roamed, and forbade us to enter it, on pain of annihilation by either Barney or himself. This became a challenge. Neither the zap from the fence, nor the lack of love displayed by Barney hindered us, particularly the boys.

Each year Thomas's jersey bull was borrowed — a nasty piece of work, if ever there was one. I am surprised that even the cows loved him. He had visitation rights to those ladies, but during his visit, stayed most of the time down in the far paddock, near the virgin bushland. He was also a challenge, but I was far more afraid of him than the pig, because he could travel fast!

In due course he would go home, and later on various calves

would appear. The Jersey calves were so pretty, with big, soft eyes, long lashes, and gentle demeanours. If they were bull calves they would be poddied with the skim milk, and fattened for market. The heifers were kept, becoming part of the herd, and in consequence they were all named. I became envious when two of the calves were called after Frances and Judith, youngsters who lived over the road from the farm. Some names which were used were Milly, Molly, Mandy, Bessie, Pansy, Patty and yes, there was even an Elaine.

The herd was docile, and rounding them up was no real trouble, it just interfered with other occupations. As Aunt milked each cow, the shed cats used to hang around awaiting the occasional squirt of milk which Aunt would direct into their waiting open mouths. They always ended up with a saucer of milk after morning and afternoon milking.

The cows were no respecters of hygiene. They would shuffle around in the milking stalls, as the milk was drawn away. Sometimes a good solid stream of urine would flow in another direction as the milk let down — still far too close to the buckets in my opinion. It was a very earthy sort of job.

Carrying the buckets back to the house we would pass the greenhouse, but I never displayed much interest in this. It was a real, original bush house, and contained treasured plants of Grandma's, but my heart had long been lost to the maidenhairs.

Next to the farmhouse, separated only by one of the orchards, was the cottage. I think it must have, in the past, before they acquired the place, been a farm labourer's cottage. I understand we lived in it for a short while, but I was too young to have any memory of this.

After the war, Uncle Sine returned to the farm, as good-natured and kind as ever, but not managerial material. Then he went away for a short visit to Kyogle to an old army mate of his. He came back, as silent and happy as ever. Then one day Grandma received a letter, which stunned the whole family. It was signed: "Your loving future daughter-in-law, Dorothy Reith". I still recall the feverish excitement that letter provoked, and the women trying to get the silent Sinclair to expand on it.

It was probably the best thing that could have happened to him. He got a loving wife, with enough sense to boss him around, so that he actually DID things, and five splendid and clever children. They took over the cottage. As we moved up to Queensland about this time, it was a blessing for Aunt Blanche and Grandma. They were able to give their love to those children, and when Uncle Sine died of a brain tumour at sixty-seven they were there for Dorothy too. My real regret is that I never really got to know them as well as I did my older cousins, of whom I saw much more.

There was an antbed tennis court as Galston too, and a splendid swing, on which one could sit and dream, or watch the cloud pictures in the sky, or weave daisy chains with the dandelions scattered everywhere. In spite of two tennis courts none of us ever made the grade in the sport — lack of instruction and partners may have had something to do with that! Gee, it was a good playing area.

Rarely, we went to Galston village for some purpose, even if it was just to post mail. I was christened in the Anglican Church there. Now a craft shop and library, I believe. This ceremony had been neglected for years until the unhappy day Dad decided it should be done. I was ten, Elaine was two and a half.

The Reverend O'Brien was one of a number of men who, over the years, had displayed an interest in my aunt, but until her fifties she never took the plunge — after Grandma's death. I suspect she stayed single because they could not have kept the farm if she were not there.

One memorable time there was a fete at Galston Hall, including a cookery contest. One section was for the best sponge cake. There were no electric beaters then. Sam had a strong wrist, and an interest in cooking. He was all of eleven years old. Under Aunt's supervision he made, and cooked, a sponge. This was entered in the competition, and to the chagrin of the local ladies, it won first prize. Even more galling for them was that, directly after it had won, Sam was showing it off and someone sat on it. As the cakes were not permitted to be taken home until the function was over, this attractive object, sporting its first prize certificate, was on view all the afternoon.

Back in the hallway at "Selhurst" was a piano. I could not play it at all, although I painstakingly taught myself to play, using one finger only, and starting from middle C, the air of "God Save the King". At other times I would, providing I thought I would not be found out, strike the keys, belting out my version of music. The discordant notes attracted a bit too much attention, usually.

As a bride I visited Aunt Blanche at Galston, with my new husband. She took me to her room, and showed me a beautiful string of pearls that Frank Shirley had given her for a Christmas present three months earlier. Then, to entertain us, Frank and Blanche, by now fifty-six years old, took us for a picnic in his car. When we got back to our room Alex said to me: "That old bloke's after your aunt." I laughed at the idea, but he was right. Within six months they were married. As indeed, was Uncle Bill. The three of us married in the same year, 1958.

The association with the Shirleys (Frank was Blanche's husband) went back for many years. Mum knew Mrs. Shirley (Frank's mother) when she was single. In fact Mrs. Shirley made her wedding dress.

The Shirleys had a daughter, Trixie, as well. When Jim's birth was imminent Mum stayed with Mrs. Shirley, as it was too far from the hospital out at the farm. Over the years the contact lapsed, doubtless through geographical separation. Then Grandma died, an old lady, and the funeral notice appeared in the Sydney Morning Herald.

Frank Shirley, himself now a widower with four adult children, attended the service for the sake of old times and fond memories. From this meeting, his friendship with Blanche was able to develop into a lasting marriage of more than twenty-five years. At the time of the wedding I was intrigued. Still young, and madly in love, I was curious as to how an elderly spinster would cope with the intimate details of a marriage. My concerns were laid to rest, when it was put to me that Aunt had spent most of her life on a farm, with lots of animals, and she would have accepted that as a perfectly natural consequence. What egoists the young are! I now know that love is not confined to just the young. "Love's Old Sweet Song."

When Grandma passed away, and Aunt's circumstances changed, she gave me a few items I loved. The tiny silver rickshaw, which moved, a souvenir of one of Grandpa's overseas voyages. The miniature Toby jug I had saved for and had purchased as a present for Grandma so long ago. Several tiny clay and porcelain figurines which I had also given Grandma in the past. I also received Aunt Becky's birthday book, which I recently gave to Jim and Mavis, because they have a true bent for family history. I would have loved the China cabinet, but I had been too long away from the centre of the family to feel any right to ask for such a thing.

Mum passed on to me two beautiful, heavy, intricately cut,

crystal bowls, matching, but one smaller than the other. The had been our grandmother's mother's. I have since passed them on to Jenny. The real reason is because in appearance, she reminds me of Mum and Grandma. If she turns out as well as those two grand old women I will be happy for her. She is still on track, fortunately.

Another part of our lives was spent at Mirrabooka. During the depression, when work was unobtainable, Dad used his savings to purchase a block of land at Mirrabooka, on Sugar Bay, part of Lake Macquarie, which had a circumference of 365 miles. He then built a cabin with his own two hands (Viola: "I will build me a cabin at the gate.") for us to dwell in. It was three feet off the ground. Its access steps on to the verandah were two very large wooden stumps, arranged like a stile. The back door had no steps at all. It just opened at the elevated floor level. There was one room and a large verandah, closed in about the lower half, which was the same size as the room. This verandah was where we children, and all visitors, slept.

Our beds were made of bush timber — crossed forked sticks at either end, each supporting two long side poles. Opened hessian bags were stitched across and over these poles to create a base for our mattresses. They were quite comfortable. Inside the room, at the end nearest the lake, was a double bed iron bedstead, with a black and white striped ticking mattress on it. This became a holiday house when living and work conditions improved. The mattress would be rolled up and stored in the rafters — there was no ceiling – only being lifted down and placed on the bed, when we came to stay.

I was too small when we used this as our permanent home, to recollect it at that time. I believe it was a disastrous episode, particularly after Dad went back to sea.

My personal recollections are almost all delightful. The furniture was the beds I have already mentioned, a triangular shelf in the far corner, from which hung a curtain. This was our wardrobe. There was a white kitchen dresser, a small deal table and wooden chairs. That was it! There was no stove. In the house was a small metho and kerosene primus, of which I was scared, because I could rarely light it without a bang. The food was cooked on the open fire, over a tripod.

There was no bath, and only a fairly small, galvanised iron tank outside. Mum would fill the white enamel baby's bath and supervise our cleanliness each day. My memories of this are such that, when I was expecting Russell, I bought a similar type of bath for my baby.

There was also a wind up gramophone in an upstanding cabinet, and a number of old 78 rpm records, the whole handed on to us by Grandpa Pearse. I bet Sam could still tell us about the firmament, the stars in the sky, the milky way and all its connotations. He loved that wretched record, though no one else liked it much, because it was just the voice of a man lecturing about the night sky. Other records had music and singing on them. "Red Wings" and "White Wings" both figured, as did "Abdul A Bulbul A Meer", and my all time favourite: "Two Black Crows in Hades". I would love to hear them again for old time's sake, and sheer enjoyment. They were a patter exchange between two Negroes; some of the conversations ran like this, each man playing a part. On this record one was the Devil, the other a reluctant entrant to his Kingdom. "If you lie, the buzzer of lies will buzz — but if you tell the truth the bells will chime melodiously", and a ding would sound. Then "Goodbye bye Mr. Debbel. Ah hopes Ah nebber sees you no more, and even that will be ebber so much too soon!"

The house was not far from the shore, and the lake was both

tidal and salt. I still enjoy the smell of rotting seaweed, as it blows of the edge of the water, because it is all so redolent of life at the lake.

To reach Mirrabooka was an event in itself. All our goods and clothing were transported in large old globite suitcases, for the school holidays. Lumbering these we would take the electric train to Hornsby. No porters, so we shifted this ourselves. At Hornsby we had to go up the stairs to another platform, using the overhead pass, then down the other side, still lumping our possessions. The boys were prepared to help Mum, but they considered me old enough to do my own thing. By the time we had shifted all of this we would be just in time for the steam train. We would show our tickets , and climb into one of two types of railway compartments. Some were boxed compartments, others were accessed through a train corridor, and into the carriage that way. There would always be an argument as to who should have the window seats; we would fling up the windows, and hang out full stretch to wave good-bye to the guards, stationmaster, and anyone else who was prepared to respond. We would pass Asquith, and settle down for the trip. It seemed as if we were travelling to the ends of the earth.

We would pass gangs of railway fettlers who would wave as we went past, calling out for any passengers to fling out newspapers if they had completed them. We had a horrible fascination with the toilets, too. These had no bottoms, and the contents would drop onto the lines below.

Two or three times during the journey we would pass through tunnels, all the black soot from the engine shooting into the carriage, if we did not get the windows closed in time. At some stage at least one of us would collect a piece of flying soot in an eye, kicking up a performance until it was removed. Usually with the corner of a handkerchief moistened with a bit of spit. We would pass Gosford, Wyong, Woy Woy, over the bridge crossing the Hawksbury River (where we could also see in the distance, the road traffic bridge), then Toronto, Tuggerah, and finally we would arrive at Morriset. I was never quite sure which was the station before Morriset, and I was convinced that the guard would forget to let us off at the station. (We had to make arrangements with the guard before we left Hornsby). He always remembered, but as it was a whistle stop we only had moments to disembark before the train chuffed off again. On many occasions we had a spare boy or girl with us as well.

At Morriset we would wait at the station whole one of the boys would be sent to the shops to find the old chap who had the solitary taxi cab. This was a very large vehicle with a soft hood; but it had one marvellous attribute. There were two folding dickey seats behind the front seat, and facing the rear seat. Most of the luggage had to be crammed into the boot, and tied on the running board — the rest was tucked in and around our persons, or else we nursed it. It has to be remembered that we had to take our food with us too, because there was only one very small general store at Sunshine, to supply the whole area. On the way to the house we would stop at the store to let them know we were there, and to purchase last minute perishable goods. Then down the winding road, to the turn off past Merrits, where we always bought our watermelons, until finally we would arrive at our idea of Heaven.

The taxi would come as close as it could. We had to hop across a small stream and welling spring before we had access to the house. One of the boys would rush around to the front, unlock the door, then open the door without steps.

Job Number One was to lift out the little boat, really a yacht tender. During our absence it was stored in the house, and would dry out. The boys would plunge down to the water, to immerse it in the lake, in order to swell the boards, so it would be watertight once more. This took at least twenty-four hours. The rafters had to be climbed and the bedding lifted down. The iron bed had to be set up, and Mum had to unpack the food. Firewood had to be collected, and the fire lighted. As the verandah faced some virgin bushland, this was not difficult.

Dad had also built a very large shed near the house. In it was the laundry tub, also doubling as a bath at times, a large mangle, and a pan toilet with a wooden seat and lid resting on top of it. At the close of each vacation someone had to take this pan into the bush, dig a hole, and bury the contents. I only ever had that job once, when I went to the lake with Mrs. Levy, Joan, and Gwenda Symonds. Normally that was not my problem.

I used to burn very quickly and very badly in the sun, especially on the water, so Mum would baste me with coconut oil, which was supposed to help one tan, not burn. Of course I fried. My fiercest memory of this is when I was still quite young, and I blistered terribly. My whole back was one big blister. I could not wear my normal pyjamas to bed, so I was clad in an old nightie. Eventually weariness overcame me, and I dropped off into slumber. When I awoke the blistered back had burst, and the garment was firmly glued to my body. It could not be eased off. The baby bath was filled with warmish water. Somehow I was draped into this with my back submerged. It took most of the day to part me from that nightie.

Swimming togs, or "cossies" weren't the pretty little items worn today. Mine were made of wool. I had a dark green woollen pair, and when I outgrew them I had some in pale yellow. I rather prized these until I saw a photo of myself wearing them. Films were black and white then. I looked naked, the yellow hadn't photographed at all well. These costumes would be left at the house from one year to the next. Mum forgot that I was a growing girl, and as a result they were often somewhat skimpy.

I always wore a hat, but this did not stop the overwhelming mass of freckles which pervaded my face. Only time and adulthood cured that. This did not stop me from testing out the bleaching qualities of hydrogen peroxide, or lemon juice. Both useless, unfortunately.

We would sleep on the verandah, watch the stars, feel the rain, unless the weather was too severe, when we would cram inside on the floor. We would sit by the firelight, with the Aladdin lamp going as well, unless Mum was trying not to waste the kerosene. If Dad was with us we would sing. It was my sorrow to possess a flat, tuneless singing voice. However, I was loud, so I would put the others off the tune, unless I was told to be quiet. We would listen to the gramophone, and finally creep into bed.

In the daytime we would launch the boat, or try our hand at fishing off the jetty. Mostly I caught little leatherjackets, which had to be skinned rather than scaled. No fish was too small for our pan.

We went swimming. I learned to swim the hard way. Dad was the perpetrator of this method. I would paddle around the shallow end of the wooden fenced baths, in amongst the thick seaweed near the shore. There were also frequent influctions of jelly fish, both the shapeless clear blobs, and the ones with caps and stubby tentacles, which always reminded me of a cows udder. I was fool enough to stand on the jetty, near the deep end, beside Dad, when he suddenly swooped on me, and hurled me into the deep water. I spluttered and dog paddled, vocalising screamingly as I did.. I certainly learned to swim, but never with any style. I also had the misfortune to be one of those people whose ears developed abscesses if water entered the canal. Consequently I have always swum with my head and neck arched out of the water. This slows progress and defies beauty. The same day I lost my glasses in the same deep water, as I clung madly to my hat, while the specs fell off into the briny. No, they were not recovered. Serve Dad right if he had to buy me another pair!

There was one gloriously exciting time. The Patricks holidayed in the house next door. Old Grandad Patrick lived there permanently, but come holiday time the extended family moved in for the duration. They were miners from Cessnock. They would arrive holus bolus, with wives, kids, furniture, crates of chocks, dogs (they followed the greyhounds, and raced some themselves), beer, nets and fishing gear. In a pantechnicon. This was a supersized removalist's van. I watched the unpacking with awe. I must have had a relatively inflated idea of my family's values, because I felt different. Also, grog was never part of our lifestyle, and these boozy, good natured folk regarded it as an essential part of their lives.

Before dawn one morning — at about four am — Mum came to our beds and woke us up. The Patricks had been prawning, and had invited us over for the feast. I had never seen prawns, far less eaten them, but the excitement was too much to miss. Over we went, well wrapped against the chill, pre-dawn winds. There was a large fire blazing. Over the flame hung a four-gallon kerosene tin, boiling water bubbling away inside. Into this was dropped the salt and the seething mass of freshly caught prawns. To me it seemed as if there were millions of them. There was also a seething mass of kids, dogs, the squawking of the chooks in the background, disturbed by the noise. The women were supervising their offspring; the men were quaffing their beer, for all I know now, it was probably rum. Whatever it was, it was the demon drink.

Then the prawns were lifted out, and we were invited to tuck in. Never averse to food, I took a prawn and bit into it. It was horrible. No one had shown me that they have to be peeled and beheaded first. My disillusionment lasted for many years. (Aunt Blanche was caught in the same way once. Uncle Bill took us both to some friend's place where prawns were on offer. Blanche did exactly the same thing. She bit into the unshelled prawn, and didn't enjoy it at all. I had to show her how to strip the shell off).

On the whole our pastimes were fairly innocent. Once, the boys and I, eager to try out the boat before it had been rendered watertight, equipped ourselves with fishing gear, and set off across Sugar Bay. We intended to call on the Lilleys — uninvited — who lived over the other side.

As we rowed over the boat began to take in water. We bailed frantically. Eventually we got it to the stage that, if we sat perfectly still, the water inside the boat was at least four inches below the rim of the boat. Suddenly a swift squall gusted across the bay. The waves it produced swamped our vessel, which promptly turned over, as we leaped out. The old flat iron we used as an anchor dropped to the seabed, and held the boat in situ. The sailors abandoned their ship, and swam to the shore, quite some distance away. They really were quite proficient swimmers, more than could be said for me. Watching the oars start to drift away, I dogpaddled after them, and seized them. By this time they were intertwined with our fishing lines. I began to flounder around, struggling to the shore, loudly demanding help from Jim and Sam, who cruelly ignored me. Finally my bellows prompted a response: "Stand up and walk." The tide was low, and I found that I could manage to drag myself armpit deep in water, through the mud to the edge of the water, with my salvage operation still under way. By the time Bob Lilley rescued the boat next morning it was well and truly watertight.

For Christmas Day we would walk up to Merrits' place and buy a watermelon. This was kept cool with a wet bag placed over it until we were ready to eat it. It was always enormous, the long stripey sort of melon, and absolutely delicious.

There was also the long walk up to the Sunshine General Store, when it became necessary to purchase anything. I did not like to make that journey, it was an uphill trek to get there, and we would be heavy with groceries on the way back. We used to obtain milk from the Merrits, which was a version of Cold Comfort Farm. it was not very arable soil.

We once had a picnic at Morriset Lunatic Asylum. We had to walk quite a few miles, carrying all the picnic gear as we did so. It was just Mum and ourselves going to this very popular picnicking spot. Families of the inmates would also visit, and make a pleasure day of the occasion. We settled down on a beautifully mowed grassed area and had our meal. Nearby was another family group, whose Grandpa was a permanent resident. The small daughter confided to us that Grandpa refused to eat anything except chicken and jelly, both delicacies in our time, so we reckoned he had the right idea.

There were also a number of confined areas, separated from the public by high, heavy, chain metal fences, which were topped by several rows of inward leaning barb and razor wire. They had cement paths around the perimeters, and smooth green lawns. I was greatly impressed by a lawn mower which was all metal (the push me pull you sort such as had removed my finger). The metal handle was completely twisted. My simple soul envisaged a maniac rending it like that with his bare hands. The public like us were free to walk along outside these areas, and gape at the unfortunates inside. It strikes me as shocking now, but this was the accepted behaviour and attitude of that era.

Jim and Sam, being older than I, and members of the scouting movement were allowed to go to Mirrabooka by THEMSELVES, with groups of friends. Sam and his pals, always including John Allen and Alan Bruce, would plan meticulously, working out the catering, and who was to take which item. The would load their rucksacks and set off on a well-planned vacation.

Jim and his pals, always including Don Lock, Alan Cunninghaam, and at times Bob Levy, had a different method. No, it wasn't even a method. They would sling a few items together, and head off. At times they would go when Sam's group was there, and sweat on their provisions. There were no flies on that mob.

Once I took Dorothy Miller and Linnea Jonsson. We were just approaching our mid-teens, and dressed accordingly. Linnea, who was nicely rounded, had an interesting sunfrock. The back was full, from the neck to the hem, but the front was separated at the waist, and tied in a knot under her breasts. It was a pretty blue floral. I would have liked a similar dress myself. We frolicked around, leaping around our somewhat unstable beds. We were acting out some songs. Dorothy flung out her hand, striking me in the mouth. Bingo! There went another of my teeth. I just accepted this, and we spent the rest of the holiday there, with no thought that the dental repair might need instant attention. People just didn't seek out the medical and dental professions unless they were very badly hurt.

The only time I went without the family was with Mrs. Levy, Joan, and Gwenda Symonds, and we have photos to prove it. For once I had certain responsibilities. I believe I handled them adequately.

Though we were on a casual holiday Mrs. Levy did not vary her normal style of dressing at all. She probably had no other type of clothing. I enjoy the photo where she is sitting in the stern of the boat, with her afternoon frock on, and sporting her narrow-brimmed hat, trimmed with flowers and veiling. She was such a nice, gentle woman, with simple, kind manners, and a soft voice. She would have had her problems with us three strongminded teenagers under her care.

Ten

Grandpa Pearse figures very little in my past. I am sure this is because he remarried and had a second family of his own just about the time of my birth. I was at the wedding, but still internally. He represented dignity, pomp and wealth. Aunt Ruth, his wife, was the niece of his first wife, which sounds almost incestuous, but of course it wasn't. She was a kin woman, always slightly breathless. The third of her sons was a severe asthmatic, Ron. My first memories of Grandpa are of his home at Balgowlah. When we visited there we were sometimes taken to the rock swimming pool at Fairlight, but I didn't like it much.

They had three sons, Alan whom I hardly knew, and who played N.S.W. representative football; Ken, whom I always liked, and of whom I hold fond memories, and Ron, the asthmatic boy. I classed him and Ken as friends. We just didn't see enough of them because of geographic and economic constraints. Being without a vehicle was so limiting.

Once I was invited to stay with them for Easter. This was not so much a holiday time as a Holy time, involving a good deal of Church. Grandpa was a church warden. Aunt Ruth, unwisely, put several Easter eggs in my room, to be taken home for distribution to Jim, Sam and Elaine. The were the size of hen eggs; each was covered with silver paper, with a fluffy chicken on top, and placed in an egg cup. Even more unwisely, she showed them to me. In short order they disappeared. I salved my conscience with the knowledge that each sibling would at least have an egg cup. Too late I began to worry. I had about sixpence to spend, so I decided to replace them with some judicious purchasing. But how could I reach a shop? The family lived in a purely residential area.

Somehow I persuaded them to leave me at home with Ron, who was younger than I, whilst they all went off to Church, as it was Good Friday.

As soon as they had driven off, I whipped Ron out of the house, setting off to find a shop. Even today shops usually respect Good Friday, and this was sixty years ago. Disconsolate, we meandered along the street, only to be overtaken by the churchgoers on their way home. We were taken up. Still I did not reveal my awful secret. When it came time for me to go home, Aunty Ruth, to my everlasting horror, decided to repack my bag for me. Thus she discovered my sin. All I remember is my ultimate shame. Doubtless she split her sides after I had left, but to this day it has somehow reflected my relationship with that family.

Grandpa and Aunt Ruth used to visit Ron in Bathurst often, during school holidays. His asthma was so severe that he had to attend boarding school there, even as a young student, and even in many of the holidays, poor child. The Balgowlah house was offered to us as a vacation occupancy to give us some pleasure, and to keep their garden watered while the family was away. It was an unmitigated disaster!

I was allowed to bring Joan Levy for company. On the first day the boys discovered the rotary clothes line. They used it as a carousel, hurling themselves around and around, as it spun madly. The design was so new that we had never seen one before. I bet Mum wished she hadn't seen one then either, because they managed to break it.

Next the bottom of the kettle just fell out. This was followed by the gas bath heater blowing up while Joan and I were using it. There was one disaster after another. The final one was the smell. Something had died somewhere. No matter how hard we looked we were unable to trace it. It pervaded the house. On the day we were due to leave for home we found a putrid mouse among and behind a number of packets of soap, which were tucked in the back of a cupboard. The stinking odour was still in the house when we departed, though the mouse had been removed.

I have never known one of these house exchanges or arrangements to be really successful. That was one holiday I did not enjoy. I must have recognised how difficult it was for poor Mum.

A couple of times Ron and Ken stayed with us. I remember those visits with pleasure. We used to try to work out how to define our relationships. Were we first cousins once removed, were we second cousins, or should we have been calling each of them Uncle? One for the genealogists, perhaps?

Once Grandpa and family took us to Wallacia for the day. He arranged for two cars, so everybody could be transported. There was suitable picnic food, and it was a delightful day. We discovered the little backwater which was Penrith, and the wonderful weeping willows sobbing over the serene waters of the Nepean River.

I was always aware that Jim felt differently about Grandpa to me. I have never asked Sam how he felt. Elaine was still further separated than I, because we left Sydney when she was only eight.

I was so envious of her, having appendicitis just before they went north. Nothing so interesting was my lot.

Just prior to our departure there was great excitement in our house. We purchased a refrigerator. Dad had been advised to get one, and have it shifted north with the rest of the furniture as, so soon after the war, it was still very hard to get appliances. We had a Cold Flame fridge. The other obtainable and popular one at that time was the Silent Knight. There was no large freezing compartment in them; just a special place where two small trays of ice blocks could be set, and a space above this where an ice cream brick could go.

A fridge like that would have been handy a couple of years before, when we held Elaine's sixth birthday party. She had a proper one, supervised by Barbara Oke and myself. Once Elaine made the discovery that presents were involved she stationed herself at the back door, meeting each guest with the request, "Presents, please." The children played a number of games and had the usual party. A cake, fairy bread, small cakes, sweets, jelly and custard. We had made lolly baskets (and lollies), paper caps, and had done the decoration bit quite successfully.

However, in the side street was a house, the back yard of which abutted the vacant lot next to our place. The back verandah overlooked our back yard. The householders were people named Sandiman. They had a plump little daughter, Judy, who was a friend of Elaine. Alas, they were members of the Closed Brethren Sect, and did not believe in such worldly things as birthday parties. Mum spoke to Mrs. Sandiman, who must have had a bit of common sense, explaining that on Elaine's birthday we intended to have some young visitors for tea. Could Judy come? That child had a wonderful time. She literally never left the table from start to finish, of that party. She wisely went home minus her party cap, having finished her basket of lollies some time beforehand.

Even as a small child Elaine was possessed of a deep love for her dolls, as was my Elaine in her turn. She also possessed the ability to create crafts. She was no more than four when she made a "carry-seat" for her doll, based on the ones in which women used to lump their babies and toddlers. This was wartime, and women had now to do so many things with which they had never had to cope before, so their hands needed to be free. There was a broad strap which crossed over the back and shoulder, culminating in a semi-rigid seat which settled to one side in front of the wearer. Elaine's effort was made with some red scrap material, and it was held together with some LARGE tacking stitches; but it worked.

I was always sorry that these talents of hers were not used in an earning capacity. I do not think that either Elaine or I was ever truly ambitious, but a respect for professionalism and higher education had been bred in us all too successfully. Other talents, such as her craft and singing abilities, and my acting skills, were regarded as lesser achievements, and amateur amusements in the adult world, rather than means of earning a living.

School, particularly high school was almost always a pleasure to me. I flourished where appearance mattered less than brains.

Who could forget the declaration that the war was over, and a period of peace lay ahead of us? By this time we had acquired a radio, and we listened avidly to the news. The radio announcer stated that there were to be addresses given by the Nation's three leaders. We gathered around the wireless set. First to speak was the Prime Minister, Robert Menzies. He was one of the world's all-time great orators, and a speech of this proportions was a wonderful thing to listen to. He was followed by Arthur Fadden, the Deputy Prime Minister. After one had listened to Bob Menzies, he sounded florid, and seemed to overdo it. Ben Chifley had a less sentimental approach to the subject. All three men were so happy to be able to confirm this initial statement that everyone was in a state of euphoria. Mum took us into Martin Place to be swept up in the excitement of the occasion, and to share the time with the hundreds of thousands of other people just milling around the streets. I can't remember doing anything in particular, just that wonderful feeling of relief that it was all over.

The only one who felt any regret in our family was Jim. He was almost old enough to join up and had been looking forward to this ascent into manhood with great fervour. Like most of the youths of his age, it had been their only real thought and expectation for several years, so it required a complete change of attitude and way of thinking for them. In the end he joined the occupation forces for a period. Doubtless this would have been to his advantage. He acquired some steady discipline and experience of working with adult men in a co-operative way, all splendid training for the adult life ahead of him.

During the war Mum had regularly and faithfully gone one day each week to the Methodist Ladies' Comforts Fund, for servicemen. What visions that name would conjure up now! She was one of the group who used to serve meals and cups of tea to the men who made use of this facility. The finale for this group of women was a morning tea, when all the workers gathered together for a final celebration. It was a huge turnout. Just about every one of them came. There were so many that it became chaotic. Some tried to help by gathering up used teacups. As was the custom, the dregs from each of a pile of cups would be poured into one cup, and the whole lot would be carried back to the serving counter for clearing and washing up. There were so many there that women, seeing full cups on the table would whisk them off to drink, not realising that they were now consuming the dregs.

After the war, Dad, who had spent the second half of it in the Royal Australian Naval Reserve (Seagoing) as an Engineer Lieutenant was due for release. Prior to that he had been in the Merchant Navy all his life.

Mum used to scan the Sydney Morning Herald each day, keeping an eye out for suitable jobs for him. One day she spotted a government advertisement which seemed to fit him to a T. Knowing how difficult it was to reach him, she applied for the job on his behalf. To his astonishment, he received a letter from the Department of Navigation and Lighthouses, awarding him the position, and giving him a choice of either Townsville or Newcastle to take it up. The job was for a Marine Surveyor. He chose Townsville, partly because he enjoyed the hot climate.

This proved for him to be a wonderful career move. He now had position, which he valued. He had his own work car (a left-over government jeep with a left-hand drive, and a mechanical yellow hand which had to be used to give hand signals to other traffic); as well as his own small, grey, second-hand Prefect car. He always liked little cars, and one could hardly have got a smaller one at that time. He also had his own offices and balcony, situated in the splendid old customs house building, facing the Strand, and the sea.

The Customs House, at the main entrance had a wonderful curved, polished, wooden staircase, which swept up in a pair of semicircular staircases, uniting halfway up, and leading to the Marrinan's private living quarters. Mr. Marrinan was the Head of the Customs Department. It was very "Gone with the Wind" or "Rebecca" like — most effective.

At the time of this momentous change in our lives, I had almost completed my final year in secondary school. The Levy's very kindly offered to keep me in their home until the school year finished. I stayed with Joan, attending school each day with her. It was a good job we were both academically minded. I was very much in awe of Mr. Levy, and did my best to avoid him, in case I should offend the poor man. He had been the West Ryde Primary School Principal when I was a student, after all.

Mrs. Levy once cooked some tripe for a meal. Aware that I should be no trouble, I manfully tried to eat some. My imagination got to work — sheep's stomach. Ugh! You can't swallow that rubbish. Don't forget where it came from! Precipitately I left the table and tore outside to the backyard toilet, where the tripe and I parted company. It must have startled the Levys for a moment.

Very shortly after my family left for the north by train, Joan Levy's brother Bob came to me on the Sunday morning. He made me get dressed, then walked with me right up to the West Ryde Newsagency. We were about to buy a Sunday paper. What sacrilege! We walked back home, I was shown the paper. Blazed across the front page was the information that the Brisbane to Cairns passenger train, following the Sunshine Route, had crashed at the town of Tiara, three people being killed. The question was, were they my family, or were they all right? I really wasn't very concerned, as I was a great believer in the "It won't happen to me" theory. Fortunately I was right.

Whilst with the Levys I found that the earth would not stop if one read anything on Sundays, that it was O.K. to buy papers and read comics without being tainted. Amazing discoveries.

Then my exams were over and I caught the train to travel to Queensland. The girl who lived over the road from me in Ryedale Road, was coming with me as well. I never really understood why, as although I knew Barbara Oke fairly well, she was a year older than I, she went to the Domestic Science High and not my school, and she was never an intimate friend of mine. I know too, that her family was not well off, but then, who was? We set off on this great adventure. Fortunately, we had sleepers, for the journey took several days.

I had read many books about the wild northern frontier towns, and had seen the occasional picture, so I knew that white girls would be a rarity. I realised that I would be the social hub of the town, and probably half the town would make the effort to be at the railway station to see this newcomer, and as a by-product, her friend. My information must have been about a hundred years out of date. The only ones to welcome us were the family. There was a very busy crowd because train travel was the commonest, and best, way to travel in those days. Where were the bands? Where the putative admirers? Alas, I never did find them.

I found I was a very small frog in a very large puddle. Townsville had, at about that time, 1947 — 1948 — about thirty-eight thousand residents. No one cared two hoots about me. Many of the young women of my class and type began to travel overseas. They all seemed to have their close personal friends already, and I was very lonely. No one thought much about girls who were absorbed in reading, or who actively liked learning. Girls who felt a bit unattractive. I realise now that I was not the enormous lump I felt I was. For this I have only Jim and Sam to blame, as they fed my well-oiled inferiority complex.

Like many older brothers they assumed they had the right to criticise me, and proceeded to do so. Had I been slim and pretty I might not have met the same fate. My glasses certainly detracted from my appearance. I was strongly short-sighted, and the outside edges of my thick, plain glasses reflected circle upon circle of repeated light, so that they made my quite nicely shaped and coloured eyes look small. I had really lovely hair, but no idea of styling, so the heavy mass gave my face a rather matronly look. The freckles (when I was small a pin could not have been placed between them all) gradually faded. I liked food, and would have been the better for, not necessarily less food, but more suitable nourishment. I did not have much idea of how to dress attractively. I was the sort of girl people described as "good". What worse epitaph could a teenager have had? I was certainly no social butterfly, though I longed for such a metamorphosis. I was low on self esteem.

In spite of all this I had the odd admirer. One such was "Chock" Archer, whose Christian name was really Charles. I met him at a dance, and could hardly believe that this tall blond footballer could display an interest in me. After a few outings he put forward a suggestion which spoiled our relationship forever. Would I do his washing every weekend? As I did my own only when I could not avoid it, I could picture the derision which such an action would produce, and I declined. I was astonished, later, to find this was a common practice in Townsville, a sort of sealing and bonding together. Perhaps the boys were testing out their girlfriends' abilities in the home?

Eleven

I had only one ability. I could act. In Townsville I joined two repertory theatre groups — The Townsville Little Theatre, and the St. James Players. Here I discovered my metier. I played a variety of roles, all character parts. I had enough ability to transform my part into the star performance each time, which was always gratifying. As a result I was accepted in the little theatre on my proven merits, not my own estimate. My eyes were opened to a different more bohemian world.

Several persons in this culture were probably bordering on the eccentric, but they accepted me, which was very important. I blossomed in that atmosphere and consequently enjoyed it. One fellow actor was Patrick Gaunt. He was a rather slim Englishman, who had been working for the Main Roads Department, north of Townsville, for a while. At this time, in Western Australia, there was a tremendous fuss, because the recently appointed professor of English in the W.A. University had disappeared. He was very young (I think in his early twenties). His folded clothes were found beside the Swan River, indicating that he had committed suicide. Other indications made the police think it was a fake suicide. I have to agree with them. I feel almost sure that the missing professor was actually Patrick Gaunt. He was my sort, with similar interests. I enjoyed his company immensely, though not romantically. There was no such suggestion in our friendship. The theatre group once went on an excursion together on the back of a truck. We began to sing in harmony. I did have the sense to sing very softly. Patrick then remembered a couple of tunes which harmonised beautifully together. I was the only other person who knew the words. One was "Molly Malone", the other "The Ashgrove". Under his tutelage, using the words of "Molly Malone" to both airs we harmonised, with much success.

Another chap I liked was John Kingston. I fell for his voice. He had the most mellifluous speaking voice I have ever heard. It was like spoken music. He was not tall, and he was rather stout, but not softly fat. He escorted me to the Townsville Show, and purchased a child-sized monkey for me to carry. Again, it was not really a romance, just the pleasure of listening to his voice. In any case he had a friend, also a bloke. I knew nothing about homosexuals, and I was not aware that such friendships existed. Eric was the younger man's name. They could both act. John had been a professional down south. In one play Eric and I played the part of two Negro servants. Because of our greasepaint we shared a dressing room. No one really wanted to come near us while we were browning up.

I had two favourite plays: one was "You Can't Take it With You"; the other "The Charm School" by Alice Duer Miller. In this play my character had a minor role, but because it suited me to a T John wrote another act to the play, especially to display my talents. I really was very good in that part. Another of the actors was John from Michael Nielsen's Hairdressing Salon. I had to change from being a dowd to a charming woman. John did my hair. I was given a chignon to create the dowdy impression; then later in the lay I had to emerge from this cocoon into the new me. However, the chignon looked so classy that we reversed the hairstyles. I also played Mrs. Bennett in one, and Lady Catherine de Burgh in another version of "Pride and Prejudice." There were other plays, but these were my favourites.

We used to hold cocktail parties too. They were the fashionable thing. The only thing against them is that there is nowhere to sit down, one just circulates. But we all had on our cocktail hats. One of the men asked me if I would mix him a gin squash. I didn't know how to do so, so I asked him. "Half gin and half squash." That's what he asked for, and that's what he got. No minor detail like water was included. He nearly choked on his first and last taste of that drink!

Some of the actors were temperamental. One lady, inflamed not by passion, but by beer, picked up one of the props. This was an Indian brass, chased,

On one trip we were approaching Queensland's highest mountain. Surely I must know that name. It also began with B. "Mount B..B..B.." I was a flop. It turned out to be Mount Bartle Frere. The footballers felt that if I had a drink I might feel a bit cosier, but I was a flop there too. I still didn't drink — my background was too strong.

When we reached Innisfail Sam was there to greet us. He took us, on foot, to the family with whom he boarded, and with whom we were to spend the weekend. They had a shop, but it was closed over the weekend. However, the son was a keen cyclist, even racing bikes. As a special treat, he, Sam and I went riding on the Saturday afternoon.

I loved Innisfail. With so much rain, it had a clean freshly washed look. The black ribbons of road threaded through the bright green cane fields, growing in brilliant red soil. I was surprised at what a neat crop sugar cane was. The patchwork created by the varying heights of the cane, the bare fields, the vivid colours of the soil the grass and the sky was extremely attractive. The one thing marring it was our locomotion. I had been provided with a semi-racer of a bike. It had a narrow saddle, as well as a horizontal bar, and the handlebars were slung low. Before the afternoon was over, I thought I was in serious damage. I felt as if I was in the process of being sawn in half, vertically.

The journey home on the train was even more exciting than the upward trip. By this time all the footballers and their fans were in a very jolly state, happily sharing, nay, insisting upon sharing, their hot chips, coffee, pieces of fish, sandwiches and whatever other food they had with them. They mourned with us that we had been unable to attend the game, hoping that next time we would be together again. I was happy to arrive back in Townsville in one piece.

Then Sam fell in love.

As his circumstances slowly improved, he purchased an old Nash car, with a fold-down top. Phyllis lived in South Townsville, and we were in North Ward, but the Hughes maintained they could hear Sam's car start up at our place, when he was off on a date with Phyllis.

She was so pretty. Her younger sister, Pat, was tall and vividly pretty. Phyll was shorter, slim, and very elegant. She carried herself with grace. I didn't know Coral very well. I came to know Joyce, the eldest, extremely well over the years. She always had my admiration, as she coped with trials and illness not very many have had to bear.

It was with great regret that I could not be Phyllis' bridesmaid. By this time in my life I had taken up teaching, and I was on my second appointment, at Camooweal. There was only a weekly plane, and a weekly mail truck, with two trains a week running between Mount Isa and Townsville, on a two-day journey. Thus, geographically, I could not get there. The date of the wedding had been brought forward from Easter, to sometime during Lent, because Sam had taken a position in Kavieng, New Ireland.

The bridesmaids' material was beautiful, pink satin, with pink and silver lace for the bodice. As Pat Hughes was to be the other bridesmaid, it was just as well that I could not get there — I would have been well and truly outshone. The fabric came in handy later for a ball gown, and in a stage play as well.

I was very much involved in the Church activities, both Methodist for old times' sake, and the St, James Youth Club, because I really was an Anglican, and this was the first time the English Church had been easily available to me.

One entertainment was a bike hike. One Saturday morning we all set off on our bikes for Blue Water, many miles to the north. The others had updated bikes, but mine was still the heavy, cumbersome black vehicle of earlier days. As I pushed at my wheels, and pedalled along the road, everyone else disappeared into the distance ahead. They had their picnic, and commenced the return journey as I came ponderously along, still on the outward trip.

Naturally I did not complete it. I turned around, and commenced the return trip, enviously watching the others as they vanished once more. We were supposed to go out that evening to the pictures. I expect the others did. I certainly didn't. I imagine I was lucky to get home in one piece.

That day recalls another in Sydney, when I was about sixteen. The church group had decided we would hike out to Berowra Waters, starting to walk from Hornsby Station. It was a long walk, and I kept up with everyone else, striding out in unaccustomed style. That, of course was the disaster — it was unaccustomed. At the end of the hike, with the others, I staggered on to the train, and settled down for the twenty-five minute journey back to Denistone, when I would get off, and walk the last stretch home. I soaked up the comfort of the leather seat, until Eastwood, the station before mine. At this stage I found I could scarcely move off the seat, I had stiffened up with the warmth and rest. The train halted at my station, and I was barely able to lurch out the door before the train took off again. I then had the painful task of tottering home the remaining distance. I suspect that most of that day's hikers had the same problem.

In Townsville, Saturday night was always dance night. I was not a good dancer, so this was no real pleasure to me, but it was the accepted thing.

During my teens Dad had insisted I attend Miss Gerrie's School of Ballroom Dancing, which was just as well. I could never have socialised if I hadn't learned. With similarly trained dancers I could dance quite well, and enjoyed it, but in the public arena it was quite different. Boys who had just picked up the steps, with a good sense of rhythm and a good band, could manage extremely well. But they didn't follow the proper steps, and these, to a tuneless learner like myself, became very confusing. I hated being a wallflower. More, I hated being the girl next to the girl who was solicited to dance. If she refused, the poor coot would then ask me. Sometimes pride would make me refuse also. Sometimes I accepted.

Before each dance I would anticipate it with either dread or joy, dreaming that this time it would be wonderful! As the evening progressed, my heart would sink. I made things worse by not wearing my glasses, which may have improved my appearance, but it didn't help my vision. I could scarcely see the lads until I was dancing. I used to carry my glasses in my purse, then put them on so I could see my way home. Most dances were held in the Y.M.C.A. Hall.

The Friday night pastime was the cinema. Our poor circumstances, when I was a child meant that I rarely saw a film. When I had the opportunity to go as a young woman, I went. Usually we went to the Olympia Theatre on the corner of Herbert Street and Sturt Street. This theatre was a combination of open air and enclosed. The rear of the picture show was covered, the front half free to the elements. The seats were deck chairs, singles, twosomes and threesomes. They too, were exposed to the elements. Many was the time when a patron dropped heavily onto a seat, to find that he or she had continued dropping onto the floor, as the rotting canvas failed to hold the weight. Just the thing to add interest to a bit of a cuddle at the pictures. Even when it was raining a few souls would watch the show from the open-air section with their brollies up. The Wintergarden was a fully enclosed building, and an alternative to the Olympia. It was further down Sturt Street.

As a child I felt a great envy of my friend Joan. She was the youngest of four — they were spread over a period of twenty years. from eldest to youngest. So Joan must have been the child of her parents' most affluent period. She had one shilling each week to go to the Saturday matinee at the West Ryde Picture Show — was it the "Rialto"? She was allowed to go every week. The afternoon's programme started with the National Anthem, when everyone rose respectfully to their feet and remained silent until it was over. There was an enormous clattering of seats as they dropped back into place and the audience settled down. Next came the Movietown News, which covered recent world events, with a presenter explaining everything as it was shown. This was followed by a cartoon. After this was the first feature picture of the afternoon. It was usually classed as a "B" Grade picture. As "The End" appeared on the screen, there was a concerted rush for the milk bar, where sustenance was purchased to see one through until the second half.

Interval over, signalled by the shrilling of an electric bell, the second half began. There was the weekly serial. This could be about the adventures of Flash Gordon or Buck Rogers, or other superheroes of the day. There were the promotions for the following week, followed by either one or more cartoons, then the main feature of the day. It was almost always of a higher standard that the first film.

My family not being film buffs, expense was the real criterion, I treasured the times when I was allowed to go. I saw Snow White and the Seven Dwarfs; Blossoms in the Dust; Bambi, Fantasia, Dumbo, Mrs. Miniver, Good-bye Mr. Chips, Sitting Pretty, Life with Father, and a few Bob Hope and Bing Crosby Road pictures. I loved Monsieur Beauclaire. I recall Johnny Weissmuller in Tarzan of the Apes. My repertoire was not large.

When I grew up and had control of my own finances, I went as often as I could afford it. Of course, once I went teaching I was again in a situation where pictures were not a regular feature of my life. When I married they were even less on tap, for geographical reasons. To make matters worse Alex did not care for them, as they had the effect of lulling him to sleep.

As I see them so rarely, I prefer comedies or suspense films. I do not enjoy blasphemy, swearing, any foul language, nor explicit violence or sexual viewing. The hot, open-mouthed kisses displayed today merely make me squirm in my seat, turning aside until they have passed. The innuendo and suggestion of cruelty and sexuality allow much more freedom for one's imagination. One just needs to see a couple heading for the privacy of a room, and a closed door, to know what is happening inside. The flash of a knife, a trickle of blood, and a steady drip, drip, drip after the deed is done, and one knows what has happened to the victim. Those ploys cannot really give ideas to mentally disturbed viewers, because they haven't seen anything.

I have been to a few unusual picture shows in my time. Once I went on Magnetic Island. It was ground, blanket or self-provided seating. There was only one projector. Each film usually had five or six reels. As each one finished a notice appeared on the screen. "Sweet music while the operator changes the reel. Have a cigarette."

Camooweal was even more interesting. Here too, one provided seating if he or she wished, although early arrivals usually got a seat that was there. It was also a one projector theatre. This was operated by either Mr. Buchanan or Young Joe Freck. Joe was the younger son of Mr. & Mrs. Freckleton, who owned a local store.

An unusual film was to be shown one Saturday night. It was a modern version of a silent movie: "The Thief'. Rita Moreno was the star. To this day it has been incomprehensible to me. Because the film ran with music only for sound effects, and because so many pictures had adopted the practice of showing the lead up to the film before the credits came on, we finished the whole of the third reel before anyone realised that it was not actually the first reel of the picture. These pictures were delivered on the mail truck, the mailman having collected them from the Star Theatre in Mount Isa, after their showing there. Occasionally he forgot to pick them, and we missed out on a showing.

The theatre was, of course, open air. It was surrounded by patchy corrugated iron, with the screen projecting well above the fence.

One local hero took offence at what was being screened once, so he shot the screen up. As far as I know the bullet holes are still there. On another occasion, an equally lively gentleman resented the way the picture was unfolding, so being upset during one scene he flung stones at the villain, and also left a permanent record there.

In cold weather several forty-four-gallon drums were set up, with fires burning in them to counteract the bite of the wind. Anyone who got there early enough was able to sit as closely as possible to them. The disadvantage was that only one side of you would be warm. There was always someone else waiting to jockey you out of a place if you stirred. Smoke from the fires would drift across the screen, often obscuring the picture.

Once Alex came courting to Camooweal. He had brought with him the family truck, on which was a crate full of wild pigs to be taken to Mount Isa for sale. In this vehicle, with full accompanying noises we went first to the pictures, where Alex, following the form he has followed ever since, went to sleep; and we went courting afterwards. There is little less conducive to romance than a herd of wild pigs crashing around on the back of a truck in which you are cuddling. My pupils reported every move next Monday during Morning Talk.

At Mary Kathleen there was another open-air picture show. This was more sophisticated. It had been erected by the mining company, and though it had canvas seating it had two projectors, so the running of each film had some continuity. At that time the first satellites had been put into space. It was exciting to try to locate them and watch them speed across the night sky. In between pictures one could get a very good view of them.

Alex visited Mary K once and took me to the pictures there. True to his usual form he fell asleep, this time with his head on my shoulder. I was thrilled to have him there, but he was a bit heavy. Next day my pupils reported; "We saw you at the pictures last night, Miss Pearse. With a man. He was lying all over the top of you." Truth in reporting?

Although I enjoyed the pictures, my real escape from reality was books. I do have to take care how I select them, though. Should I read a depressing tale, I feel personally depressed for some time afterwards.

Twelve

Once, in Townsville, the family went to Mt. Spec overnight. I was left at home. My reader's choice that night was "Dr. Jekyll and Mr. Hyde." The setting was perfect. There was no moon. The house was an old Queenslander, the wood creaking and talking as it does in old homes. An enormous mango tree grew next to the house, shedding leaves all over the ground. I cannot now understand why we never thought to clear those leaves away. As a result they dried, and became crusty, crackling as anyone walked on them. In the tree lived a happy family of possums, which would visit us as the whim took them.

This night I read compulsively. The hour grew late. I knew perfectly well that I should go to bed. At half past one I began to make the effort. Stop! I could hear footsteps. Someone was walking stealthily over the mango leaves on the ground. I could hear light thumps. Was I about to be attacked? Was that a door being quietly opened? My legs refused to move. Nothing happened. All right, I would stay in the lounge room and finish my book. The tale grew more vivid, so did my fear. My bed remained unused. The light remained on. I slept in the chair, that is when I eventually did sleep. And the possums continued to enjoy their usual nightly patrol over the mango leaves. Now, if I want to read anything with a bit of fear, or spice, I go to bed first. I was really pleased to see the family come home that day.

When my father took up his position in Townsville, he achieved something he had always craved. Position. He became a fairly big frog in a middle-sized pool. His position was of some importance, as the town was a large commercial port. His area of jurisdiction extended from Thursday Island down past Mackay and the Whitsunday Islands.

He had a lovely office with imposing fittings, and he was obviously very happy. He became part of a group of men around his own age group and station in the area. Each day half a dozen of them would meet for morning tea in front of the Ozone Cafe on the Strand. This group became known as the "Millionaires' Club", because a couple of its members were very affluent. Dad was just coming into his most financial period, so he was comfortable, without heavy debts, and able to relax about money for the first time in his life.

We were a family of non-drinkers. In the relaxed northern atmosphere my father occasionally shared a whiskey and soda with friends. One Christmas morning he awoke with a terrible headache, convinced that he was dying, certain he had a fatal attack of influenza. Judicious questioning showed that he and Bob Hayles had quaffed one too many whiskey and sodas the evening before. He must have been suffering from his first hangover.

In Townsville he was able to resume his love affair with the Masonic Lodge, indeed, becoming Master of the Lodge in his due turn. He also became a member of Rotary, and had quite a big input there too. Because of his seagoing life he had never been able to participate fully in any such clubs before. He was also a member of the Queensland Club.

By virtue of his job he was given a place on the Board of the Missions to Seamen, and this is where I became involved.

Each year Townsville conducted a number of Debutante Balls, a practice I did not care for. I did change my mind however, as I saw what it did for a girl's social life. The Catholics and the Anglicans each held a ball, so did the Amateur Racing Club, and so did the Missions to Seamen.

I was just the right age, straight out from school, thus a perfect candidate. My misfortune was that I didn't know any local boys whom I could ask to be my partner. Later I realised that this was an equally big event for the boys too. Salvation came. One of Jim's friends, quite a pleasant-looking, and tall youth, was staying with us for an extended period – Alan Cunningham. He always reminded me of Prince Philip in appearance. We trotted off to practice each week, learning the social mores of Townsville, as well as the selected dance for the Presentation. As the Mission to Seamen was an offshoot of the Anglican Church the local Bishop was the Guest of Honour. There were eight of us debutantes, all affiliated in some way with the Mission. The only venue for balls was the Exhibition HQII. Our last practices took place there.

Certain dress requirements were standard. Everyone attending the ball was in full evening dress, save the Bishop, who wore his robes. The partners were in full evening dress, hired if necessary, and all wore white gloves, presumably to keep the girls' dresses clean. Each deb was in white, her gown could not be off the shoulder, nor could it be sleeveless. The necklines had to be modest. The only acceptable jewellery was pearls. Flowers could be worn in the hair, and elbow length mittens covered the arms, while a posy was to be carried. The frocks were to be an inch off the floor, sensible really, no one could trip on them in that case.

I was lucky, a neighbour, who was a dressmaker, made my frock. She had the sense to encourage me to dress fairly plainly, which suited me. I had toyed with the idea of a Scarlett O'Hara frock, with a hoop.

As so often happened on my special days, it rained (no, it wasn't the wet season). The plane carrying my posy did not land until midnight, so I had to do some quick substitute work. In my slip, but minus my ballgown, I tore up the back yard, into the fowl run and picked the last four frangipanni flowers off the tree. The fowls roosted in that tree each night, in preference to roosting in their house. I threaded those flowers onto wire, so they could not fall off. I took three fronds of fishbone fern, and a few scraps of white taffeta, left over from my petticoat. I frissoned this into a bouquet, retaining one flower for my hair. I was amazed to see it looked quite well in the subsequent photos, while some of the other debs had posies which resembled full gardens.

We were arranged in order of height, smallest first. I was somewhere in the middle. Each girl in turn was announced, whereupon she had to parade alone, right up the centre of the hall to the official party. At this stage the Matron of Honour came forward, introducing the girl to the Bishop. She then dropped into a full curtsey — the hardest thing to do properly. She rose, the Bishop extended his hand and she saluted his ring. She then took a few paces backwards. By this time her partner was in place behind her. She took his arm, gratefully, and moved off to form part of a semi-circle. When all the girls were presented the Bishop gave them a homily about the great Adventure of Life. The music struck up, and they swept off into the Debutante Waltz.

We proceeded around the hall, watched by admiring relatives. When each girl reached her parents, she was told to stop, and curtsey to them, as to the Bishop. As usual, my vanity had prevented me from wearing my glasses — they really were thick, reflective, and ugly. I spotted Mum and Dad, stopped, swept into the required curtsey, then danced on again. Later I realised they had been in an entirely different place. I have no idea whom I actually acknowledged.

As one girl caught chicken pox the night before the ball, another was partnered by her brother, and another had a rather tubby gentleman as her partner, I was well satisfied with mine. A shame he knew me so well, and treated me as he had always done, the same as my brothers, a lowly girl!

During the year most girls attended several balls. I went, of course, but I didn't really like them much, as I did not know anyone very well. My academic background didn't quite fit in with the local social set.

Brains did not seem to be necessary. The real criterion was to be a member of a well-established local family, having attended St, Pat's Catholic School or St. Anne's Anglican School.

Over a number of years my opinion of St. Anne's didn't rate highly. (I had nothing to do with St, Pat's, so I suspend judgement there.) If a girl actually received a senior pass, it was considered worthy of an accolade in the local newspaper, no matter how poor the result. I was shocked when I learned that a girl could be a pupil at the school one year and a teacher there the next!

As a result, even though all my children attended private schools for their secondary education, I have a leaning towards State Schools and their trained staff. When I was planning to send the children away, I would study the Junior and Senior results of various schools, to see where I would prefer to send them. In the end this, together with Joan's health, helped me to make the final decisions.

Enjoyment was discovered by me in the Central Methodist, and St James' Youth Groups. I spread myself quite liberally here. My real interest and ability in the acting sphere was my salvation.

The Central and Hermit Park Methodist Churches had vigorous and successful youth groups in Townsville, when I was in my late teens. I remember with admiration Reverends. Les Vickery, Ron Howe and Jim Mitchell. They were sincere, active and responsible leaders who guided their flocks well.

The Methodists had acquired a parcel of land at Nell Bay, on Magnetic Island, on which they placed three ex-army huts. One hut was for boys' accommodation; one was for the girls, while the central hut became the kitchen/dining room/community and recreation centre. The facilities were ultra-simple. A large number of ex-army double and treble chain wire bunks had been installed with a fibre mattress on each, for sleeping. The windows were the push-out, wooden shutter variety, while at each end there was a double door, and in the middle of each side, a single door. The buildings were two or three steps, off the ground.

The central hut was partitioned off at one end, where there was a kitchen and servery. The main part was a dining room, the tables able to be pushed to one side to leave an open area. At the far end were a couple of rooms for those in charge, and the cook, to sleep. The cook was the only paid employee. (In parenthesis, years later, while living on Planet, I met one of these cooks again, now employed on Lawn Hill Station — Bev Lucas. She vividly remembered those camps.)

Dozens of us would pay the required fee to cover costs, never excessive. We would catch the evening ferry over to Arcadia. From there we would head for Nelly Bay. We were organised, fed, supervised, our spiritual needs received attention, and we were entertained, and provided much of the entertainment ourselves, very simply and effectively. Long weekends were the best times, or times when we could snatch an extra day from the work force. It is a shame that such simple pleasures and innocent amusements are no longer adequate.

We had concerts, hikes, swims, campfires by the beach, church activities, which certainly never hurt us, and a thousand and one acts of impishness and devilment perpetrated by lively spirits. A student minister, who did not have the happy knack of endearing himself to the rest of us, once made the mistake of sleeping too soundly. He was due to catch the ferry back to the mainland to take a morning service, one Sunday. The boys carefully fastened ropes to his bed — he had chosen to sleep on a single bunk in the centre of the hut — and silently and in unison they raised it to the rafters. He couldn't believe where he was when he woke up.

Another hapless student minister was unable to find his suitcase for a while, because a Papua-New Guinean amongst us, one who could easily scale coconut palms, had scaled a high branchless tree, where he fastened the suitcase well out of reach. The students were frequently fair game because, although some were delightful companions, a few felt they were a cut above the populace, who thereupon took great delight in cutting them down to size.

Once the boys banded together, arrayed themselves in swimming trunks and singlets, with their leaders sporting ties as well. They arranged themselves into a marching group, proceeding to march as one, right through the girls' dormitory, from one end to the other, and out. This brought forth the anticipated squeals of mingled horror and delight.

Not to be outdone, a couple of days later, the girls robed themselves in their bedsheets, covered their heads and shoulders with their towels, masking their faces with their washers, apart from their eyes which they needed for vision. They lined themselves one behind the other, each girl placing her hand on the shoulder of the lass in front of her. Thus they shuffled silently through the boys' dorm, whose reactions were different. They sat down and tried to identify each girl under her swathes of linen.

We held concerts, one in particular was my success story. There were no plays, just variety items. Not able to sing or dance, not able to recite any elocutionary pieces, because I had never had access to any of them, I stood up and recited: "! watched the birdie in the sky. It dropped its message from on high, And as I wiped it from my eye, I thanked the Lord, that cows can't fly." It was the hit of the evening. Commonplace now, that verse was virtually unheard of at that time.

Water was always a problem. The shower facility was under a tank, which had to be filled through the medium of a pump. This had the quality of frequently breaking down. It did so while Hazel Graham was taking a shower. She was a lass, whose practice it was to wet her body all over, then work up a rich lather with soap, after which she would sluice it all off. This time she had reached the stage where she was covered in lather, and the pump broke down again. While those in charge worked to repair the pump, Hazel's faithful fiancé, Keith, stayed outside the bathroom door, to keep her company for an hour and a half, until she finished her wash. Nowadays he would go in and help her.

There was a time when the girls decided to try out various beauty treatments. The yolk of an egg is not recommended in the hair if hot water is used. Washing blue in the final rinse is successful. Several girls had an assortment of face packs. Not having one of these I bethought me of the breakfast oatmeal in the kitchen. I helped myself to some of this, stirring it into a thick paste, which I plastered over my face, as had done everyone else with their brews. As it dried I could feel it stiffening on my skin. I decided to check it out in the mirror. I looked. I looked again. My face was alive. All the little grubs which must have been in that porridge were now wriggling over my face. None of us ate porridge from then on.

I had a good friend, Margaret Gherke. She was exceptionally pretty, with a charming manner, which endeared her to all of us. She wasn't quite well enough to come to that year's camp. When we returned from camp, we were met by the news that Margaret had died, the sudden victim of a liver complaint. It was shattering. This was one of our few encounters with an early and unexpected death. Her funeral was heartbreaking, as are those of all young people.

Most of my friends had been given twenty-first birthday parties. Mum was not a party giver by any means, but I must have had the gene in me. Tentative suggestions had been given a cool reception. Then I had a brainwave. I would have a surprise party. The twist was that it would be my parents who were surprised. I therefore organized it. Various friends made and brought different dishes. I did a bit of housework, which must have surprised Mum also. On the appropriate evening all my friends turned up. Some even brought presents. I had always had visions of three wonderful gifts — a bottle of Chanel No. 5 perfume, a rare cattelya orchid to wear, and an imposing box of luxurious chocolates to eat. That night I nearly made the grade. My current admirer, Tom, brought me a whopping great bottle of 4711 eau de cologne, another guest had a bunch of flowers from her garden, and someone else had made some fudge for the party. Tom used to sing me a song popular at that time: "When you are dancing, and you are dangerously near me, I get ideas, I get ideas." I felt that this was rather racy.

Our next door neighbours were the Thompsons, who became very good, and close, friends. There were Mr. & Mrs. Thompson, Dorothy and Claude, their son Jim, and their daughter Claudia. Claudia became Elaine's close friend, she even named her daughter after her. Claudia contracted Bright's Disease, and died when she was seventeen. Jim was an articled law clerk like me, in the same firm.

Once I heard Mr. Thompson complaining about his place in his wife's priorities, which he listed in this order: 1. Jim; 2. Claudia: 3 the house; 4. the cat, Felix; 5. the dog; 6. the ferns; 7. the garden; last. himself. He was a very kind man with the patience of Job.

Jim was a great friend of mine too. There was a stir in town when Princess Alexandra was to make a Royal visit. She was young and attractive, and had to be entertained accordingly. The City Council chose to put on a ball for her. A number of young men had to be vetted, so that she would have young partners. Jim was one of these. There was one problem. He was no dancer. He had to attend a number of dancing lessons before he was entirely acceptable. At the first State reception Princess Alexandra attended pavlova was served. This dish had never come her way before, and she commented on how delicious it was. By the end of her visit she was wishing she had never seen the dish, as it was presented to her on every possible occasion from then on.

Royal visits were few and far between. The Queen and Prince Philip once came to Townsville, where all the local dignitaries were anxious to be on the presentation list. My parents were part of that hallowed group. At the same time an epidemic of dengue fever swept the town. No one realised how serious an illness it could be. About half the populace succumbed, including my parents. As one, the mob rose from their sick beds to attend this reception. I was surprised that the Queen was not ill for weeks afterwards.

When we moved to 106 Stanley Street, Dad decided that the outside of the house needed painting. I was co-opted into helping him. Week after week he attacked it with a blow torch and scraper. Week after week I followed him, putting on two undercoats and a topcoat of paint. (This was after work hours, and weekends for both of us.) I really did work at that job and was ultimately rewarded when Dad had Grandma Miller's closed face nursing watch repaired and suspended on a brooch for me to own. I treasured it for many years until it came to a distressing end many years later.

Because it was so hot in Townsville, I slept on a cyclone stretcher, on the verandah, covered only by a mosquito net to keep the insects at bay. As I lay fast asleep one hot night, I was jerked out of slumber by a sound like an explosion. A great bar of wood came crashing down onto my face. I let out a scream of terror, which brought the family running. I had been unaware that there was a rat problem in the house. Dad had put a heavy board cornerwise through the verandah rafters, right above my bed. On this he had set a rat trap. A rat had been trapped, hurled itself around, dislodged the plank, and the whole caboodle had landed on top of me.

Life with father was always exciting. Not always happy, but never dull!

Thirteen

Mum and Dad had married, as he was fond of telling us, on 9th October, 1926. Therefore their silver wedding anniversary fell during our Townsville sojourn, on 9th October, 1951. Sam and I conceived the idea of giving them a surprise party to celebrate this. By this time they had established a number of good friends who were only too happy to be part of the scheme.

Mrs. Roy Goldring made an enormous, many layered sponge cake, which she decorated appropriately; various people brought plates of food, while Sam and I also provided some. A few people even gave presents.

We had trouble in preventing our parents from going to bed before the guests arrived, and in making them wear suitable clothes, without giving the surprise away. It was worth the effort for a splendid and successful evening. Only two other anniversaries ever overshadowed that one — the golden and diamond celebrations many years later.

When Jim and Mavis married there was a good deal of excitement in our household. The wedding took place in Bowen, and we were to drive down on the wedding day, Mum, Dad, Elaine and me. I was important, I was to be a bridesmaid.

We made up a picnic hamper, while Dad got the car ready.

However, there had been earlier preparations also. Dad admired sophisticated women. At that time a pale blue rinse was favoured for silver haired women. Mum reluctantly agreed to this embellishment. I prepared to give the rinse. We lined up at the kitchen sink. As it was stainless steel we thought it would not stain the metal, and we were right. The hair was shampooed and readied for the Magic Silver White. The instructions were explicit. Only enough powder to cover a threepence. I stirred this into the water, and began to sluice it through the hair. At this stage Dad passed by. He was interested because the whole thing had been his idea. He stopped, looking at the solution washing through her hair.

"That's not enough!" he exclaimed as he took the bottle and gave it a good shake, sending a large blob of powder into the sink. It immediately turned a deep indigo blue. I wailed in dismay. Dad moved in to finish the job. Cup after cup of rich blue liquid he poured over Mum's head. Only then did he stand aside. I was permitted to finish off.

We drained the blue water away, and started rinsing her hair, which was now a bright, deep, biro blue. We washed it again and again. We reshampooed it yet a few more times. She still sported a head of rich blue hair. Finally we gave up. Her only consolation was that women always wore hats to weddings.

On the morning of the wedding Dad packed the car. It was the Austin soft top. Unable to control his impatience with women in general, he hurried us up. He hurled a suitcase in on top of the bridesmaid's frock. I protested, and rescued the dress. We were bundled into the car, and set off on the trip. The road was appalling, and the travelling was slow. Dad was one of those who believed you should ease your way over every corrugation so we felt every bump.

In due course it was time for a snack. Where was the hamper? Back at home on the kitchen table. This set the tone for the whole journey.

We arrived in Bowen: gritty, grotty and grumpy. I was delivered to the Ayles family home for a bath, and to get ready for the wedding. The others departed for their accommodation.

How things have changed! None of us bothered about hairdressers; we were quite satisfied with our hair as it was. Jean Ayles and I were both fairly solid girls, we matched quite well. Jean's frock was of pale blue, mine of peach pink. Both were covered with dainty sprays of white flowers, though they never showed out on my dress in the photos afterwards.

Mavis was enchantingly pretty. Jim sported his Flight Lieutenant's uniform. I am ashamed to say that I do not recall who were the male attendants. Neither Jean nor I sported much of a smile in the wedding photos.

This was the only wedding in which I had any involvement until my own a number of years later.

As time passed I got some real wear out of my bridesmaid's dress. I removed the diamente trim, opened the frock all the way down the front, following seams already there, added some ribbon ties, and turned it into a charming negligee.

So often did Dad try to glamorize Mum, but the basic material and interest were not there.

For a long time he tried to persuade her to smoke. Thankfully he failed. He wanted her to paint her nails in vivid hues. Eventually she compromised. He was permitted to paint her toenails if he left the hands alone. One day he had completed this service — purple was the colour of choice — and her toenails were partly dry when the doorbell rang. She opened the door bare footed. There was the local Methodist minister come to pay his respects. No one could have missed those toenails. An embarrassed mother welcomed him inside.

At that time most women wore nighties to bed. Then the era of baby doll pyjamas came in. Home from work came Dad, bearing a pair of bright yellow seersucker baby doll pyjamas as a gift for his wife. They contrasted so beautifully with the heavily purple-veined legs she sported. They were nevertheless successful, as they were cool to wear.

The veins in one leg were cured shortly afterwards. Dad had for some time been replacing the front verandah floor. He had completed the task, save for one board outside the bathroom door. Mum blithely stepped into this space and her leg plunged through the hole. She had the quickest bit of skin abrading anyone ever had. When the thigh eventually healed every capillary vein had gone, and her upper leg was smooth and white.

She always maintained that what Dad had really wanted was a blonde showgirl from the Tivoli Theatre. He never realised just how lucky he was to get her, until he grew old.

When they had been married for fifty-seven years, he and Mum went to Sydney to visit Blanche and Frank Shirley in Castle Hill, Sydney. One day he dressed himself up, and announced he was going out, without revealing his destination.

What happened, served him right.

Over the years he must have cherished a fantasy of a blue-eyed, ash-blonde beauty he had known as a youth — the daughter of a Methodist family in his family's congregation. Apparently he had kept some sort of a tab on her, for he knew where she lived, and whom she had married.

He drove to this lady's home, somewhere in Concord. He knocked at the door, which was opened by a woman, who explained that her mother was out, but was expected home shortly. Would he like to wait?

Wisely he chose to wait in his car.

Finally, along came an elderly lady, enormously stout, puffing as she lugged a couple of plastic bags. She entered the house. The white knight slipped away. When he got back to Castle Hill Mum was hanging out a load of washing. He walked out to the line and said, "Thank God you're not fat!"

Understandably Mum was wild, mostly because he had not trusted her sufficiently to say where he was going. When she recovered from the hurt, she learned to enjoy the episode immensely, even if he didn't.

When I first arrived in Townsville I had to hunt for a job. I did not like the idea, and did not know how to go about it. Then I saw an advertisement in the Townsville Daily Bulletin, for a filing clerk at Burns Philp. I made an appointment to be interviewed, and was seen by Mr. Ruffle, the deputy manager, who gave me the job.

For a week I learned how to file invoices, and make tea for the rest of the staff, while doing all the other tasks very junior employees are always given.

A week or so later the General Manager returned from his vacation and called me into his office. This was Mr. C.P. Swan. I felt as if I had been summoned by the headmaster. He looked me over, then just about accused me of pulling strings to get the job because of Dad's work connections. I hotly denied this. I could hardly say that Dad did not approve of me working there at all. I had that job for some time.

I thought Dad's idea about employment was magnificent. He wanted me to stay at home and help Mum. She had other ideas.

"I will never speak to you again, if you choose to stay at home and become a household drudge!" She could easily have added the words "Like me", but refrained. As a girl she had no opportunity for gainful employment, so she felt very, very strongly on the subject. Therefore, I worked.

An odd thing happened in Townsville one weekend. Someone in the family, who was obviously feeling pretty fed up with parental control, put a carbide light in our parents' bedroom, with water to activate the carbide, but no flame to burn off the resultant gas. No harm could possibly have come to them, because the house was so open, and the climate so warm, that windows and doors were rarely closed. However, I received the blame for this, and was suitably punished — the last hiding I ever received. I still protest my innocence. Until I went to Planet and saw the men there using carbide lamps at Kamarga, I had no idea what they were, or how they worked. I do know that we had an opened bag of carbide under the Townsville house, though I don't know why it was there.

When I went to Teacher's College at Kelvin Grove, I rediscovered the pleasures of learning, and studying. I felt as if I were once again in my own metier. Through the church connection, I obtained accommodation, boarding with an elderly widow, Mrs. Jarrett. Because the welfare system did not at that time, make much provision for impoverished widows in her situation, she had divided her home into two flats. One she rented out to the two Miss Williamsons, one of whom went to work, while the other maintained their home. She also took in a female boarder. She felt responsible for me. To my horror, on the day I was to enrol at the Teachers' College, she accompanied me, just as one would a child going to a new school for the first time. I tried to dissuade her, but her sense of duty was too strong. Heaven knows what the principal thought when I saddled up for my interview with Mrs. Jarrett in tow. I did not even know her myself.

This was the year after the murder of Betty Shanks, still unsolved. Brisbane was in a state of fear. In winter, night falls early there, and often I would not get off my tram until well after dark. Loch Street, where I lived was a steep hilly street, and had Peacock's Furniture Factory in it, which was unlit, and very lonesome at night. One night I left the tram, as did another traveller. I walked on bravely, becoming more uneasy by the minute. I was definitely being followed. Into my mind kept coming visons of poor Betty Shanks. It is surprising how one's legs can develop wings, as did mine that night. I sped past the furniture factory, and turned with thanks into my own front yard.

Some of the students were extraordinary. There was a very pleasant German chap, Ralph Schroeder. Alas, he could only speak in a very broken accent, so I would feel sorry for his pupils in the future. One extraordinary woman was Fenell. She cultivated a rather witchlike appearance. In one memorable session the lecturer finally asked her to withdraw from the class, as he could no longer bear to see her sitting high in the back row, sucking raw eggs. Such was her quality, that her scholarship was withdrawn at the end of the year.

On the day of our induction, we gathered in a lecture room with the professor of music, Mr. Hall, and his second in charge, a lady. He asked everyone to stand up. Then he explained that his assistant would play on the piano, her left hand playing the melody, and her right hand the accompaniment. As soon as anyone recognised the air, he or she was to sit down. One by one the students sat. When there were only four left standing, I suddenly sat too. I knew it – "Pop Goes the Weasel". It was a good job I was not the student he asked to identify the tune, because it turned out to be "God Save the Queen."

I became very friendly with a group of other young adults like myself, at college and settled into a different and contented way of life. Towards the end of the year my teaching skills were recognised by the headmaster at Ascot School, where I had been doing some practical teaching. One of his staff became ill, so he asked me to take her class for the last three weeks of the school year, as there were no such things as supply teachers then.

I really didn't mind where I would be sent to take up an appointment. My only problem was that I did not know where my first appointment was. I had only heard of Richmond, New South Wales up till that time. To Richmond, Queensland, I eventually went, and found I was the lower half of a two teacher school.

Ted Maris was the principal, and I had the misfortune to follow hard on the heels of a respected teacher who had been at the school for several years – a much admired "Miss Tickle".

My accommodation was upstairs, above the bar, at one of the hotels. Unfortunately my room provided the access path for the son of the publican to visit, and presumably, receive the favours of the young barmaid in residence. I was too green to challenge his right of way, but my shock made him thereafter find another entrance to the enclosed veranda where she slept.

I was given the lower Grades (previously Miss Tickle's, where I suffered in comparison to a well-loved efficient teacher of many years experience.) But my enthusiasm was great, and I did my level best, involving hours of preparation, and a desire to improve the world. At that time religious instruction was still given by the teacher, from a set book, and also at that time the town had been rained and flooded in from the day of my arrival – was it weeping for the loss of Miss Tickle? The set topic for religion one morning was Noah and the flood. Graphically I described the torrents of rain, and the flooding. A query was raised by an impressed pupil. "Was it bigger than the bore drain?" Another query, "Were you there?" followed by the realization by one child that if I wasn't on the Ark with Noah, I would have been drowned. I was appalled to discover that many of these youngsters had never seen the sea, so its size was beyond their comprehension, though I did, with words, try to give them a picture of it.

This was my first experience of a Western town, and wondered what I was to do about lunch each day. I could not believe it when a pupil arrived in the lunch hour, carrying a tea towel wrapped meal. There was a main course — a hot meal — covered by an inverted soup plate. On top of this was balanced a bowl of soup, covered by a plate, and topping the lot was yet another covered bowl – a dessert dish, full of sweet pudding. This was brought to me every day that I remained at Richmond.

A small town with a very limited young female population, I became fairly popular, and enjoyed myself. I also became very friendly with Garth Baker, a teacher from the neighbouring whistle stop of Maxwellton. Further beyond, on the railway line, was Gordon Le Pia, who had been at college with me, and who now ran the Nelia School. While at Richmond, I went to the pictures three times a week, and whenever there was a ball I attended it also.

Fourteen

My next appointment was to Camooweal, where the school had just been upgraded from a one to a two teacher school. I arrived in Mount Isa by train and waited at an hotel until the weekly run of the Camooweal mail. The mailman collected me, and I was finally delivered to the home of one of the local residents, the Buchanans, where I discovered I was to become a boarder.

The experience of teaching here was as novel to my pupils as to me. They had never had a female teacher before, and a novice at that. Once a week I had to take the sewing class for all the girls (I was never much as a seamstress). I also had to teach my young pupils singing. My family can testify this was never a strong point either. In fact a school inspector, on his annual visit asked the children to sing. When they had finished he turned to me and said, "Congratulations Miss Pearse. Sixteen children, and sixteen different tunes."

My grades, from one to four, were a mixed bag. Some of the

aboriginal youngsters lived on the reserve. They and their parents had no conception of school time. They would stay awake till all hours of the night. As a result, they would often not rise until school time. Their breakfast would often be very substandard. This also gave them no time for ablutions as I knew them. When this happened they would droop around throughout the day, occasionally even falling into an exhausted sleep.

A child arrived at school one day, entirely untutored, hitherto unexposed to our society, and aged twelve. Lily's hair had never seen a comb, but she had a wide smile, and was extremely likeable. I was surprised how quickly she moved from Grade 1 to 2, then 3 within one year.

Each Thursday morning I was given the older classes to teach. I loved poetry and reading in general, and was able to imbue several thirteen and twenty-four year olds with a similar passion. In recent years I have been in touch with quite a few of them, and most of them remember "The Forsaken Merman" and other touching pieces.

From the Buchanans, who worked for the Department of Civil Aviation, I moved into a partly furnished hostel type accommodation, supplied by the C.W.A., which was attached to the side of the Buffaloes Hall. This building was next to the Police Station, and the single constable's barracks. The Police Sergeant lived next door again.

I became good friends with Ron Rooke, the cop. As time went by we decided to have our evening meal together, for company. There was nowhere in my quarters for this, so I would go over to his place and cook when it was my turn. He had a big kitchen. A number of young Stock Inspectors from both Queensland and the Northern Territory used to bunk in with Ron when they were in town, so I acquired a number of good friends. The only single girls in town besides me were Joy and Beryl Beaumont. Joy was engaged to John White, so we didn't see much of her. Beryl had an unwanted, but steadfast admirer, so we didn't see all that much of her either. She was an exceptionally attractive girl, who later married another chap.

Ronnie Rooke flew an aeroplane. It was his passion. He told me that until the expected visit of Queen Elizabeth to Australia he had been unable to join the police force. However, at that time an urgent need was felt for more men, so, in spite of being no speller, he was accepted, and became a very good country policeman.

If Ron thought I was late getting up he would hurl a few stones onto my roof. I sometimes wonder just what the town thought about me. I did not realise that every action of every person in town was known to every resident in that town. Only my complete innocence saved me from undesirable effects.

One night, while at tea at Ron's, as usual, we had a Northern Territory stock inspector for the evening. Then I went home. I used an old battery as a steppingstone over the fence between our two houses. This young chap was on his way down south to get married. About midnight I heard a discreet knocking on my door. I struggled up from sleep and opened it. There was this young man. He had thought I was an easy mark and had come by to seek a favour or two. It didn't take me long to rout him, once I realised what he was after. He had long gone from Camooweal before the morning broke. Once in a while I would ponder on what sort of a life his wife was going to have.

I became friends with a number of young drovers too, notably Bruce Simpson, also known as "Twenty one." He acquired this nickname because he was in Lennons Hotel Bar, in Brisbane, at the same time as a Courier Mail reporter. He had a very young appearance. When he asked for a beer, it was refused as the barman thought he was too young. Used to this Bruce produced his birth certificate. The journalist snapped a photo of him holding the certificate in one hand and a beer in the other. This was then printed in the paper with the caption, "He says he's Twenty-one." Thus was a legend born.

When his brother Keith joined him he became "Twenty-two."

Bruce was a true Bush Poet, in the style of Banjo Paterson, in that he wrote ballads. I found some of his verses very moving. One at least was put to music, but the well-known balladeer who sang it did so in a dreary fashion, which spoiled its impact. He had a touch of humour too, in other of his poetry. I am fortunate to still possess the original of one of his poems about an old stockhorse.

There were various other young men who became friends, but whose friendship I had to pass, once I met Alex. He did not really appreciate my close association with these others. Over the years I had had plenty of practice with brothers, and this helped me in my relationship with a number of them. There just were not the girls around with whom I might have become good friends.

One slightly unbalanced man, who was still suffering from the aftereffects of the war, had a set on the police. Quite often he would approach the police sergeant's house in the small hours, and proceed to hurl heavy stones on the roof, disappearing into the night as the sergeant roared out in wrath.

Some of the pupils at the school were fourteen and fifteen years old. They had no intention of advancing beyond primary school. In a town of that size they were young men, and built like it.

Each year the school ran a fancy-dress ball, which started with a display of marching by the children, who were all dressed up in their fancy outfits. Plastic had novelty value at that time. Dorrie Finlay created a spaceman outfit for young Max. It was made entirely of blue plastic, save for the visor, which was made of clear plastic. No one had allowed for the fact that plastic doesn't breathe. The poor child had to be released from his costume before he passed out.

For weeks prior to the ball we had to usher the children down to the Shire Hall for practices. The Head Teacher was up front, and I was bringing up the rear, making sure the children marched in line. I would tap their legs with a ruler if they lost step. These practices also included ballroom dancing. Most of the children were better at it than I. They had grown up dancing. Nevertheless it was my job to teach the boys the steps, and Mr. Thorne's to teach the girls. I still get a laugh when I think of John Malony as my partner. A tall, strapping youth, he had finished the dance, and was escorting me back to my seat (as part of the process of learning social behaviour). As he led me back he said, "Thank you Miss Pearse. You dance very well for a big woman".

We learned spiral marching, Figure of Eight, Snail formation, Diagonal Cross, and others, all to the tune of either Colonel Bogey or The Teddy Bears' Picnic. Yes, I had to learn them too. I had never witnessed anything like this before.

On the big night, all available parents and residents of the town were in the hall to watch these wonderful displays. The costumes had to be judged. Then the ball was open for everyone to join in.

Wagga Darcy was notorious for the size of his feet. He rode barefooted, keeping his big toe only, inside the stirrup iron. When he came to a dance, he wore Roman, or Box, sandals, the only footwear he could manage. This did not stop him from being a very pleasant chap.

The women really dressed up for these occasions. They had

CRIPPLED.

YOU MAY RUB YOUR HEAD ON MY COAT OLD CHAP
 AS YOU STAND BY THE GATE IN PAIN
AND I LOOSE THE KNOT IN THE GREEN HIDE STRAP
 THAT YOU NEVER SHALL WEAR AGAIN.
YOU MAY NUZZLE MY HAND AS YOU'VE DONE SO OFT
 IN THE DAYS THAT HAVE GONE FOR AYE
FOR YOU'LL CARRY ME NEVER AGAIN ON WATCH
 ROUND THE CAMP ERE THE BREAK OF DAY

YOU WILL WAIT NO MORE FOR THE STORES TO SPLASH
 BY THE LIGHT OF THE STORM LASHED SKY
WHEN THE SCRUBS REECHO THE THUNDER'S CRASH
 'ROUND THE CAMPS ON THE MORANGI
NO MORE BY THE NIGHT-HORSE BREAK YOU'LL DOZE
 IN THE CHILL OF THE WINTERS NIGHT
WHEN THE BRANCHES STIR AND THE BACK-LOG GLOWS
 AND THE STARS WINK COLD AND WHITE

YOU WILL DRAUGHT ME MORE AS THE GREY DUST SWINGS
 FROM THE CAMP AND NEAR AGAIN
WILL YOU WHEEL THE ROUGES BY THE STOCKYARD WINGS
 WHEN WE YARD FOR THE CATTLE TRAINS
WE MAY FIND ANOTHER WITH SWINGING GAIT
 TO RIDE THRU THE TRUCKING TOWN
AND THERE WILL BE OTHERS WHO'LL QUIETLY WAIT
 BY THE PEG AS THE STARS LOOK DOWN—

WE MAY FIND ANOTHER TO MATCH YOUR PACE
    THRO THE SCRUB WHEN THE FIREWORKS START
BUT NEVER ANOTHER TO TAKE THE PLACE
    THAT YOU HOLD IN A DROVER'S HEART
YOUR MATES HAVE STOOD ON THE CAMP SINCE DAWN
    YOU'RE WATCHING ALERT AND KEEN
THE PACKS ARE ON AND THE GIRTHS ARE DRAWN
    BUT THE FENCE STANDS THERE BETWEEN

    " — "

THE PLANT IS OFF ON THE ROAD AGAIN
    AND HERE BY THE PADDOCK GATE
WE DAYS TO FOLLOW AND ASK IN VAIN

AND OFTEN IF ON THE WESTERN TRACK
    WHEN THE EVENING SHADOWS FALL
OUR THOUGHTS WILL TURN TO THE GAMEST HACK
    AND THE BEST NIGHT HORSE OF ALL

    " — "

ACTOR FAREWELL, THRU YOUR LAST LONG SLEEP
    MAY NEVER THE CREEK GROW DRY
MAY THE GRASS BE WHISPERING FETLOCK DEEP
    FOREVER; OLD CHAP GOOD BYE.

on beautiful gowns, dainty shoes, and looked altogether lovely. The country girls would also come into town for these events, so there were enough single girls to be able to hold a Belle of the Ball. The most romantic dance was held, just before supper — the twilight waltz. The lights would be dimmed, and young couples could mooch around the dance floor, feeing as if they were floating. Next to this, the medley at the end of the dance was most popular. That was the dance girls would perform with the youths who would be expected to escort them home. For the livelier souls there were the Barn Dance, the Jolly Miller, the Mexican Hat Dance, and later, the Hokey Pokey. Most people danced for the pure love of the movement and music. It was once described to me as poetry in motion. Not a bad description either.

Fortunately I had the ability to teach the small children, a number of whom had illiterate parents who had always lived out of town, to read. One school inspector asked them all to read to him. He could not fault them, so he became suspicious that they had learned by rote He then instructed them to turn to the back of the book and read backwards. The kids did me proud. They were all up to the task.

Fifteen

After three years I moved to Mary Kathleen, one of four teachers. I had the middle grades. These children were all the offspring of a much more sophisticated group of people.

They loved school, and again did me proud. Promotion was then incumbent on the inspector's visit. The day he was due to arrive I had a bad dose of flu. but struggled off to work, anxious not to miss any opportunity to improve my lot. The visitor was a nice man — he sent me home, and took my class for the day. I was lucky enough to receive an excellent report. God bless those kids!

Those inspectors loomed large in my life. On one occasion the principal was out attending a house auction for a departing resident. In his absence the school dentist arrived, unexpectedly accompanied by the school inspector who had sought a lift with him. I surreptitiously sent one of the older boys off to advise my boss and give him time to return with a suitable cover story. We also acted as an unofficial childcare centre for the single mother matron of the local hospital. Her four-year-old had to be despatched home also before he was noticed.

A few of these older boys were merely filling in time until they could officially leave school. At times a frustrated head teacher would administer the cane. The boys expected nothing less and respected his action. At times one would be sent outside to pick a suitable stick from the large stool of bamboo growing in the school yard. In spite of the boys' best efforts, bringing to school matchboxes full of termites, which they released into the middle of the stand, the bamboo showed no sign of destruction.

Each day, on my way to school I would walk past an extraordinary pile of old cars, machinery and collected junk. It was many weeks before I realised there was actually a house at the centre of this rubbish, and several of my pupils lived there.

When Vince Gair was the Premier of Queensland he came to our school for an afternoon. I have to commend him for this. At that time Camooweal was difficult to access. and a visit was very time consuming. Some will remember that Premier Gair was a stout man. The school made quite a ceremony of his visit, culminating with a gathering in the classroom. A row of canvas director's chairs was lined up in front of the assembly. A delightful part-Aboriginal youngster named Arthur, who had a wide beaming grin, decided that Mr. Gair was a nice chap, so he went to sit on his lap, and stayed there until the programme concluded. The finale was the singing of the National Anthem. Everyone was upstanding, including the premier, and his chair, which rose with him.

Mary Kathleen was a different experience altogether. Once again I was a boarder. There was no accommodation for single women. When the town was built it provided lanes at the back of all homes, so that children did not have to walk on the roads.

The mentality of those who designed the town was very much of its period. I remember that all homes were designed in a similar fashion, to maximise any breezes, with louvres everywhere. There were two, three and four bedroomed houses. The latter were mostly for the executive class. All the houses were furnished, but again. there were certain class distinctions. All the furniture was similar in design. However, the blue-collar workers had silky oak furniture, white collars accessed golden maple, and the elite had mountain ash.

I went to Planet Downs once with Bid Conlan, prior to my marriage to Alex. The races were on, which also meant two nights of dancing. The dance floor was one of the more unusual variety. The side wall of the store attached to the Gregory Hotel was taken down. Inside the store was permanently stored a piano. There were quite a number of floor stumps beside the store. At this time, floorboards, which had been stored out of the way for the rest of the year, were hauled out, and nailed on these stumps to make a floor. Pops, dressing, talcum powder and kerosene mixed with sawdust, were then tossed onto the floor, and the younger generation worked at putting a polish of the boards. For safety's sake a light timber railing was erected, so that the dancers would not slide over the edge too easily.

Some musicians or a band of some type was always hired to play while the partygoers danced the night away. It is hard to visualise anything more potently romantic that gay dance music playing, while a couple is dancing, with a golden moon glowing down from a clear night sky. There were always more men than women at these affairs. Consequently there were plenty of tap dances, where young men could tap a dancing friend on the shoulder, and take his place while the dance continued. Naturally, if one of the men was in the middle of a romance at the time, the others would take a fiendish delight in robbing him of his partner, again and again. Social mores permitted this, so he would just have to swallow his gall, and return the favour.

The following year, while I was teaching at Mary Kathleen, I again attended the Gregory Races. I had come to the conclusion that Alex possibly liked me, but that the affair would go no further than that, so I intended to tell him that I would not be seeing him again. (In all the four years until we actually married, I had only ever seen him for a total of six weeks.) He spent most of the two weeks out bush, sinking a dam, so I did not see him very often. Then one night he came into the homestead and asked me to marry him. I was stunned because I had not thought such a thing was going to happen. The poor wretch had to ask a second time, before I felt able to give an answer. His birthday was on the day of the races, so we decided to wait until then to announce the engagement.

Beverly Schaffert, a former neighbour and friend of the Carringtons, was at the race meeting. She was sporting a very new engagement ring, which she displayed to Alex, inviting him to her wedding early the next year. Regretfully(?) we had to decline because we had set the same date for our wedding.

While still at Planet I wrote to my family, advising them of the change in my future. In short order I received a telegram from my brother Jim, which read: "Congratulations! I have always wanted a cattle station holiday." Normally this would have been just amusing, but because all telegraphic traffic, inward and outward, to all stations, was read out loud by the radio officers in Cloncurry, our intentions were thus immediately broadcast to the whole of the North-west.

Dad's reaction was also typical. He wrote back, expressing his good wishes. Then he continued. "You will be married from St.

James' Cathedral — it was our parish church — There will be sixty guests, thirty of whom your mother has already invited, the other thirty are for the Carringtons."

The result was one hundred and twenty attending. I was in a very difficult position. I would have dearly liked to invite my Camooweal friends, but I was in no position to do so. Nor was my fiancé pleased with the idea of having as guests several young men, with whom I had been very friendly, so I had to leave them off the guest list. Alex was part of a very large family, too, most of whom still lived in and around the north, so they had to be invited, for courtesy's sake, and because he liked them. We did not have many relations there, because our family, other than the immediate members, lived in New South Wales still, and it wasn't all that easy to travel north in the wet season.

I had become very fond of Alex by this time but was not certain of his reaction. The women stayed at the station, eleven miles from the racecourse, while the men camped by the river, near the track with their horses for a week. The animals had been all put into one paddock seven weeks before the race meeting, so that they would all be starting from a level playing field, at the meet. One week prior to the big event, they were taken out by their proud owners, trained, and fed with grain and grasses until the actual day. Consequently, all the men stayed with them and trained them. Nancy, John Carrington's wife, would cook up meals for the Planet Camp, and we would drive down to the river to give it to them, and join them for a meal.

My treasure would come up to the table, cut himself off some corned beef and bread, then retire behind a tree alone to eat. This made me wonder if I was imagining any interest on his part. This year a young female pianist had been engaged to play for the dances, Val Charles. She happened to be nearby when Alex invited me to come with him to the airstrip to cut some grass for the horses. Quick as a flash Val leapt up and seated herself in the middle of the seat of the Customline utility which Alex drove. Rather subdued, I sat near the door. We collected the grass and returned without much conversation. Could I have been imagining that he liked me? Fortunately, Val had to play the music all night, and didn't get a chance to go near Alex, so I was safe. Like any other girl in the same circumstances, I revelled in the music, the stars, the romance, and equally enjoyed it when the other ringers continually "tapped" my partner, time after time.

Nicknames abounded, Spider O'Keefe, Black Georgie and White Georgie, Pic (short for Picaninny), Twenty-one and Twenty-two, Honest John Matey, and Wagga.

The first baby in the next generation of the family was David, Sam and Phyllis' first son. He was loved and admired by everyone of us. It was such a pity that we missed his first two and a half years, which he spent in New Ireland. At that age he was a charming little scrap of humanity. When Sam and Phyll lived in Cook Street, Townsville, for a while, he broadly invited the lot of us to share with them a meal of "worms" (spaghetti), which he loved. Another time he offered to share his "prawks" (prawns) also. Once he got hold of a roll of caps to fit a toy gun. When we called in he had a stone and a brick. He was busily engaged in making each cap explode and having a ton of fun at the same time.

Little Jim had equal pleasure. Where David had been a grave-faced little blond, Jim was a dark-eyed, merry little boy, with a mop of curly hair. When Alex arrived in Townsville just prior to our wedding, we were walking Denham Street when he saw a small head peeping over the shoulder of a young woman ahead of us. I was astonished when he recognised Jimmy. The young woman was his mother, Mavis.

On this same visit, Alex and I had been to the Post Office to ring up a friend of his, Alan Greene. Alan was signing on the dotted line on the same day as Alex, and they were comparing notes. I enjoyed Alan's explanation of why he was being married at 1.30 p.m., in Brisbane, instead of 5 p.m. as originally planned; the time we married. His fiancée had discovered that he intended to spend that afternoon at the races. Suspicious of in what condition he might return from the races, she opted for an earlier time slot, to prevent any mishap.

After we left the post office we wandered back to the Blue Bird Cafe, meeting Jim and Mavis on the way. All of us decided to have a snack. Suddenly Alex leaped up from the table and tore outside. Some time later he reappeared with a satisfied smirk on his face, and sixty pounds in his hand. As we were sitting down he had spotted a bookmaker who had welshed on a bet at the Boulia races some time previously. He had followed him out, demanding his money. To everyone's astonishment he received it. He felt rich, I thought he was wonderful, and Jim and Mavis were suitably impressed.

On 15th February, 1958, I arose early to overcast skies, followed by heavy, incessant rain. I expect this served me right, for choosing the middle of the wet season for my wedding. One reason for my choice was that all my teaching entitlements ceased on my marriage, so it seemed good sense not to lose all that Christmas vacation pay. But the main reason was that Alex was free from most of his duties on the station at that time of the year. I forgot to consult with providence, however, because it continued to pour all day (nine and a half inches fell). No planes could land, so no southern flowers could be brought in, and rain-affected local produce had to be used. The only flowers available were some dark red, rather scabby looking gladioli. The orchids I had arranged for the mothers of the bride and groom were disastrous. As far as I knew orchids were great gorgeous cattelyas in shades of lavender. What we got were some yellowish-brown, thin twisted petalled golden orchids. The bridal bouquets were delivered about an hour before the ceremony. We were advised not to open them until just before we left, because the humidity might cause them to wilt. They too were disastrous. My bouquet was pretty enough, but the bridesmaids' flowers were deep purple asters, tied with magenta ribbons. As their dresses were both in an apricot/rockmelon shade the contrast was shocking. At first both girls thought they would rather carry nothing. Then I seized some scraps left over from the making of their most beautiful gowns, and cut them into strips. This replaced the magenta ribbon at least, and they agreed to carry them. I didn't even have time to iron out the creases in the ribbon, as Dad was harrying us by that time.

That was the flowers.

During the morning we had to go to the C.W.A. Hall to see that the tables were set appropriately for the reception. Just as well I did. The top table was set, with Dad having arranged the seating. He had placed himself and Mum as the central figures, working on the theory that as they were giving the reception, they were the most important people there. He had seated the Archdeacon on one side of him, and the Chairman for the evening, Jack Ashe, on the other.

We did a bit of place card re-arranging, but until we actually arrived at the reception we had no idea whether Dad would have made some further re-adjustments. Fortunately Mum kept him out of the way.

Because of the weather, and at that time no air-conditioning, garments tended to have a limp look about them, including the wedding dress. That dress had caused me much anguish. As I had been living at Mary Kathleen, I had ordered the frock through the Bride magazine. I was disappointed when it arrived as it had no train, which I had ordered. I did not wake up to the fact that I could have returned it. As I had already paid for it I assumed that that was that! A friend had offered to make my veil. It was waist length, and I did not really like it much, but how could I reject a friend's kindness? I did buy a pretty headdress, and later re-attached the veil to that.

I was totally inexperienced in weddings. I had been a bridesmaid for Mavis and Jim in Bowen, but all I had had to do there was to turn up on the day of the wedding, and wear a pretty dress, while standing near Mavis — quite simple.

Appalled at the cost of a wedding cake, I decided to ice my own. In my High School days I had once iced a Christmas cake, so that was good enough for me. I was not aware that only pure icing sugar should be used, so I opted for icing sugar mixture because it was much easier to manipulate. I also did not know what an important part these cakes play at the receptions either. The weather was such that the cake had begun to absorb moisture, and the colour was beginning to seep out of the cake and into the icing. There is no way it could have lasted another day. The best thing I can say about it is that it saved me sixty pounds. What my in-laws, who had a lot of wedding experience, thought, I was never game to ask, in case, in a moment of truth they told me.

As the day wore on the causeway flooded, and any guests living on the southern side of town were automatically excluded from the party. A couple of northside guests rang up to say that they had unexpected guests of their own, and could they please bring them? Normally this would have been a disaster, but they filled the seats of the guests cut off by water.

The rain continued. Alex, instead of being the one looked after, had spent the week looking after his handsome and susceptible younger brother, Neville, who was the groomsman. His brother Ron was the best man. I think the family stiffened up the bridegroom's courage with a whiskey or two that afternoon.

At that time it was not deemed necessary to hold wedding rehearsals. When I had made such a suggestion to Archdeacon Hohenhouse, who was a friend of my father, he explained that he had already managed over two thousand weddings, so he felt competent to stage manage this one. (He only thought he knew Dad!)

There had been another two weddings before ours, that afternoon. At about this stage the rain ceased, and a watery sun peeped through the clouds. A rich humid atmosphere now prevailed. When Dad finally hustled us into the wedding taxis, we arrived at St. James Cathedral to discover that the previous wedding was still in progress. We therefore drove away, and came back some time later, as the guests were streaming out of the church. This time we had a shorter drive.

For once in my life, I showed a bit of sense. Instead of carrying my glasses, I wore them, afraid of tripping if I didn't.

The wedding march sounded out its peals, and I prepared to walk in. I hadn't bargained on Dad, who was now orchestrating our entrance. We were met at the door by the Archdeacon, who lined us up. Then he proceeded in stately fashion down the aisle. Dad counted loudly to ten, and allowed Dell to proceed. He again counted to ten, and Elaine stepped it out. He counted to ten yet again, after which he took a couple of tries to work out on which of his arms I should walk, and we stepped into the church. By this time the organist had completed the wedding march, and was providing some quiet background music, on the understanding that the procession had finished some minutes before. She didn't know Dad either.

Alex looking very handsome, spoke his piece clearly. I, who normally would have sounded out well, spoke in a subdued voice. The moment came to put the ring on my finger. It was laid on the Bible, blessed, after which Alex took it in his hand and tried to slide it on. It wouldn't go. Then the Archdeacon whispered, "Bend your finger", and it slipped on quite easily. We retired to the vestry to sign the register. When we came out the sun was still shining. By this time the hem of my frock was becoming very soiled from muddy water splashing up. Off we went for the official photographs.

Once again vanity got the better of me, and off came the glasses. In every photo they were there, but safely hidden under my bouquet. Also, at that time photographers had not learned how to avoid the flash reflecting on glasses, so often two pools of light were all that were seen instead of eyes.

The reception hall was about a hundred yards from the Cathedral, so the guests only had a short walk from one venue to the other, which would have given them plenty of time to look at the cake! After the usual marathon photo session — Arch Fraley Studios — we returned to the C.W.A. Hall.

I don't remember all that much about it, as I was concentrating on what scheme Dad might have thought up next. Jack Ashe was a good chairman. He also sang a whimsical little ditty: "I'm a little pixie, living in the glen. Sitting down, and standing up, and sitting down again. With a Hocus Pocus, hiding in a crocus, had too many mushrooms, and hope they will not choke us!" It was funny, and I wish I knew the rest of it.

Elaine sang "Waltz of my Heart" and "You Are My Heart's Delight". Reg Murray gave the toast to Alex's parents. Dad made a wonderful speech — he always did that sort of thing so well. When the toast was given to the bride and groom I bent my head in embarrassment. My new husband whispered fiercely, "Hold your head up".

As the bridesmaids were having too good a time for me to drag them away from the party, when it was time for me to leave and change into my "going away" outfit, Alex and I headed off for my parents' home without them, so I could change from my lovely dress forever.

I chose to look in the large circular mirror in the sitting room for one last glimpse of myself as a bride. I looked lovingly — then I looked again, and again. Hanging from my headdress, dangling over my left ear was a small needle, suspended from a thread of cotton. Horrified, I took off the curvette, and looked again. All along the top of the cap, still holding the veil in place, as well as the stitching, was a row of pins. Now I enjoy the episode, but at that time …

My pretty blue frock, which had embossed embroidered white daisies on it was slipped over my head. I took up my white handbag and gloves, kept on my pretty white pearlised sandals, and put the charming white straw hat on my head — this was at ten thirty at night. We headed back to the party. This was the custom. No one left a wedding reception until the bride and groom had left for the night. We were farewelled by the guests, and set off for the Queen's Hotel, and the start of our married life.

My dress, in spite of no train, was quite attractive and suitable. It had a fairly low, round neck, but not decolletage. Made from heavy slipper satin, it had a dropped waist. Veed at the front, zippered down the back, the bodice was covered with chantilly lace,

Pat at Planet Downs

Jim, Elaine, Pat and Sam with their parents Edwin and Marion in front

Pat and Russell and unknown woman in the river at Planet Downs

Pat with Russell and Alex and unknown woman and child

Pat and Family at her parents Golden Wedding in Brisbane. Joan, Elaine, Pat, Jenny, Alex, Stephen and

Pat seated between two unknown women

The Carrington family gathered at the Gregory Hall to celebrate Ted and Annie Carrington's Golden wedding anniversary

Pat with Russell and Joan at Planet

the long sleeves being lace only. The skirt was not overly full. My dress has been used a number of times over the years in bridal displays. A bridal dressmaker once commented to me at one of these showings, that mine was the only true classical line frock, which could still be worn, and still be in fashion.

My bridesmaids wore the prettiest dresses I have ever seen to this day. I let them choose them themselves. I made one stipulation, I wanted apricot as the colour. It turned out to be a cross between apricot and rockmelon, a lovely shade. The skirts came to below the knees The underskirts were of heavy duchess satin, as were their shoes. The bodices, almost off the shoulder, were covered in heavy guipere lace, with dropped waistlines. The overskirts were of fine, fine chiffon, intensely gathered, the same chiffon being swathed in a shirred fashion around the wide necklines. Each frock had two floating panels drifting from the back of the neckline to the hemline. They were made by a wonderful dressmaker, a Mrs. Brennan. On their hair they wore circlets of apricot tinted flowers. The whole effect was delightful. When the proofs of the photos were eventually sent to us for selection some weeks later, we had trouble in choosing the best ones. It was astonishing how expensive they were. There was no such thing as a colour photo, so if coloured pictures were wanted they had to be hand tinted, and this made the price soar accordingly. I regret it now, but I opted for just the sepia toned photos because of the added expense, and that is what we have.

Sixteen

Several years after our 1958 marriage we found it necessary to build an airstrip. This, of course, enabled us to participate in the visit of the Royal Flying Doctor Service, and gave us a much greater sense of security than we had possessed before. I am sure that it gave the R.F.D.S. a greater sense of security too because those men were required to land in some outlandish places, before air strips could be built at many properties.

Our strip was about a kilometre below the houses, and the weaner paddock was used for the purpose. The mandatory cleared strip was prepared, chosen at that spot because it was flat land, running beside the river, easily prepared, and not too far away from the homestead.

This was a necessity, because cattle also used the paddock for grazing, as did about what seemed to be half the population of wallabies in Australia, (presumably because of its proximity to the river). Whenever a plane arrived unexpectedly, which was on most occasions, the pilot would buzz the houses, and whoever was at home (usually the women of the house) would abandon her current job, leap into a nearby vehicle, and drive to the strip to clear off any cattle or other wildlife which had been resting there. Meanwhile the plane would be circling overhead to see if it were yet safe to land. As mobs of a hundred or more were par for the course this took quite a time. Only then would the pilot bring his vehicle in to a safe landing. Then of course, the housewife would drive over and see what he wanted.

If the visit was prescheduled none of this drama would occur, the strip having been cleared earlier. But until the plane flew overhead, a waiting game would ensue in the household. All the children would be keen to see who could hear the plane first. As they grew older, and learned to drive, it became the aim of each new driver in the family to be the one who cleared the drome of its wildlife. Each child in turn was taught to drive on that airstrip. The cattle became unwilling participants in the learning process. They were regarded as parked cars, or moving traffic. The calves became unwary pedestrians, darting out from cover unexpectedly, and the children all became proficient drivers as a result. The roof of the big shed had the name of the property emblazoned in bold letters for the sake of passing planes, a practice followed by most property owners.

Many times it was put to use. On one occasion, returning, during the wet season, with my second baby, it was necessary for me to engage a light aircraft in Normanton, and fly over two hundred miles with my toddler of fifteen months, and his new sister, the general appurtenances of a housewife who has been away for several weeks, a small chair – donated to No. 1 boy by a doting grandparent, an enormous ball via the same means, a box of BOUGHT bread, at that time an almost unheard of luxury, a box of FRESH fruit and vegetables, also a treat, and various pieces of equipment required for various vehicles and engines, as well as an enormous bag of unwashed nappies the journey having to that time taken three days (and disposable nappies had not come my way).

After our honeymoon in Sydney we returned to Brisbane to stay with Alex's parents for a short time. My education continued to proceed.

Dell, Alex's youngest sister, was still living at home, and Biddy Conlan, his eldest sister was down from Camooweal, on a visit. Like a good daughter-in-law, I tried very hard to fit in. On washday I helped with the washing. Now, my mother was one of the old school which believed that there were more important things in life than washing. She did a clean wash, but she hung clothes out on the line, as she pulled them form the laundry basket – a sheet could be aligned to a shirt or a towel.

Not so my new mother-in-law. She really did a precise wash, and her children knew it.

Each sheet was hung so that the lower end was nine inches from the ground, allowing the breeze to catch and lift both sides of the sheet. Each sheet was placed next to the other. Each towel was pegged side by side, as was each type of linen or clothing. I could see the logic of it. It not only looked neat, it made it easier folding when the clothes were taken dry from the line.

Alas, I was used to slinging the sheets over the so that the two lower edges matched.

This seemed logical to me – they were already partly folded when removed from the line.

Along came my new mother-in-law. "Who hung those sheets like that?"

"I did, Mrs. Carrington." I replied in a meek voice.

"Hmmph!"

A few minutes later I hung out the pillowcases. Certain by now, that if I hung them out in the ordinary way it would be wrong. I pegged them out from the bottom instead. Along came my boss. "And who hung pillowcases like that on the line."

"I did, Mrs. Carrington."

"Well you certainly, don't know much about washing, do you?"

I made a vow to myself that, for Alex's sake, and future harmony, I would wash in a way that would please Mrs. Carrington. I put a great deal of effort into this, with the result that my daughters now complain that I am much too fussy. At times it may seem so, but often, when I was alone at home, or feeling sorry for myself when things went wrong, concentrating on doing a simple job like the laundry to the best of my ability, would help me. I could take pride in it.

My mother-in-law was an indomitable person, and was a real matriarch. Over the years I became very fond of her, though there were times when I felt unable to please her. No doubt she sometimes felt the same about me.

Biddy did one thing for which I was grateful. She heard me addressing my new mother-in-law as "Mrs. Carrington."

"You can't call Mum that for the rest of your life," she said, "Start right now and call her Mum."

And although I found it difficult at first, I did so. I never regretted it. Alex's father was "Pop". And this was entirely different to Dad, it flowed more easily. In such ways I gradually became and felt, part of the family.

Had Mum just criticized me when I did something she didn't like, I would have hated it even more, but she was equally critical of her own girls. Like most people I resent criticism, even when it is justified. What many people forget is that different is not wrong

– it is just another way.

While in Brisbane we were taken out to visit Aunt Lottie, a skinny little woman with a somewhat sharp tongue. She and her husband Fred, lived right out of Brisbane. They had two adult married sons, and a third, Billy, who lived with them. It was not until we were in the car, driving out to Fruitgrove, that I heard about Billy. He was, unhappily retarded. This had ruined his parents' lives.

They could not contemplate putting him into an institution, so they bore the brunt of his upbringing themselves. As his behaviour became more socially unacceptable they converted all their inner doors to stable doors – upper and lower halves swing separately. Billy could thus be part of the social scene with intruding entirely. He a had the engaging habit of spitting on people he liked, so everyone hoped like mad that Billy would not take a fancy to them. His father used to shave him. At times Billy got fed up halfway through the shave, and would not allow his father to complete it. On winter nights he would not keep bedclothes on, so they would dress him in three sets of winter pyjamas. He favoured sweet jellies and puddings for food, and he was able to recognize instantly, any tune he heard played on the radio. When his father died Aunt Lottie had no option but to put him in a home, and when she died soon afterwards, Billy also died, of a broken heart.

After a wonderful five weeks of getting to know each other, Alex and I returned home.

This was an event in itself. The wet had set in about the time we were married, and roads had become impassable, which explains the length of our honeymoon.

Stopping at Townsville on the way back, we had used our wedding present money to buy a china cabinet, among other items.

This was to house some of our lovely wedding gifts.

The trick was to get them home in one piece.

In Cloncurry we left the train, and Alex went off, to return with his Ford Mainline Utility, which he had left with a friend during his absence. We unloaded our luggage, our china cabinet and nine tea packing cases of goods. They were as heavy as could be. The bottom of each was covered in several layers of books. I had realized that I had to bring my treasures with me, as Alex's family were not devotees of reading.

It was a titanic journey, there were no four-wheel drive vehicles, the roads were almost all unformed, and many patches were through red or black mud, detouring through long grass and bushland, around parts of road which were impassable. We stopped frequently to see that our piece of furniture was intact, and that the rest of the load had not shifted.

Alex decided to call into stations on the way, places that he had never called into before or afterwards, to show off his new bride. In consequence the journey was interminable, taking all day.

When we reached Sandy Creek, near Nardoo, water covered the whole area. The road disappeared into water, and in the distance I could see, in a totally different direction, where it emerged. It was hard to envisage how my hero knew where to drive. He covered the front of the engine with canvas, and entered the water cautiously. I had visions of lost luggage, a drowned car, and a smashed china cabinet. But no, he carefully snaked his way over a rocky path hidden by filthy water, which was flowing quite fast, and drove out victoriously at the other side. After that I felt he could do anything.

It was after dark when we arrived at my new home. The Aboriginal workers were in their quarters, and other than them, there was only old Jack MacDougall, the Gregory Downs boundary rider, who lived at the twenty-mile, an out-station of Gregory Downs, but who used to ride over to Planet Downs for his weekends.

My new sister-in-law, Nancy, had been taken ill ten days earlier, and her husband John, Alex's older brother, who also lived on Planet (in the same house we were to occupy) had taken her away.

Alex, by this time feeling the need for some food, said he would cook some steak. The stove was a big, black, double-ovened wood burning range, with a number of circular hot plates on the top. It was also graced by a large, but soot covered, copper sheath around the chimney – the hot water system- and had two enormous black kettles, full of boiling water, on its surface. Alex stoked up the fire, and rummaged around in the refrigerator to produce a whole rump of beef.

Out of compassion for my exhausted state, and my ignorance, he announced that he would the cooking that night. Expertly he sliced off enough meat for himself, Jack and me. Then he took out the most enormous frying pan I had ever seen, removed the hot plate over the centre of the firebox in the stove, and rapidly cooked the meat. After that he turned to me and said, "You can make the gravy."

Used to smaller equipment, and electric stove, and controlled heat, I valiantly tried. I strewed some flour over the pan, added water, and stirred furiously. Alas, the heat, and the ignorant cook, proved too much, I burned the gravy. Kind Jack tried to eat it, but Alex had no such inhibitions.

John was not absent for much longer, which was probably just as well, or he would not have been able to return at all for some time.

There had been some heavy falls of rain. As they had little else to do because of the weather, numbers of the station owners and managers in the district spent a lot of time communicating with each other over the Flying Doctor radio network. This was one of John's favourite wet weather pastimes. He came downstairs one morning, from where he had been conversing with Billy Foster on Riversleigh Station, which was much nearer to the headwaters of the Gregory River. The Gregory River was a beautiful permanent stream of hard, but lovely, water which was the chief source of our supply at the house, supplemented only by a couple of rainwater tanks for drinking and hairwashing. Billy had just told John that fourteen inches of rain had fallen overnight up there, and the river was now in major flood. We could expect it at any time. The men did what they could to secure everything, or to put things out of reach of the expected floodwaters.

Slowly but surely we watched the river rise until it broke the banks of the little tributary, or runner, which passed next to the house, joining the main stream some couple of hundred yards further beyond.

At this stage the men realized that the herd of over one hundred goats was on the island between the two streams trapped.

John swam through the current to try to hunt them into the water, and back to the mainland.

So did the dogs, which caused great havoc amongst the frightened animals.

Alex tried to swim across too, but was unable to do so, because of the lack of muscle in his left leg, where he had suffered polio several years earlier. His right arm was also somewhat weak, for the same reason. A few goats struggled to the shore, but we had to watch in horror as the swirling floodwater swept most of them away, bleating pitifully as they went. A couple of days later the men went seeking the animals, to find only seven of the herd, including one nanny which had given birth to twins after she reached the land.

The water kept on rising. I watched in a fascinated way, as the insidious stream of mud, silt and liquid spread itself over the stone floor under the house. I saw a wallaby, a snake and the dogs, as well as Linda and Jimmy the Aborigines who lived at Planet, perched up on the elevated floor of the laundry. We did persuade the two latter to come into the kitchen instead, but did not welcome the other visitors.

Night fell. There was a full moon, so there was plenty of light. Both men climbed up onto the verandah railings, and even clambered up onto the rood to examine the full extent of the floodwaters. The silver light of the moon made the ground look as if we were in the middle of an enormous silvery, shimmering lake. No land could be seen – just the shining reflection of the moonlike liquid satin!

I learned to cook in, probably the best, but certainly the hardest way. Experience taught me how to cope. Bread-making was appalling. Nancy had been kind enough to leave me a recipe. I took it as gospel, never realizing that it could be adapted, that quantities could be slightly more or less, and nothing terrible would happen. I would set the yeast before the evening meal. After tea I would take this enormous enamel bread dish, pile into it eight large sifters full of plain flour, add salt, sometimes rubbing a bit of dripping. Then I would make a well in the centre, and pour in the warm yeast, and enough tepid water to create a bread dough. This I would cover with a tea towel and allow it to rise overnight. In the morning my first job would be to knock down the dough, and allow it to rise again. Of course, Nancy did not expect to be away for so long, so she had omitted to say that, as the weather became cooler the bread need to be kept warm, with a blanket over it. The end result was that each week the bread took longer to make, and I would still be at it in the middle of the afternoon. Alex would look at me struggling in the kitchen and expostulate, "But Nancy always had it cooked before lunch".

With a great deal of useful advice from Jack, I learned to make cakes in baking dishes.

Each cake contained at least five cups of flour. Biscuits were made by the multiple dozens. Very early in my stay, Alex asked me if I would make some biscuits for his brother, Ron to take on the road, when he set out on his droving trip. No one explained to me that he wanted a number of six-pound tea tins filled with many dozens of biscuits.

Therefore, I, delighted to help, made several dozen fancy little biscuits, which I made with a biscuit pusher to give them a nice shape. I then packed them neatly in a large square biscuit time, with grease-proof paper separating each layer, so they would not get broken on the road.

These I handed with pride to the amazed Ron, who had on entirely different vision of the food. It took just as much time as would have dozens of Anzacs, Ginger-nuts and Jam Drops, which would, of course, have travelled much better, and filled many empty stomachs.

One day I took a closer look at the flour. It seemed to have little dark specks in it. It had come to life. From that day onwards I had to doubly and trebly sift each cup of flour. We received our flour twice a year, in a very large hessian bags. As each bag was opened it was poured into a large bin, which had once housed carbide. Over time the seal on the lid became less than perfect as it was dropped, or banged into place with a hammer.

The results were the wildlife in the ground flour.

Meat caused me a lot of trouble too. The men would go out bush and kill a beast for food. It would be bled where it was killed, and skinned and quartered before it came back to the house. Like all stations we had a butcher's shop. The one we had when I arrived had a cement floor, with a drain. A wooden bench, composed of heavy slats, and another bench where the men could work on the meat. There were a couple of steel cross bars from which hung savage looking meat hooks. The butcher's knives and steel were also kept here. The whole area was gauzed in.

Because there was little refrigeration – two kerosene refrigerators of household size provided the cold space- most of the meat was salted. They would rub Kwikcurit and salt into the flesh – to colour and preserve it. It was then placed on the other bench, where it would drain into a five-gallon drum placed below the drain provided just for that purpose.

As the men had to leave for work early in the mornings it was one of my less pleasant jobs to go over to the butcher's shop twice each day, and turn the meat, so that it would drain evenly.

Occasionally a piece would not be salted properly, and I would find it going to be rotten, with maggots on it.

All the meat had some form of black beetle crawling around it- but that was acceptable.

Shortly after I married Alex I found that I was expecting my first child.

Unfortunately, I was one of those who suffered from morning sickness, and that, severely. That was difficult enough to cope with, but when I combined it with the station cooking, the bread baking, the living flour and lively meat, I found life very hard.

After each killer two four-gallon drums of fat would be brought into the kitchen and placed on the stove for me to render into dripping, which was our cooking fat, as well as being the fat used to rub into the saddles and other leather gear.

It had a smell all of its own.

What was I supposed to do with it, when it had been rendered?

(Rendering the fat required that it be melted down slowly, so that it separated from all the bits of membrane which encased the pieces of lard, without allowing it to catch to the bottom of the container and burn. This took several hours of slow heating.)

"All you have to do is strain it into these other drums, just pour it on top of the old fat."

There were several blue drums lined up in the stove recess beside the range.

I got splashed and burned, but I prepared it as instructed, and poured it off. Sometimes I burnt it a bit. Then it began to develop a strong rancid odour. It got worse and worse – it smelled rotten. No one was home to tell me what to do. I thought perhaps if I re-rendered it that would correct the problem. The smell grew stronger. The kitchen was a separate unit to the rest of the house. It was on low blocks, while the house was high, with access by a set of high steps.

I went to bed. Alex was away sinking a dam, but John and their father were both home. I was in the room I shared with my husband.

Pop was across the hall in the other room, and John was on the verandah at the far side of the house. A detail like different rooms made no reason to cease bedtime conversations between the men.

I heard all sorts of things, which it would have been better had I not.

At the time of the rotten fat, the smell had pervaded the house upstairs (not even the same building as the house), prompting John to bellow out to his father. "What's that frightful stink?"

"It's the fat gone rotten in the kitchen."

"Can't she do anything right?"

"Doesn't she even know how to render fat?"

I cowered in my bed. "She's learning; She'll be all right when she's done a bit more."

"It can't come too soon for me … it stinks."

Seventeen

The day Nancy came home was welcomed by everyone. Certainly by me. She would now resume the cooking and I would assume the duties of teaching two of her children by correspondence.

I walked into the kitchen after she had once again resumed the reins. To my astonishment the black kettle and the copper sheath around the stove chimney were clean and gleaming.

Linda, the dark woman, who lived on the property with her husband Jimmy, who was the houseboy, and cowboy, had been put to work, during my period as chatelaine, she had done the washing up for me after each meal, and had helped me a bit with the washing. I had not been aware that she had other duties. The men had spent most of their time away mustering or dam sinking, so they had not instructed me on any of this. Linda's halcyon period was alas, now over. But these dark girls, who lived with their husbands on the property and with their younger children, were never overworked on Planet. They had basic duties in return for generous pocket money, meals prepared for them, and clothing provided. The women of our house also looked after their medical problems, and acted as relay when the Flying Doctor was called for advice. The families were only with us during the mustering periods, unless they wished to extend their stay. As a result, we had a very good relationship with almost all of our employees, be they white or black.

One of my first experiences as the unofficial medico on the station concerned Maurice Aplin. Maurice was a genial part-Aboriginal gentleman, who had been brought up as one of the family. He shared the housing with the other members, and was as kind as he looked. He had a perennial and engaging smile. On this occasion he had slaughtered a pig for food. In the process the animal had bitten his thumb to the bone, which was actually visible. Maurice came to me, "Quick, Missus, pour some kerosene over it." I gagged at the thought. There was a flying doctor medical kit, inside the office, and I prepared to get it.

"No Missus, kerosene."

Under the force of a stronger personality, I went to the engine shed, pumped out a cup or so of kero, into a container, took him outside, and poured this liquid over the mauled digit, after which, he permitted me to dress the injury with a stoicism I found hard to comprehend.

In spite of this treatment his thumb healed. Apparently it was the standard method of handling unexpected wounds out bush. I was never a supporter of the kerosene method, but after this incident I never knocked it. These people were brave alright.

Sam Hobbs, the head stockman over at Lawn Hills Station later received a savage gash, which tore the full length of his forearm. As this occurred in the wet season, while Sam was alone on the place, he took a needle and black thread from his sewing and kit, and sewed the opening up himself – all twenty-nine stitches, a type of broad based over-sewing. This also healed without complications.

My next learning experience was how to deal with the snake problem. As a young man Alex had been bitten on the ankle by a brown snake. Consequently, he had a very jaundiced view of the "Live and Let Live" Theory. He was a follower of the idea, that the only good snake was a dead snake. One-day old Jimmy Walden who was the cowboy gardener at the time of my arrival on Planet, called out to me from the garden. He was in the process of preparing the garden for the years' produce. While digging and turning the soil, he had found a large brown snake, coiled around itself like a series of figure eights. It was objecting to being disturbed, so Jimmy had called in re-enforcements – me – to dispose of it. At the time the only reptile I had seen had been in Taronga Park Zoo, Sydney, so I was not really qualified. Like most people I had a fear of the unknown, and snakes were definitely on the unknown list. Bravely (at least that is how I felt) I seized the long-handled shovel, Jimmy was proffering, and went into action. I chopped and chopped, until the creature was in dozens of inch long pieces. I could hardly wait until the men came back to tell them of my courage and my defence of their property! At last Alex and John come back.

"How big was it?"

They would have a look.

Over they went to see the kill. There was absolutely no way they could even estimate the length of the deceased such was the carnage I had created.

Over the years I had many herpetology experiences, mostly with the unfortunate snake as the loser. Some of these experiences are vivid in my memory – one or two are remarkable in

Alex's memory.

The most frightening of all was the incident when he and his brother John went out across the horse paddock, in the afternoon to round up the cows for milking. John led the way. Following, Alex felt like a stick jab at his ankle. He tried to shake it off. When it would not shift he glance down. There, fastened to his leg like a limpet, was a very large brown snake. He finally shook himself free, and both youths ran back to the house.

His father was away, putting a corduroy in the river. His mother was at a loss as to the best remedy. At this time the recommended treatment was to cut a cross through the bite and suck out the poison. After this the patient, was not to be allowed to sleep until seen by the doctor. Fortunately, the Flying Doctor Service had recently been established, so it was possible to arrange for him to come out. However, he would not be able to take off from Cloncurry until daybreak, the next day.

Dusk was drawing in, and the only help to hand was the old fencer, Johnny Paterson. Mrs. Carrington called on his expertise. Johnny took out a razor, tried to steady his hand to incise the puncture marks, and wavered.

"No", he just could not nerve himself to cut the flesh. Mum then sent down to the river, where the men were working. Back came his father, running. Aware of the perilous situation, Dad took out his castrating knife and made a bold cross at the site. He then sucked and sucked, spitting out the debris. By this time the area had coagulated, and a large clots of a black substance were spat out.

Finally satisfied that he had got out as much as he could, condes crystals were poured into the wound, which was bound, and the doctor was radioed for assistance.

The next problems were to transport the patient to the closest airfield – thirteen miles away, then he had to be kept awake all night.

He was taken to the Gregory Hotel, and all night someone walked Alex up and down, while the others gave him black coffee to drink, all with the estimable purpose of keeping him alert.

The fear was that once the patient lapsed into unconsciousness he might not come out of the coma.

Present day treatment is diametrically opposite to this way of thinking.

At daybreak the plane and doctor left Cloncurry. The weather was overcast, but they arrived in good time. The doctor examined the boy, then prepared to take him back to the Curry. The hospital there had, at that time, a very poor reputation, and the patient was reluctant to leave. I am surprised he was awake. In any case Dr. Al Berry, satisfied that Alex would recover, consented to leave him behind. After this, he and his pilot set off in the plane, for the return journey.

Because of the distance, there was insufficient fuel for the return trip to Cloncurry unless they flew first to Burketown, and topped off the fuel tanks. However, the cloud cover was low, and the pilot chose to follow the river northward to the coastal town. He made a serious error in his tracking, and took the wrong branch of the river, veering to the left branch. By the next day the news spread over the outback radio – the doctor's plane had not reached Burketown. The men were presumed to be lost.

The whole district was activated. All able-bodied men, including the patient, joined in the search, mostly on horseback, to seek the plane. Various persons on a number of properties announced that they had heard a plane flying overhead, in a variety of directions. All this information had to be checked out. Other aircraft were also brought into the search.

Ultimately it was Punjaub Station, and the Scholes family, whose reports were correct.

The missing men were very lucky. Finally realizing that he was lost, the pilot had found a bare claypan, and brought his aeroplane down without mishap, but also without any idea of where he was, because he was still totally unaware that he had followed the wrong branch of the river.

A message was dropped from another plane, in a small tin wax vesta matchbox. Actually the only problems suffered by the two men were, a) hunger, and b) (because of the open cockpit, and the doctor's bald scalp), a bad case of sunburn on the exposed areas, as well as numerous mosquito and sandfly bites.

For years the children in the Carrington family were held paralysed by the tale of the Gregory River in deep flood, and Grandpa, having been swept away by the flooding water, saving himself by seizing a large tree as he was being dragged past by the current. He was trapped with only a large snake for company, both waiting until the river subsided. By the close of the second day Grandpa was extremely hunger and afraid of becoming too weak to hold onto the branches of the tree. He took off his belt, and grabbed the snake, tying it with his belt, and fastening the other end of the belt to the tree. He thereupon cut off a bit of the snake's tail and ate it. By this means he was able to have fresh food until he was finally rescued.

This same story was told to me by a husband and father-in-law with totally straight faces, and it wasn't until I heard it elsewhere that I knew I had been gulled once again by one of the great Australian myths.

When Russell was born it was at the beginning of an extremely hot summer. As often happened, I was alone at the homestead, apart from my 21-year-old, brother-in-law Neville. The other men were all away working for the day at one of the yards.

At the front of the house there was an ancient bougainvillea, in full bloom, growing over a high metal arch. I placed my baby in his stroller under this bush, as it seemed the coolest place for him. I would go into the kitchen to prepare something, then go outside and on the child. My last visit showed me an appalling sight. There, swinging down from the arch, over the infant, was an enormous water python, (I am talking about a ten to twelve feet reptile, who thought it had found a free meal). I dragged the pram away, and shrieked for Neville.

The terror in my voice brought him running.

The snake was still swinging down, as Neville grabbed a spear belonging to one of the Aborigines and struck the creature. He finally killed it and left it to show the men on their return. To our astonishment, when the time to display it came, both the snake, and the spear which was embedded in its body, had disappeared forever.

Because the river was so close we often saw these snakes. They would come up to the fowl yard, slide through the K wire fence and seize a fowl for a meal. At this stage they would slime the trophy all over, stretch it in their coils, then swallow it. By this time the rest of the residents of the yard would make such a cacophony of noise that one of the men would head down to see what the problem was. The snake, realizing that it was in trouble, would then try to escape back through the wire. The difficulty was that the size of its body had expanded with the meal inside and it could not get out. It is hard to estimate just how often this scenario was played out over the years. Goannas would also sneak into the fowl yard, but they were mostly after the eggs, or any chickens running around. Chicken hawks were also a problem. Nevertheless, without the fowls there would be no eggs for cooking or eating, nor would there be roosters fattened up for Christmas.

We used to have boxes containing 100-day-old chicks flown out on the DC3 aeroplane. Someone would be there to meet the plane, returning with this box of cheeping chicks. A wired in area would have been prepared for them, containing chicken feed and water. The downy little birds would be released into paradise – that is all except those who had been squashed on the journey out in the plane. However, most of these also recovered every time – a feat which amazed me. I would not have given them a hope, but a bit of air to breathe and room to move, after being coddled for a while in a warm cloth wadded into an old shoe box, and they would revive to join their companions, in the garden, to pick at the grass and play. As usual snakes had to be watched for. Each night the babies would be gathered in and popped back into the box in which they had arrived. They would then be locked in the office, away from predators, overnight. It did create a rich aroma by morning. This procedure would be followed until they were old enough and large enough to be left out all night.

At one time and aviary had been built, when Glen had been interested in cage birds. This was a cage large enough for an adult to stand in. It had a protective roof, chicken wire walls, and even a nesting box.

It was decided to keep the chickens in there, once it was no longer used for its original purpose.

Once again, while the men were away, Nancy and I heard a frightful commotion coming from this area. There inside, on the beam supporting the roof was a children's python, which had a chick in its mouth, and a suspicious bulge in the middle of it body, while the other 98 downy chicks squealed in terror.

Neither Nancy nor I had ever held a gun, but Nancy found

the .410 shotgun, loaded it with a cartridge, and returned to the cage, my job was to keep an eye on the snake encase it tried to escape. Fortunately, it remained in situ. Nancy aimed the gun in the general direction of the snake, and scored a shot, right in the middle.

It dropped the now deceased chicken from its mouth, and as it did so, the first chicken, which it had already swallowed, fell out from the hole in the middle. We were very proud of this effort.

When Alex saw it he decided to give us lesson in how to shoot. Nancy did quite well, but he refused to teach me, after the first shot at a tin can, maintaining that the only thing I would hit would be myself, or some other member of family. Oh, ye of little faith!

There were many incidents with snakes.

A 9ft 6inch python paid a visit to our front bedroom when Joan was an infant. It actually had to pass under her cot to enter the room, and it was slithering around on the floor, when Alex arose in the dawn. It had been joined by the one-year-old Russell, who was also playing on the floor of the same room.

Our house was still very new at this time, and the floor was covered by a shiny new linoleum, which gave little purchase to the snake. The proud house owner sent me out on the lawn with the children in my arms, while he disposed of the python. He was about to whack it with a shovel when he realized that he would mark his branded new floor covering. This gave him pause to think. Suddenly he seized the animal and hurled it outside, right next to the spot where I had been standing nursing the babies, safely out of the way.

We found snakes in beds, in the toilet, around the window frames. There is little more unnerving than to be standing naked in the bath, than to look out the window, only to see a serpent gliding along the window sill.

Our youngest girl, Jenny, liked animals. Her chief pets were her poddy calves, and "Loud", the rooster, though Brandy the Labrador dog had a large portion of her affection also. She did apparently seem to be carrying things a bit too far when she discovered a clutch of small eggs in the woodchips under the woodheap.

She rescued these. Finding an old cigarette tin, she placed the eggs within, covering them with woodchips. For several days she monitored these, until her uncle asked what she had there. Lovingly she carried the tin over to him.

"I think we had better see just what is inside an egg," said Uncle John, taking one of the clutch and breaking it open.

Out wriggled the tiniest brown snake which could be imagined, just ready to hatch. In spite of their would-be foster mother's anguished pleas, the rest of the clutch was also destroyed.

Margery McWhirter was a lass, working on our property as a ringer, at one time.

She was not with the stockmen, but at our home. The weather was so hot, that nearly everyone slept on the verandahs, to escape the stifling feeling of the heat in the enclosed rooms. Margery was on a stretcher on the verandah, encased by a mosquito net. Further along the same area was Alex's nephew, Gary Sturmfels, also bedded down inside the cocoon of his net.

Alex and I were heavily asleep inside our small bedroom which was at the enclosed end of the same verandah. I was aroused by squeals and yells, muffled by the mosquito nets and closed doors. Struggling awake I listened a bit more closely. Then I shook my hero awake.

"You'd better see what is happening!"

He scrambled out of bed, as did I, and we opened the door, to an amazing sight. There was both Margery and Gary, perched like birds on a tree branch, clutching the verandah posts and bellowing for our assistance.

"What the hell is up?"

"Snake! A Snake!"

"Where is it? I can't see anything."

I switched on the flashlight. There was no electricity, as the power was turned off about 10 pm each night, to conserve fuel.

Alex seized the torch from my hand, and looked closer.

"It was climbing in bed with me," uttered Margery.

"I felt it under the net, near the pillow."

Now he had some direction Alex looked. The snake had indeed joined Margery in bed, for there it was still. Her re-action had been sensible. In the darkness on one would have had any idea what type of snake it was, venomous, or non-venomous. It was quickly dispatched and the two new age birds were able to descend at last. After that everyone on the property made quite sure that nets were tucked in very securely when each person took to his bed.

Eighteen

Many years later another incident occurred at John and Nancy's home. They were both asleep upstairs, also on the verandah. It was just breaking daylight, and Nancy had thrown off her net, and covering, lying quietly on her bed to await the world's awakening.

All at once she felt her arm seized and discovered that she was being attacked by another of the enormous water pythons. Her cry woke John, who pulled her over towards him. Her son Graeme heard her, and he came running out to see what had happened. Her son-in-law, Lionel White, who was visiting with Lyndell, rushed out. He grabbed her upper arm and tried to use his hands as a tourniquet, until help could be summonsed.

John dashed over to our house to call me, to work the radio, to get medical help, and Graeme when on a snake catching hunt. He caught the snake and threw it downstairs, where it lay still in the old bougainvillea bush.

We organized the proper treatment first, before calling the doctor.

"We need some wood as a splint," I instructed, as I raided the medical kit for crepe bandages.

Back came someone with a large paling four foot long. We could not wait until another was found, so we bound the arm, then put the splint in place, and bound it on also.

Nancy was told to rest while the doctor was called. She could do little else with this great piece of wood attached to her arm. She said later that it was monstrously heavy.

I had difficulty in raising the doctor. The airwaves are not always co-operative. Although we were within the Mount Isa area, it was a Charleville radio officer who finally responded to the call. He rang the Mt. Isa Base, and we were able to obtain a connection.

We explained the problem, and yes, it turned out we had treated the bite as we should.

"You had better keep the snake, so we can take it to Mt. Isa for identification," said the doctor.

"Some snakes cross breed, and it could have venom. With regard to the treatment, you had better give the patient an injection of adrenaline."

An old conversation of mine with Nancy filtered back into my mind. "I can't, she is allergic to it."

"Well, just watch her, monitor her progress, and we'll be out as soon as we can."

In due course the plane arrived, and the doctor was taken up to see her. He decided to take her back to Mt. Isa, as, knowing what other foods snakes targeted, he was certain that, if nothing else, she would get a severe infection from the bite. Certainly I was astonished at just how long she was required to stay in hospital and town, before she was declared well again.

Just prior to the departure of the plane the men looked around for the aggressor. It had recovered somewhat, and was on the move out of the way. However, it was safely secured in a sack bag, and joined the party in the cabin, still protesting its innocence.

My most recent personal experience with a snake involved doing some sewing at my machine downstairs. I had a long tape measure around my neck, only to feel that it had slipped between my legs. I reached down to retrieve it. My hand brushed up against something else. What I had thought was the tape measure was a snake, rearing up between my thighs, which were spread apart for coolness.

Sheer terror kept me still. I had no idea what it looked like, as my dress covered it. That same terror must have conveyed itself to my husband, for once in his life actually heard me calling out.

"What's happened? Are you all right?"

Still, as only a paralysed object can be, I breathed. "It's between my legs"

"I can't see anything," he claimed as he pushed me out of the way.

The chair fell over with a clatter. There was the snake, doing its best to escape. As quickly as Alex struck at it, it dodged, finally whipping out the front door.

Brought up to observe a "No meat" day on Good Fridays, I assumed this would also be the case for the men. We started the day with a curry from tinned salmon and rice. Lunchtime came. Alex had gone fishing that morning, and we had plenty of bream for everyone. Came time for the evening meal. I served up a very large dish of macaroni cheese, using a couple of my wedding present dishes. It looked yummy, providing one wasn't a dedicated meat eater.

John Molony, a young chap who had recently started working

for us, looked at it and said something that warmed the cockles of my heart. "Miss Pearse, it looks like something out of the Women's Weekly." John had, about three years earlier been one of my pupils at Camooweal, which explained his form of address. Indeed, he still addresses me in this style. The food was eaten and enjoyed. True to my beliefs I have never served meat on Good Friday. I reckon that it won't hurt anyone to think about something other than their food for one day of the year.

When I had only been at Planet for only a short time Alex constructed a most efficient barbecue from half a forty-four-gallon drum, sliced lengthwise. On this was a very strong steel plate. The drum was set on strong legs. It became the practice, on the days when a beast was killed for meat, that we held a barbecue.

Skirt steak was always cooked – small pieces of steak which danced over the barbecue plate as they were heating. Another gourmet delight – for them – was the milk gut. Sweetbreads from the pancreas and the back of the tongue were considered appetizing, as was the fresh liver. If these were to be eaten at all, it was necessary to eat them soon after killing, because of refrigeration was not a strong point on the station at that point.

Cold rooms were still regarded as luxuries, and only a few properties boasted them. Our refrigeration consisted of two kerosene refrigerators, much smaller than the present domestic fridge in suburban households. The fresh meat was jammed into these containers, whilst the corned beef was left to drain and cure in the butcher's shop.

This fresh meat was perforce eaten before the corned beef. The menfolk loved the way the refrigerators could make ice, in a group of three trays of ice cubes, suspended in the centre of the cabinet. Many a time I seethed as someone come along, remove a tray, and either take out the ice cubes, or drink the icy water, which had not yet set. This continual opening of the fridge door did nothing to help the meat remain in a very cold condition. On many an occasion either Nancy or I would have to wash the fresh meat in vinegar to remove the slightly greenish tinge which covered the cut of meat we wished to use. Alternatively, if it was too strong, we would carve off the outer layer of the meat, and use the centre. If nothing else, the meat, treated in this way, was always tender.

In time we graduated to a cold room. Not big enough to walk into, it had on full length door, behind which could be hung the whole fore or hindquarters of the beast which had been slaughtered. Before hanging the carcass would be butchered in various sections, such as the rumps, buttocks (topside), blades, fillets, roasts and so on. These were then laid out on a series of shelves in the cold room, accessible through small doors. The piece de resistance was a whole area where things could actually be frozen hard. Alas, at times this might be a six pack of beer, placed in there for quick chilling, then not rescued in time, before exploding, and making a frightful mess of the area.

It took me a long time to familiarise myself with the various portions of meat.

Buttock and rump all looked the same to untrained eye.

Using the whole buttock, I made a mouth-watering stew, which proved very popular, and for which I was amply praised. I glowed with pleasure.

A couple of days later it was decided to hold a barbecue, as we had guests coming.

"I can't seem to find the rump, "exclaimed Alex. We haven't used one since the last kill."

He searched through the meat, pulling it this way and that, without success.

He never did find that rump, and I never gave him a chance to make the connection. He was forced to use topside steak for the barbecue, but we survived.

I found myself unable to cook tripe either. On most occasions this was dumped, but rarely, it was decided to have a go at cooking it. An unusual solution to cleaning the tissue was to scrub it, then put it in the washing machine. This was a process strongly objected to by the mistresses of the house, although the men thought it was a wonderful idea.

The idea of having to clean the machine after such a use, getting rid of all the fat and smell, before it could return to normal duties was enough to defy the butchering gang. Instead it was boiled in the copper, quite a number of times, before it was considered acceptable to bring into the kitchen for preparation for human consumption.

I never cared for offal meats, though many found them a delicacy.

By the same token, when a pig, was slaughtered I found myself unable to use the head to make brawn. I was just too upsetting to take off the lid of the saucepan to see a head apparently appealing piteously up to me, snout to the ceiling.

Neither could I cook a sucking pig as a whole entity. If the head had been removed it reduced the meat to a lump of meat. With the head still there my imagination prevented me from letting the carcass baste in the oven.

I eventually became very good at cooking barramundi, and blue peas, but there were a few problems while I learned.

I had not much exposure to pressure cookers prior to taking over my share of the Planet kitchen. I learned the hard way how careful one has to be with the replacement of the rubber pressure valves and rings securing the lid.

Nancy had shown me how to use the saucepan, and it became a very useful tool in shortening the time it took to cook many dishes. One notable example was dried peas, often called "blue peas" because of their bluish tinge when dry, also known as "blue boilers."

She was away and I had taken over the cooking, as was our normal arrangement. Blue peas were a favourite side dish served with hot corned beef, which I proposed to serve at the evening meal. I had soaked a packet of peas, using bi-carb soda to soften them up. They were then placed in the pressure cooker. Its sealing ring had perished a day previously, so I had replaced this. What I didn't allow for was that, as the rubber had deteriorated in the ring, it probably had in the pressure valve also. In the light of later knowledge, I found out that if one piece of rubber is replaced, it is to replace them all.

I put the pressure cooker on the stove and left it to reach boiling point. After this I slipped on the bob, which kept the pressure valve under control, and allowed the pot to simmer away.

Suddenly I heard an almighty explosion. I whipped around to see that the bob had blasted off the lid, and a steady stream of mushy pea mixture was jetting up to the ceiling, where it was coagulating all over the place.

That which did not adhere to the ceiling fell back all over the stove, where it made a stinking, black mess. Anyone who has had anything to do with dried peas, would be aware that once they are set hard onto a cooking vessel (or anywhere, for that matter), it is almost impossible to remove the mixture unless it was protracted soaking. The ceiling was high. In the big kitchen it had been made of pressed tin, and over the years it had been painted.

Perforce, I stood on a chair, on a table, trying to soften the pea paste to a more gluey consistency, and wipe it off.

I tried to scrape it off. All I did was remove the paint from the ceiling (that is when I discovered the tin surface). It took hours of work, and many caustic comments by the men of the house, who made no attempt to help me. I had done it; I could clean it up! The stench of the burning peas on the stove was also practically unbearable. It was years before I trusted a pressure cooker again.

The ceiling got another touch up when the boys came home from boarding school. During one holiday they decided to cook pancakes for lunch, and what is more, they intended to toss them. I had a recipe book which had two pancake recipes, one for "Perfect Pancakes", the other "Family Pancakes". I was requested not to interfere, so, as the stock camp was out for the day, I let them have their way.

The mixtures were made, the pans were heated, batter was poured into Stephen's frying pan. Rapidly the underside was cooked. Now the moment of truth. He gingerly held the pan in both hands, and tossed. The pancake turned over, but landed back in the pan half in and half out. It was now Russell's turn. He took his pan, cooked the underside, and flipped the cake over. Up it went, and he moved the pan to catch it. It was a misjudgment. Down came the pancake, flat onto the stove, which had to be cleaned. The final straw came when the batter was tossed once again, and it soared up to the ceiling, where it stayed, as if held there by glue.

This time it was not I who cleaned the ceiling!

When Alex was to be married the family had had a discussion, which resulted in a decision to build a second homestead, where he and his family would be able to live, without the two families interfering with each other too much.

Mrs. Carrington had a brother J.P. Muller, living in Proserpine, who was a carpenter and builder. His youngest son, Gordon, was in partnership with his father. They were given the job of building the new house. I had no input into it whatever. This was probably just as well, as had I given suggestions which were used, and unsuccessful, I would never have been able to live the fact down. In this way I was uncompromised, and would have been able to criticize as much as I liked. Fairly easy going, I did not find it necessary to complain, though, in the light of later knowledge I would have done some things differently.

The house was to be bungalow style, in fact, an old Queenslander style, with three central bedrooms, and a lounge room, surrounded by a wide verandah, one corner of which was to be closed in, to become the kitchen.

The house was to be built on high blocks, which were to be cut by my husband.

The bathroom and toilet downstairs. In his spare time Alex searched for trees tall enough to be stumps for the house.

This proved more difficult than had been expected.

After four trees had been cut, a major reappraisal was made.

The house would now be low stumped, with just a few steps, leading up to the verandah. The back verandah was now to be closed in, with the kitchen at one end, and bathroom at the other.

As the house was being constructed it dawned on the future resident, that the inner lounge room, would be very hot. A discussion with Uncle Jack resulted in the removal of the whole of the back lounge room wall, so that this room opened into the now enclosed back verandah.

The room could now be accessed through the door, which remained, or through the large square arched area, which replaced the wall.

Every wall now had an opening or door in it, making the placement of any furniture very awkward.

But it was rendered much cooler as a result.

We still had only thirty-two-volt electricity, and each home had only one desk fan.

Household air-conditioning was considered too new an innovation to even be considered.

Nineteen

As the building of the house progressed, so did the interest of both Alex and John, as well as everyone in the district.

One-day John came to me and said, "You know it hasn't been decided yet just who will live in that house. I might want to there myself".

I had no argument with him. I really didn't care, so long as I had a roof over my head.

Obviously he decided to remain where he was in the old homestead. I guess it was the practical decision, because Nancy was the cook at that time, the radio was over there, and any business emanated from that home.

Theirs' was an interesting house, built in 1929. I had never before seen a home made entirely of tin. The walls were all constructed of ripple iron, with a galvanized corrugated iron roof. There were two sets of stairs, in that they rose onto an enclosed verandah up top.

This house, too, was in the style of an old Queenslander, but the toilet and bathroom were both downstairs.

An amateur attempt had, many years before been made to create two bedrooms from part of the verandah, one at each end of the back section of the house. I say amateur, because when these rooms, which were both long and narrow, had the floors put in, there was a slight step right across the middle of the rooms. An unsuspecting person would often get a shock as he stumbled at the unexpected drop. The floors were covered by linoleum, a floor covering similar to vinyl, which gave the preliminary illusion that the floor was level. At the time of my arrival at Planet there were still some pieces of homemade furniture, around the place. Chief among these were bedroom seats which had been constructed from wooden kerosene packing cases, which had been nailed together, then padded with wadding, and covered with cretonne material.

There was also an old car seat, which had been stripped of leather to its basic shape, and mounted on some bent iron legs.

It had a hard padded cushion for its seat, and it was painted to match the floor downstairs, where it rested beside the internal stairs.

Years before the kitchen had been under the house, but when the grandparents retired their old home it was shifted to the back of the building, and converted it into a large kitchen and dining room with a scullery out the back on the verandah.

This building was on low stumps.

The floor under the big house had formerly been kept hard and cleaned by application of water thrown on to the dirt, then it was beaten with bags tied to long handles. It was surprising just how effective this was.

Years before my arrival, the two older Carrington men had

gone to the river with horses and a wagon, dragging back many enormous stones, which they set deep into the ground, as flagstones.

The rocks had not been split to make them thin and easy to handle, but they made a wonderful floor base, and during the whole of my lifetime at Planet they were painted red, with the mortar joining them deep green. It was quite a spectacular floor.

I was disappointed when I learned that the subsequent owner just cemented them over. A few of the stones had fossil footprints of birds on them, and fossilized leaves.

This area was where everyone congregated to relax. There were some iron chairs, which had fine chain wire slung like canvas to make extremely comfortable seats. They were virtually indestructible, though red back spiders did have a habit of building under the wire, as Nancy could testify.

She called for my assistance once. She had received a bite at the extreme top of the back of her thigh, and it was beginning to hurt. One of the red backs had bitten her! Of course similar rules to the treatment of snake bite had to be used. The poor woman lay prone on her stomach, while I took a brand-new razor blade, which I sterilised. I swabbed the area, which was, by this time becoming red and inflamed, and then found it very difficult to make an incision. Would it be tough to cut? Would it bleed excessively? I nerved myself to do it, and found that the flesh parted easily, and because there was a bit of fatty tissue in that area, it did not bleed too much. We cleaned up, then checked with the Flying Doctor. Fortunately she recovered without any complications.

At this time the men kept their swag rolls under the house, and after a hard and long

morning's work, they would come up for lunch, then go outside, unroll the swags and stretch themselves out for a rest during the great heat of midday. It was, of course, far too hot to work the cattle through the extreme heat as well.

Nancy had enhanced the area with a number of pot plants. Many were suspended in half tyres, which acted as hanging baskets. This created an area of coolness. Most of the plants were "water plants" — a type of philodendron. One day a local resident of the area called, and asked me if she could have a plant. There appeared to me to be a multitude of pots, so I selected one and gave it to her. She was duly grateful, which was just as well, because when Nancy returned to Planet after her illness one of the first things she noticed was the absence of this plant. I had assumed that among so many, one would not be missed. I had not bargained on the hand and eye of a true gardener.

Later, two sides of the underhouse area were enclosed with glass louvres on the top, and metal louvres on the lower half. This was to counteract the prevailing rainfall, and at times the vicious winds, which could blow so unpleasantly. Later still the whole area that was not covered with stones was cemented, so that the area for entertaining and resting became pleasanter still. A half-sized pool table was bought and installed under the house, which gave the stockmen something to do in their spare time. The children of the household all became fairly expert too, at shooting balls. Because people seem to have a habit of placing objects on any available clear space, very heavy duty vinyl cover was made, and this was kept on the table when not in use.

A ping pong table was also obtained, which rested on top of the pool table, but it never had the same impact, although, of course, it was well used in its time.

Before dinner at night the men would gather in this recreational area, for a beer and a bit of relaxation. Once I was living in my own home it would gall me to hear my husband's voice taking part in conversations over the way, while I was at home with the children waiting for his arrival so that we could share our evening meal with him. He obviously did not realise that I was lonely, as my previous lifestyle had not included long periods alone. I did not take into account the fact that he, too needed to unwind after a heavy day's physical work.

The truth is that as long as he was at Planet he was really more of a son of the house, and younger brother, rather than a husband and father, which were of secondary importance in the scheme of things.

The kitchen/dining room, which was an adaptation of the family's first home on Planet, had an interesting history. While they still dwelt in it, the family rapidly grew. In short order there were six children, Fred, Biddy, Midge, John, Ron and Vera (Pat).

Their mother was once again expecting, and had passed her seventh month She was cooking a roast dinner when she realised that her labour had commenced. At this stage Harry Foster, from Gregory Station arrived at the house. He was in a horse and buggy, and suggested that Mum travel with him to Burketown, which was seventy miles away.

Common sense made her say that this was an impossible solution. She did ask him to bring back the midwife, whom she had booked some time previously, to come out and stay with her at the time of the expected birth.

Grandma Carrington was at the other house on the premises, so her daughter-in-law called her to come and help. As activity became more urgent the older children began to wonder what was happening. They were sent outside with promises of a picnic.

Editor's note:

The above are the last known words written by Pat as part of her memoirs.

Russ informed me that, "She is speaking about when my father was born. He is one of twins, unfortunately his brother William did not live beyond eight days. His grave is on Planet Downs.

I remember finding on the net a report written by a Constable from Turn-off Lagoon who was sent over to Planet to officiate at the burial saying that it was a very touching and pitiful burial. It was a practise in our family to name the children who were not expected to live one Christian name only, hence William and Alexander Carrington. One of our family historians said that in our family history the name William appears 700 times, and the name Alexander 400 times."

Russ's Uncle Neville Carrington also died on the property, in a horse-riding accident.

Appendix One

Here is a list of most of the Cattle Stations upon which Russ has conducted mustering operations.
Seven Emus, Abingdon, Albinia, Alcala, Alehavale, Alice Downs, Almora, Alroy, Amaroo, Anthony's Lagoon, Ardmore, Armraynald, Arnhemland, Ashover, Augustus Downs, Austral, Avon Downs via Camooweal, Avon Downs via Mt. Coolon, Balgo Hill, Banchory, Bar Creek, Barkly Downs, Beamesbrook, Bedford Downs, Benmarra, Biralee, Boomarra, Bowthorn, Brighton Downs, Brinawa, Brookdale, Brunette Downs, Buckingham Downs, Bullita, Calvert Hills Station, Camfield, Canobie, Centaur Park, Carlton Hills, Carrum, Cassiopeia, Cerito, Chatsworth, Cliffdale, Clonagh, Conway, Coolibah, Coolullah, Coralie, Corinda, Cowan Downs, Dalgonally, Davenport, Delamere, Delta, Donors Hill, Doomadgee, Dorunda, Dotswood, Double Lagoon, Dugald River, Dunbar, Eaglefield, Egilabra, Elgin Downs, Elsey Station, Epping Forest, Escott, Eureka Springs, Eva Downs, Fig Tree, Flora Downs, Flora Valley, Fort Constantine, Fort Cooper, Fox River, Frankfield, Gallipoli, Gleeson, Gregory Downs, Hanging Rock, Haslingden,

Havilah, Headingly, Heidelberg, Herbert Vale, Old Hidden Valley, Highland Plains, Hodgson River Downs, Inkerman, Innes vale, Islay Plains, Kalmeta, Kamilaroi. Katherine Research Station, Lake Elphinstone, Lake Nash, Laurel Hills, Lawn Hill, Lorella Springs, Lorraine, Lotusvale, Lyrian, Magoura, Malbonvale, Manbullo, Margaret Downs, May Downs, Macalister, Mellish Park, Milungera, Miranda, Mittebah, Monstraven, Montejinni, Moola Bulla, Morestone, Mt. Hope, Mt. Guide, Nappa Merrie, Nardoo, Nelson Springs, Neumeyer Valley, Nobbies, Norfolk, Nosnillor, Numil Downs, Oban, Parada, Pandanus, Plain Creek, Planet Downs, Punjab, Rifle Creek, Riversleigh, Robinson River, Rockhampton Downs, Rocklands Station, Rocktare Park, Rocky Glen, Rosebud, Rosetta, Ruby Plains, Rutland Plains, Sophie Downs, South Galway, Split Rock, Spoonbill, Springvale, St. Ann's, Staaten National Park, Stanbroke, Stratford, Strathmore via Georgetown, Strathmore via Collinsville, Surveyors, Sutherland, Talawanta, Taldora, Tanbar, The 10 Mile, Thorntonia, Tobermorey, Trenton, Twin Hills, Undilla, Vacquera, Van Rook, Walhallow, Warrenvale, Waterhouse River, Wentworth, Wernadinga, West Inverleigh, West Leichardt, Westmoreland, Whynot, Willeroo, Willesly, Wilsons Hut, Wollogorang, Wondoola, Woodhouse, Woodstock, Wrotham Park, Yacamunda, Yarromere and Yelvertoft.

Appendix Two

Carrington Family Timeline

1828- William Carrington born 29th February in Westminster, England (my Great Great Grandfather)
1846- William Carrington arrives in Australia
1854- William Carrington marries Eliza Hooker in Melbourne
1854- William Carrington is wounded at the Eureka Stockade whilst fighting beside Peter Lalor.

William and Eliza go on to have 10 children
1856- Birth of William (2), Note a Son of this William (2) -John Carrington KIA 1915 Anzac Cove, Gallipoli.
1858- Birth of Eliza (2)
1861- Birth of Sarah
1863- Birth of John (Jack) Carrington (My Great Grandfather)
1865- Birth of Henry
1868- Birth of Harriet
1870- Birth of Emma (married 1915 to Robert Anderson of

Ragged 13 fame)

1873- Birth of Eliza (3), note, this is the 2nd Eliza born to this family

1874- Birth of George, served at Gallipoli, also in France

1875- Birth of Frederick (Flood), so named as he was born on the roof of a flooded house

1878- William Carrington Started a Hotel at Comet called the All Nations Hotel.

1885- John (Jack) Carrington travelled to Camooweal with wagons in company with his sister Sarah Beaumont and her Husband William Beaumont as well as their sisters Harriet and Emma Carrington

1889- William and Emily Barrett (nee Austin) bought the Gregory Downs Hotel

John (Jack) Carrington met his wife Anne (nee Austin) while carrying past the Gregory Downs Hotel

where she was working as a cook for her sister Emily Barrett.

1889- Jack Carrington marries Anne Austin at Camooweal.

Jack and Anne Carrington had 10 children

1890- Birth of William (3)

1891- Birth of Dora

1893- Birth of Charlotte

1895- Birth of Frederick (Ted) my Grandfather

1898- Birth of Annie

1900- Birth of Alexander

1901- Birth of Clare

1905- Birth of Leonard

1908- Birth of Eva

1914- Birth of Arthur

1892- William Barrett held the licence for the Gregory Downs Hotel until 1892, when his wife Emily took over the Licence and held the title, till her death in 1933.

1916- Frederick (Ted) Married Annie Muller. They had 10 children.

1917- Birth of Frederick (Served WW2)
1918- Birth of Lila (Bid)
1919- Birth of Edna (Midge)
1921- Birth of John Carrington
1922- Birth of Ronald (Served WW2)
1924- Birth of Vera (Pat)
1926- Birth of Alexander (my Father)
1926- Birth of William (Dec at 8 days) twin brother of Alexander
1929- Birth of Joan
1931- Birth of Dell
1934- Birth of Neville

1921- In 1921 Jack Carrington along with his son Frederick (Ted) and their families, purchased off Emily Barrett, a block of land 13 miles from the Gregory River and east of the Hotel, this was the original Planet Downs and is still known as Old Planet. I have the original Planet Downs Horse Book from those days with the first entry being on the 20th November 1900.

The two men Jack and Ted for many years plied their trade as Carriers, carting to and from the Burketown Port and the Stations in the Gulf and far into the Northern Territory, carting Wool and other goods and other properties as well as ore from the various mines in the area.

To augment their income, Ted took on the Burketown to Camooweal Packhorse Mail Run with the stretch from the Lily

Waterhole to Camooweal, subcontracted.

My Great Uncle Len was also an integral part of the family workforce, and played an important part, taking his turn at running the Teams and the Mail.

1922- William Barrett died in 1922

1933- Emily Barrett passes away at the Gregory Hotel and she is buried at the Gregory Downs Hotel Cemetery along with her husband William..

Emily Barrett became a legend in her own lifetime, known to everyone as 'Aunty Barrett'

1924- Gregory Downs let a couple of blocks lapse and they were taken up by various Pioneers, these included the Carrington men. Drawing the Tagassa block on the eastern bank of the Gregory River in a land ballot they later included the blocks of Kunkulla and Kamarga to this.

1925- The family shifts the house from the Old Planet Well in onto the Gregory River and erects another homestead as well.

Appendix Three

William Carrington Obituary
Northern Miner 27th February 1907
Death of an Old Colonist
("Rockhampton Record")

On Saturday last there died in the Rockhampton Hospital, at the age of 79 Mr. William Carrington, the well-known contractor etc. of Comet and Blackwater, who had been ailing for some time as the consequence of an operation he had to undergo previously. Mr. Carrington has been a respected resident of the Central District for some 40 years, and when his remains were removed to the Railway Station on Sunday, preparatory to their being conveyed to Comet for internment there the next day, they were followed to the station by a number of well-known citizens.

On the following day the remains were laid alongside those of Mrs. Carrington, who had predeceased her husband at Comet 24 years ago, the Rev. J. A. White, of Emerald, officiating at the grave.

Deceased, who had been the father of 10 children, seven of whom were born in Queensland, has left a grown-up family of four sons and three daughters, who are more or less scattered around the district, the deceased gentleman had had an adventurous career.

Born at Westminster, London on the 29th March 1828, he would have been 80 years old next year, and 18 of his birthdays would have fallen on leap years.

At eight years of age he ran away from home and took ship to New Brunswick, but he deserted the vessel there, and for some time worked his way, in one way or another, into the States.

Returning home for a while he took a ship for Australia, and deserted at Melbourne. From that time he was then 18 years of age (1846) – Australia claimed him as her own.

He became a miner on the Victorian goldfields, and had strange tales to tell of the life by the gold-seekers in the early days, and of the big money that would be made at great risk and labour – only to be spent in riotous recklessness afterwards.

The deceased was went on to say that he and his mates could clear £2000 a month easily in those early days, and that he himself lost as much as £1000 of money made by hard work in one night's gambling.

Previous to the great discovery of gold at Ballarat and Bendigo, men of the immigrant class were content to work on stations; at all sorts of occupations, for as low as £15 per year and tucker; when the rushes were in full swing, however, it was difficult to obtain good artisans and tradesmen at less than 15s a day .

Mr. Carrington was at the side of Peter Lalor when that worthy was wounded, and he himself (deceased) was shot in the leg.

They were helped in running the gauntlet by two girls dressed as men who were assisting the miners by loading their rifles, Mr. Carrington used to tell another story of those stirring times.

The police then used to travel about the goldfields for the purpose of ascertaining who had and who had not miner's rights.

On one of these occasions, a miner down a shaft refused to show his permit to the Inspector, and a mounted trooper was sent to find out how things were. As he was descending the shaft, by some means never explained, his revolver went off, and the bullet killed the quarry.

The Trooper was immediately surrounded, and a rope was put around his neck. He begged for a hearing, and explained that the affair was an accident, but this statement was not accepted and the Trooper was about to be lynched when Mr. Carrington and his mate rushed up and said they would shoot the first man that pulled the rope.

Eventually the man was released. In 1861, Mr. Carrington came to Queensland, where he made his home ever since. But in these 45 years he followed his occupation as a miner in New Zealand and Tasmania and in many parts of Australia.

He was on the Palmer, and witnessed many curious scenes there and elsewhere in North Queensland. On the Palmer he used to say he had paid as much as £100, and even more than that, for a horse to convey his stuff to the ship's side.

Deceased eldest daughter, Mrs. McNicol, who acted as mother to her younger brothers and sisters, died last year. For the past seven years Mr. Carrington has resided at Comet with his youngest son, Mr. Frederick Flood Carrington.

Glossary

ASI – Air Speed Indicator

Attending – often shortened to tendering means to attend your neighbours muster to assist and also to ensure that the correct distribution of cattle was carried out. Usually only practiced where there were unfenced boundaries.

BTEC – Brucellosis and Tuberculosis Eradication Campaign. This was an extensive campaign carried out by the Agricultural Departments of all the states in Australia to test every beast and to eradicate the unmusterable or uneconomical feral herds.

Catcher – Bull catching vehicle modified with bars to enable it to scrub bash without damage, also some were fitted with mechanical arms to catch bulls around the neck.

Cleanskin – Unbranded feral cattle.

Dynamic Rollover – A condition of helicopter flight where the machine rotates laterally over a stuck skid

HAAMC – Head of Aircraft Airworthiness and Maintenance

Controller

Horrors – Delirium tremens, an advanced case of alcohol poisoning.

Land Ballot – as the properties started to develop, some very large places were broken up and suitable applicants were invited to compete for the land in a ballot

OAT – Outside Air Temperature Gauge

Tanksinker – Earthmoving contractor

Trough – A vessel to hold water above the ground that enables stock to get a good clean drink.

Turkeys Nest – An earth tank that is constructed above ground to hold water and to enable the water to reticulate via gravity.

VSI – Vertical Speed Indicator

www.ingramcontent.com/pod-product-compliance
Lightning Source LLC
Chambersburg PA
CBHW011802090426
42811CB00037B/2355/J